Praise fo

Love and the Mystery of Betrayal

Next Generation 2015 Indie Book Awards Finalist, Spirituality
Foreword Reviews' INDIEFAB 2014 Book of the Year Finalist, Psychology
USA Best Book Awards 2014 Finalist, Non-fiction Narrative

"What Sandra Lee Dennis tells us about the transformative power of suffering is so important and so true. She makes it clear that the price is high, but the reward of a heart broken open to a deeper love is worth the cost. I hope that many read this book; many surely are in need of it."

> —**Fr. Richard Rohr**, author of *Silent Compassion* and *Job and The Mystery of Suffering*

"*Love and the Mystery of Betrayal* is a rare and beautiful book, a powerful guide to anyone sincerely interested in recovering wholeheartedness after the shocking pain of a relationship rupture. With remarkable courage, intelligence, and humanity, Sandra weaves her own journey through the many dimensions of personal devastation. She guides the reader through a compelling journey of the soul with up-to-date psychological understanding and spiritual wisdom to support true reemergence. This will be invaluable for anyone interested in harnessing the deepest human heartbreak as a crucible for spiritual awakening. This book is a triumph of spirit. I wish for it to find its way into the hands of all who could benefit. I cannot recommend it highly enough."

> —**Miranda Macpherson**, author of *Boundless Love*

"I was moved by many passages in this deep, engaging book. Sandy Dennis shows us the way to surrender to the mysteries of grief and pain. In doing so, she must go against our happiness-obsessed culture and the self-images that equate suffering with weakness and indulgence. She does not look away or sugar-coat the experience of abandonment and betrayal with easy tips on getting over it or with any spiritual bypass sleight of hand. This book offers instead an invaluable chronicling of 'the whole catastrophe' from breakdown to breakthrough. A much-needed contribution to our collective healing I am pleased to recommend."

> —**Francis Weller**, author of *Entering the Healing Ground*

"Discover how the excruciating pain of betrayal can become a portal to unconditioned love and deep inner freedom… A powerful book that will serve many."
  —**Tara Brach, PhD**, author of *Radical Acceptance* and
  True Refuge

"This story of heartbreak has a rare quality: it is absolutely honest. Sandra Lee Dennis initially lost her faith in love, in life, in God. She endured and mined the ordeal for its deepest truth for more than four years. Coming out of the desert of heartbreak, she regained her life, her God, and her vitality. Pointing out perils and signposts along the way, she takes us with her, on a poignant voyage through those transforming depths. A wonderful accomplishment."
  —**Ginette Paris, PhD**, author of *Heartbreak*

"Sandra Lee Dennis validates and illuminates with authenticity, courage, and sensitivity the devastating impact of broken trust, and shows what it takes to clear a healing path right through the pain to emotional and spiritual awakening…"
  —**Susan Anderson, CSW**, author of *Journey from Abandonment to Healing*

"In this compelling and well-written book, Sandra takes us on a poignant journey into the dark night of the soul. She courageously reveals her authentic feelings and heroic efforts to find meaning, healing, and wisdom by engaging with the darkness of broken trust. This is an inspiring book that offers guidance and hope for those struggling to heal and grow from one of life's most painful experiences."
  —**John Amodeo, PhD**, author of *Love & Betrayal*

"Sandra Dennis offers original insights into the energetic, sexual, psychic, and neurological workings that make the experience of love betrayed so devastating. Written from the heart, this very personal tribute to the dark goddess encourages those who feel deeply (and wonder if there is something wrong with them) to stay true to their own feelings, which, in the author's case, ultimately brings about a transformation and awakening into the heart of love and equanimity."
  —**Beth Hedva, PhD**, author of *Betrayal, Trust and Forgiveness*

Love and the Mystery of Betrayal

Also by Sandra Lee Dennis

Embrace of the Daimon:
Healing through the Subtle Energy Body,
Jungian Psychology & the Dark Feminine

Love and the Mystery of Betrayal

Grieving the Loss:
Tending the Trauma,
Healing the Heartbreak,
Restoring Trust in Life

Sandra Lee Dennis, PhD

WEST COUNTY PRESS

Published by
West County Press
Sebastopol, CA 95472
westcountypress@gmail.com

Cover design and interior design: by Joel Friedlander (thebookdesigner.com)
Printed in the United States of America

Library of Congress Cataloging-in-Publication Data
Sandra Lee Dennis
Love and the Mystery of Betrayal: Grieving the Loss: Tending the Trauma, Healing the Heartbreak, Restoring Trust in Life
Includes bibliographical references.
ISBN: 978-0-9860684-3-0.
LCCCN: 2013956564

"The Dark Stone" by Rebecca del Rio, reprinted by permission of the author.

"Sacred Wine" by Greg Kimura, excerpt reprinted by permission of the author.

"Two Hearts" by Michael J. Green from Celtic Blessings Calendar 2007 (Portland, OR: Amber Lotus, 2007), reprinted with permission of the author.

*To my greatest blessing
—my daughter Rachael—
that she may ever more deeply trust in
the wisdom of her own heart.*

Contents

Preface to the Second Edition

SINCE THE ORIGINAL PUBLICATION of *Love and the Mystery of Betrayal*, I have been deeply gratified by the many reviews and notes of appreciation I have received. One of the most moving messages came from a woman who several years ago lost her young son.

> "…people should know, your book is a book primarily about grief. I lost my son nine years ago and have lived with a profound sense of betrayal by God. Your book describes my experience better than anything I have read or heard, and your descriptions have helped me—like nothing else has—to move through my feelings towards a loving acceptance."

With the passage of time, I, too, have come to understand that this is a book "primarily about grief". Once I tell my personal story in the first two chapters, the book opens up. I dive into the collective realms of grief and despair. I do my best to describe that sense of betrayal by life—by God, if you use this language—that accompanies encounters with what we experience as evil.

Events that bring us to such despair range widely for each of us, from seemingly minor disappointments, barely acknowledged in our culture, to what we all recognize as major loss: loss of child, spouse, home, health, work. For me, it was a seemingly pedestrian, though abrupt, abandonment by a man I loved, trusted and was about to marry that brought me to this dark passage.

Recently, another man who, showed me that I could love again after this traumatic loss, died unexpectedly. As the grieving waves for him began to pull me into the depths again, I was moved to re-release this book. I wanted to help it reach the broader audience I have been encouraged to believe it deserves.

I already thought I wanted to share an experience I had shortly before he died as an epilogue to the book. One morning, I awoke in a black mood. My mind was running pictures, not only of my own moral failures, but of some of the worst sides of human nature—genocide, beheadings, rape, genital mutilation, sex trafficking, child abuse. With this grim lineup of atrocities, I was falling down a dark rabbit hole, indeed. In this state of mind, perhaps you can relate? I was certain of the utter unlikelihood of any God of goodness or meaning behind the workings of the world.

Suddenly, in my clouded mind's eye, I saw a flash of blue sky open and heard a kind voice saying, "Thou art with me." This I recognized immediately as a line from the 23rd Psalm: "The Lord is my Shepherd; I shall not want…. Yea, though I walk through the valley of the shadow of death: I will fear no evil; for thou art with me…." (King James). In that moment, what I can only call, my faith took flight. My heart softened, tears filled my eyes, and I felt in my bones, not just with my mind, the limitations, the hubris, of my despairing point of view.

Who was I, after all, to make these judgments? We are so small here, our perspective so limited in the face of the cosmos. Trust in life as it is unfolding, no matter what, opens the heart to a deeper truth, to the miracle of grace. My cries of 'no, no, no' to things I do not want, I do not approve of, I cannot tolerate, are only too natural, too human. I protest and I grieve the suffering and cruelty and loss and hatred and betrayal and sickness and death.

But finally, even with the best intentions, I cannot know the purpose of life, of birth and death, of suffering; Nor the results of my or anyone else's actions. It took researching and writing this entire book, devising myriad theories and explanations, then living five years more life for me to arrive at this one hard-earned truth: "I do not know." In awe and wonder, grief and joy, I surrender to the mysteries of life with a keenly felt surrender to this truth. Now, I ask you, isn't this the greatest accomplishment of the mind— this bowing to the tenderness, wisdom and humility of the heart's truth?

To this end, I want to re-dedicate this writing.

September 2018

Preface

I WANT TO SHARE WITH you some of the backdrop for the writing of this book. Primarily, I want to tell you a few things I know about its author that I believe inform these pages. When she came to me three years ago for spiritual direction, Sandra Dennis was already two years into grappling with the traumatic aftereffects of an emotionally devastating abandonment. Because she had been involved in Eastern meditation for many years, it was with some trepidation that she turned to me for help from the Christian tradition. Several dreams and synchronicities concerning the cross, along with spontaneous prayer, had made a strong impression on her.

I was aware right away that she was an intelligent, warm, competent, gifted, and deeply spiritual woman. As I listened to her struggles to reclaim her inner life from pits of grief and despair, it became apparent that she was in the midst of an intense unraveling of all she had believed important and secure in her life. In addition to the loss of this central relationship, her long-time spiritual practices and beliefs that had formerly sustained her were falling away. They either were no longer helping her or were impossible to carry out. Her sense of herself as a kind of spiritual "adept" had all but collapsed in the face of the ongoing pain, confusion, and preoccupation with the loss.

Sandy would laugh if she heard me describe her as a courageous person of deep faith, for so often these past few years she has experienced herself as a terrified, lost soul. Time and again, she questioned her right to suggest anything that hinted at helping anyone else restore lost trust and faith. Yet, I have watched with respectful awe, as over and over she has been willing to engage the paradoxical suffering that emerges when God is so close that the only experience is of utter darkness and aloneness. Like the Desert Mothers of 1,800 years ago, this is a woman who in faith has welcomed the denizens of the shadow world that besieged her.

As we worked together, it struck me how much her experience had the earmarks of a classic "dark night of the soul." The Holy Spirit seemed to be inviting her to sink deeper and deeper into frightening, unknown waters, dissolving all that held her back from the depths of her own being. I witnessed with admiration and reverence as sink she did, in offering and obedience to that invitation. As brave as anyone traveling into a fearsome and inhospitable wilderness, Sandy was rigorous in her willingness to keep going deeper into the truth of her experience, despite the sometimes intense suffering, grief, and disillusionment it entailed. While she felt certain her faith had abandoned her, she yearned for some sign that it had not. I was with her when the time came for intimations of a divine presence to quicken in her soul, and it brought tears of relief and gratitude to her eyes,

I only work with those with whom I feel a deep bond, and so it is with Sandy. I hold her as an *anam cara*, a precious soul friend. Being a spiritual director is an incredible privilege. My work is to witness the many ways in which Spirit comes into people's lives. There are plenty of general maps that can be helpful in charting the ways of God, but they can never fully describe the stunning reality of *this* person on *this* path in *this* moment with the Holy Spirit showing up in *this* way. During the years we have been meeting, I have had the great blessing of sitting in sacred space with a woman facing her demons and receiving the gifts of Spirit with astounding courage and faithfulness.

During our time together, she has been writing *Love and the Mystery of Betrayal* as an inquiry and chronicle of this inner journey. Written straight from her broken-open heart, this well-crafted book is infused with the numinous atmosphere of the time-out-of-time she has been living. As she struggles in these pages to find the meaning and purpose of what seemed utterly meaningless to her, you cannot help but feel her devotion, dedication, and love for the deepest truth she is seeking, whatever that truth may reveal. I feel certain this book will offer great inspiration and encouragement to anyone who is walking the path of heartbreak and betrayal, or any crisis of faith. It galvanizes you with its insight, vulnerability, faith, and with a hard-won humility about the limits of our capacity to understand the deepest mysteries of life, including both suffering and grace.

I was with her, praying, when she hit up against places of existential terror and faced the emptiness of nonexistence. I saw her enter repeatedly into the shame of the betrayal, the terror of losing her sense of competency and control, the anguish of having the most confident trust in the person she loved proved worse than false. Often she was left hanging on her version of the cross as all she considered to be safe and true dissolved before her. Even in this crucifixion of her spirit, in the most intense loneliness and abandonment, she somehow (I believe by the grace of the Holy Spirit) trusted enough to keep going, exploring, sensing into the holiness of each outpost of her suffering. This is why I understand her as a woman of deep faith.

Sandy has been graced with the gift of being able to put into words both the chaos and the preciousness we all carry, but generally keep hidden from ourselves until crisis strikes. She translates feelings, insights and images from the depths into words that point the way in and through what can seem impossibly obscure when life brings us to our knees. While Sandy is an insightful and skilled psychological and spiritual guide—her background comes through brilliantly in her writing—to me her most powerful credential is her passion for and commitment to the truths of inner life

When someone works at this depth, they work not only for themselves; they help to lighten the burden for all of us and clear a way for others to follow. *Love and the Mystery of Betrayal* shines a light in the dark turmoil of betrayal and abandonment that only such a commitment to and love of truth can. As she discovers how grace comes in the midst of suffering, her heart will speak directly to your own, as it has to mine. It will inspire and help you find your way through confusion and loss to the lasting love and trust in God, that invisible Source we all long for.

As I write this preface in June of 2014, Sandy is still engaged in this work. The spiritual process of a dark night of the soul, of the dying of the ego/false self is never easy, but when it is precipitated by such a close personal trauma, it is particularly challenging and can take years to navigate. Sitting with her and the God who loves her was and continues to be a blessed and powerful experience for me. While I have watched her willingness to move into deep and turbulent waters, I have felt the palpable presence of the loving, but also fearsome One who pulled her under. When she was ready to give up hope, that One sustained her and encouraged her to bring back treasures from this underworld journey to offer to those who need encouragement when all seems lost. This book is the result—a chronicle of that sacred descent into the mysteries of the dark light that shines from the heart broken in love.

While I often prayed for it not to be so difficult and protracted an ordeal for her, I believe the Holy Spirit led Sandy into this trial with purpose and caring for those who will benefit from her work. She went with eyes wide open into this nighttime of her soul and shares with us what she found. She has met the beings of luminous darkness that inhabit these shadow realms. I feel privileged that she has introduced many of them to me along the way. Being with her has expanded the capacities of my heart and soul. She will never be the same after this descent into "the mystery of betrayal," loss, and longing. Neither will I.

Ruah Bull, PhD, Spiritual Director
Petaluma, CA,
June 1, 2014

Foreword

*L*OVE AND THE *MYSTERY OF BETRAYAL* has been showered with praise, being described as "courageous, deep, honest, pioneering, superb, heart-centered, authentic, intelligent, triumphant, wise," and more. All are fitting attributes for this outstanding and powerful book, in which Sandra Dennis takes us with her on a descent into the mostly uncharted depths of the psyche that open when a deeply bonded relationship is severed by broken trust.

Specifically, she explores a particular brand of betrayal—those "life-exploding disclosures that break your heart, fracture your world, and threaten to destroy your soul." The betrayal trauma described in this book is not necessarily the result of infidelity, although it often includes unfaithfulness. The trauma is created more subtly, through ongoing deception, hypocrisy and manipulation, and the slow erosion of identity and self-confidence that result, rather than stemming solely from abandonment or infidelity. In a relationship of presumed mutual respect, commitment, and caring, disclosure of deception comes only as the final step in the gradual undermining of the betrayed.

From my own experience, and from my therapeutic work with clients, I can only resonate with Sandra's observations. What others see as an "ordinary" breakup or divorce can hide insidious emotional abuse, which, albeit not always immediately recognizable, amounts to a soul-threatening trauma. Such a shock can erode the quality of a person's life for years to come. The severe attachment rupture from your source of safety, protection and love alone is utterly painful. The loss combined with what she calls the "time-release poison" that floods you as you realize the extent of the deception creates a unique emotional and existential crisis. When we are emerged in such a crisis it feels as if we have fallen into a kind of disaster area, a soulless twilight zone where all we see is devastation.

Accompanying Sandra into this "dark night of the soul," the reader enters the disaster zone of a broken heart, a shattered mind, a mortified identity, and a suffering soul. We join in a journey of reluctant surrender to the generally unrecognized, yet excruciating circumstances of betrayal—from the devastation of breakdown to the grace of breakthrough. Rather than describing the passage through this initiatory ordeal as a theoretician or a detached observer, she speaks with the passion and despair of one abandoned and betrayed by the person she saw as her soul mate and life partner.

To trace the plunge into the abyss is in itself an extraordinary accomplishment. However, Sandra provides much more than a personal chronicle, as we travel with her into the liminal land of the betrayed soul. Research, including up-to-date psychological, neurophysiological, and contemplative/ spiritual references and reflections are interwoven skillfully, offering background knowledge and information about the little understood subject of betrayal trauma. These insights, along with the precision and thoughtfulness of the writing, will help others to connect their body frozen in time to their bewildered, confused and out-of-control mind, which is a vital step in the process of recovery.

Without help, in this liminal twilight zone, the shocking event of the betrayal continues to recur, as it does with any unresolved trauma. It is as if it was happening now, and it is difficult to escape its grip. Caught in this frightening wasteland, you feel as if your soul has taken flight, and you may be losing your mind. On top of the heartbreaking rupture of the attachment, the neurophysiology of rejection causes you to powerlessly crave the person who has hurt you, much as a drug addict craves a drug. The deception, rejection and abandonment combined produce highly charged, conflicting physiological and emotional states. These extreme, primal emotions, including rage, terror, longing, grief and despair are utterly confusing and add to the sense of being lost and out of control.

As Sandra confirms, only those who have been through this soul wreckage can fully comprehend what it can do a person. But it can happen to anyone, no matter how strong, independent or "spiritually advanced" we are. She likens the shock to falling into a dark vortex, an extraordinary state of consciousness where you sense that your soul has been damaged to the core and where you wonder if you will be able to survive, let alone recover.

Nevertheless, and this shines through even the worst times like the light of a candle burning at various strengths, we also find infusions of grace, deep insights and eternal love rising from the suffering. And whilst Sandra reports the full range of feelings she experiences, from murderous rage at the betrayer and at God to primal grief and terror, she also catches glimpses of light, cosmic tenderness and love, and does not hesitate to report on how these glimmers plant the seeds of renewed trust and faith.

In the transformational process she documents, we see how enduring humiliation and suffering can, paradoxically, open a door to the Mystery some of us call God. In our powerlessness and pain, we have an extraordinary chance to find, at last, a true North Star to guide us through the rest of our lives. She suggests, following Rumi, that when the world pushes us to our knees, we are in the perfect position to pray. With that, the primary message of the book emerges fully: Betrayal is a spiritual crisis that breaks us open and takes us down where spiritual forces can reach and guide us home.

For those of us who are spiritual seekers, the experience of being helplessly broken down in order "to wake up" is not at all what we have been hoping for or want. Sandra chronicles her own failures at living up to her expectations. She describes how, despite her spiritual knowing and practice, goals such as getting beyond blame and vengeance, forgiving, "moving on," and rising above the seemingly bottomless pits of rage and despair continually eluded her earnest efforts to be the evolved person she imagined herself to be.

Yet, despite her many failures to "let go and forgive," using her resources of Buddhist mindfulness as well as Christian contemplative practices, depth psychological explorations, shamanic journeying, deep-diving somatic immersion and more, she finds her way. She shows how by being blow apart we are brought to surrender the borrowed self-images our psyche has struggled our entire lives to hold together. Without giving us easy answers—which, as every experienced therapist knows, do not exist when it comes to the deep psyche—this book provides us with a map to help find our way in the dark along this unwelcome, yet ultimately blessed, path to greater authenticity.

Written by someone who is clearly familiar with the dynamics of the inner world, this book speaks from many different perspectives—those of observer, victim, avenger, child, lover, scholar, psychologist, and mystic. Whilst we read, identify and digest the different voices, we begin to viscerally understand how the ego self in its many guises fights the necessary darkness that dissolves its dreams and self-images. We feel how the subtle body of the deeply bonded victim continues to throb and resonate with the betraying partner. And we recognize how betrayal re-opens our earliest wounds to cook up a mental and emotional torture chamber, difficult to imagine for those who have not experienced it.

Anyone going through the trauma, disillusionment and psychic dismemberment of love lost through betrayal can benefit from the soul work shared in this book. In these deep-diving explorations, Sandra Dennis offers validation of the complexity of the human mental/emotional body in a world that requires us increasingly to be emotionally flat, to "keep functioning" and "get on with things," and puts us on medication if we don't succeed. She provides a map and a hand to hold as we move through our own devastation, encouraging us to value our feelings, stay with our confusions, endure the loss of our selves and accept the grace bestowed upon the heroine who has made it through the empty meaninglessness that betrayal and abandonment so often bring.

As I write these last sentences I can see a deer in our garden, reminding me of the fragility of the human heart and the gentleness it requires for thriving. For those who are struggling with the painful, archetypal experience of a current or past betrayal, you have here a book that will help you hold your hurting self with more tenderness and understanding. This book was forged in the fires of the very shame and suffering you may be experiencing yourself. It will help to soothe your broken heart, collect your confused mind and accept with grace the veiled, but loving, spiritual transformation you are undergoing.

For the healers among us, to develop an understanding of the depth of the soul-suffering, to better recover ourselves and to help our clients, friends and families survive the traumatic shock of intimate betrayal, we need to listen to those who have been there. We need more well-documented, direct reports like this one. We have here an important contribution to the development of a modern-day phenomenology of emotional suffering and its transformation we cannot afford to overlook.

Christa Mackinnon, MSc
Psychologist and Teaching Fellow at University of Exeter (UK)
Author of: "Shamanism and Spirituality in Therapeutic Practice"

Introduction

If you have not lived through something, it is not true.—Kabir

I N THE MESSINESS AND IGNORANCE of our humanity we struggle to cope with the demands of being human. We all make mistakes, especially in our closest relationships. Everyone can recall times of disappointment with friends, companions, family members, advisors, teachers, or coworkers when we have felt betrayed or betrayed others or ourselves. We gain self-knowledge and learn to apologize and to forgive as we work through the many ways we let each other down. There are minor, everyday betrayals, and then there are the life-exploding disclosures that I explore in this book, the ones that break your heart, fracture your world, and threaten to destroy your soul. I specifically address betrayal in love—a shattering of trust by the one you have been most intimate with and relied on to protect you from harm.

If you are suffering from an intimate betrayal, you know. Betrayal is stunning. It is mind-boggling. It traumatizes you and upends your life. Mostly, it hurts. Betrayal inflicts a unique, unprecedented pain you can only comprehend once you have experienced it. Interpersonal trauma changes you. It lifts a veil from your eyes, and you can never see the world in the same way again. Yet we live in a culture that is blind to both the depth of wounding and the heart-expanding potential of such a blow.

Before your trust was shattered, you lived shielded from the indescribable pain you feel now that the veil has lifted. Such havoc betrayal wreaks, the multilayered torments of body, mind, and soul are so extreme that it can feel like nothing less than torture. No wonder we tend to turn away, minimize, and bury the hurt. If you are like me, you also do not want anyone to know what is happening to you. It is humiliating and maddening to be in pain, obsessing about someone that has left, deceived, or cheated on you. You can begin to feel like a character in *One Flew over the Cuckoo's Nest*. Friends and family tend to look the other way, too. No one likes to see a person so out of control of their destiny.

I know because I had the veil lifted from my eyes, in a familiar way known to many. The man I loved left me. With virtually no warning, my partner of six years walked out a few weeks before a big wedding we had planned. When he went from "I'll love you forever" one day to "I'm finished with you" the next, it stopped my world. His wholly unanticipated exit from our home and my life led me to suffer more than I believed was humanly possible. At the same time, the distress awakened depths of my heart that took my capacity to love into uncharted territory.

Meanwhile, friends and family advised me to get over it and move on as quickly as possible. They were right, I reasoned, I would move on...I tried, but it was not to be. Once the initial shock lessened, I began to grasp that my trust in life had disappeared. My entire world had suddenly turned hostile, or so it seemed, because of the faithlessness of one person—albeit one very central person, the one I had counted most in the world to be there and care for me. His abrupt about-face marked a cataclysmic divide in my life.

Prior to the moment he walked out, I had considered myself a together, self-aware person. After he left, I was more like a delusional broken heap. I put on a self-assured face, but wandered around like a Swiss cheese, shot full of holes, bewildered, with a secret, stabbing pain in my heart. I vacillated between rage, panic, and bouts of grief. Often I could not stop crying. Falling apart was to be expected—"everybody has been there"—after a tough breakup. But the problem was, as time went on, my condition got worse, not better. Instead of a few weeks or months, it went on for years.

I could not comprehend why I had gone from competent professional to terrified, whimpering child, unable to do much of anything, let alone "move on." It was only later that I realized *this was no ordinary breakup*. Eventually, I realized how deeply I had been traumatized, and that the nightmare of post-traumatic stress had set in.

Mine is not an obvious or sensational horror story of betrayal and abuse. I was not hit, or cheated on, raped or stolen from, yelled at, or bullied into submission, not even abandoned dramatically at the altar. I wrote this book to help show how relational trauma these days is often not obvious. Many of us have become too educated, smooth, or sophisticated for such overt aggression. The damage to my trust and the erosion of the quality of my life came from mind-bending subtleties, primarily half-truths concealed as exceptional honesty: from bouts of seduction and warmth laced with withholding and withdrawal; insincere profusions of praise, affection and loyalty, interspersed with blame and criticism; important omissions of personal history; sexual manipulation masked as the deepest love; systematic devaluation; and finally a complete Jekyll-and-Hyde character reversal. Abandonment and replacement were only the final and most obvious blows to my sanity and stability.

Emotional abuse and mental cruelty can be more damaging than blatant physical abuse because, at least when someone beats you, or cheats on you, it is clearly their problem. When you have a dagger plunged into your heart while being held in a loving embrace, on the other hand, you do not know what hit you. When you are betrayed with charm and a smile, it is stunning and crazy making. If you have given the benefit of the doubt to and believed in your partner, it can take a long time to get the hook out and make sense of your world again. Meanwhile, you wonder if you are fit any longer for human company, or if you should have yourself committed for observation.

As I tried to make sense of what happened, my mind flooded with questions. Perhaps the most painful was, "How could I not have seen this coming?" When you believe in someone so completely and then realize they have been deceiving you about their love and loyalty, the worst thing happens: Your faith in yourself crumbles. The instincts you relied on to perceive and understand your world have misled you, and you do not know how you will ever be able to trust yourself again. It alarmed me when I realized I had lost faith, not only in myself, but also in other people—and, most disturbingly, in life itself.

My heart goes out to you if you are in a similar situation. Perhaps what I share will help you sort through the bewilderment and confusion, regain trust in your own perceptions, and get through the worst. I had lived a lot of life and had a lot of psychological experience and inner resources when this ax fell. If anyone "should" have seen this coming and been prepared when it did, it was I. But I was not at all prepared.

To make it through this ordeal, I turned instinctively to my spiritual practices: mindfulness meditation, inquiry, yoga. I coped by sitting for hours each day, breathing and watching the chaos, tracking sensations, thoughts, and feelings. I was astonished at how much I learned—more, I thought, in two years than I had in the ten previous. As a former college psychology professor, and a teacher at heart, passing on what I learn comes almost as second nature.

I did a lot of research in the effort to understand what I was going through. I read hundreds of books and talked to scores of people. I researched a wide range of subjects and touch on many here—trauma, posttraumatic stress, domestic violence, subtle-body experiences, attachment theory, projection and splitting, death and dying, faith and conscience, grief and forgiveness, Buddhist meditation and Christian contemplation and prayer. I found that prescriptions and advice abound on how to survive the loss of love, to heal from a broken heart, to endure a dark night of the soul, to put your life back together, and to move on after being betrayed or abandoned. But for a long time, I found little that validated my extreme experiences.

Those around me, and even I, considered being abandoned by the person I intended to spend the rest of my life with an unfortunate, but minor event to be swept aside and forgotten, the sooner, the better. After all, people readily recover from far worse things. Conventional wisdom, I discovered, was way off with its clichéd treatment of heartbreak and betrayal as minor blips on the screen of life that you tend to for a while before moving on to better things.

The shame I felt about the depth and duration of the pain, along with the fact my friends, family, and even counselors did not understand, encouraged my silence. The lingering effects on those of us who receive such a shock become a secret we do not want to share with anyone. We even want to hide the life-changing repercussions from ourselves. Amidst my struggle to recover, I recognized that many who had undergone similar experiences had simply shut down. For a time, I feared I would do the same. The continuing torment of having my heart torn out by someone I believed loved me deeply and to whom I had committed my love and life was just too much to bear.

When you hurt this much, instinctively you want to help make it less difficult for anyone else in pain. I never set out to write this book, but once it started pouring out of me, I felt how much I wanted to bring more light to the facts of what an experience like this actually does to a person. There was so much to learn about this underrated trauma—the "most difficult of all woundings," as one author put it. I decided to base this book first on immersion into the lived experience, a type of phenomenological research. I believe this approach led to the emergence of a more nuanced perspective and a deeper understanding than a study based on analysis and theory alone could offer.

The orientation that guided me was to turn with curiosity toward the suffering, rather than stifling the pain or distracting myself. This approach will be familiar to many spiritual seekers and to those who have struggled to come to terms with great loss—the way out is through the darkness. What it takes to make this turn, to go from theory to practice in the midst of prolonged psychological pain, tells an unforeseen story for each of us.

Taken to heart this way, I found betrayal to be an initiation into an unknown self. The shock launches the betrayed on a "night sea journey," that stage in spiritual growth known in mystical traditions as a dark night of the soul. In this mythological descent you are taken suddenly into deep waters and swallowed up by a sea dragon. Like Jonah, you are stripped bare and robbed of what is dearest to your heart. The metaphors of darkness and night apply because you do not know what is happening. You feel as if you must be dying and you are. Some part of your old nature is being shorn away to make way for the new you cannot imagine, and over which you have no control.

Ultimately, we each have to find our own way in the dark, until we are thrown back onto land and the light of day. I share my truth, knowing no one can tell another what it takes to welcome this unwanted journey. It took me years to recover myself, and I fought it all the way, but I finally came to recognize that betrayal and trust form two poles of experience. Apparently, we cannot embrace one until we have drunk deeply of the other. Through destroying my trust, and taking me into more suffering than I had ever known, betrayal catalyzed a transformation inside that awakened qualities of faith, compassion, and love I barely imagined were possible.

During the long days and nights of blame and rage, of tears and staring off into space, beneath my awareness, strange mystic moments penetrated through the pain. These elusive flashes of truth, fleeting at first, but arresting, planted seeds of renewed faith and trust in the ground of my own raw heart. With time, against all instinct, I learned to embrace the humiliation and heartbreak as the terrain I needed to pass through in order to deepen into secrets of a love my soul was hungry to taste.

Never before had I felt such intimate kinship with life around me. Never had my heart beaten in such rhythm with others in pain. Never had I sensed such a fervent need not to harm anyone else with my actions. Never had I felt the vast sadness I had carried in my bones my entire life. Never before had I sensed the touch of the "hands of light" comforting me, or the gentle power of the earth and sky supporting me, or the tender stirrings in my heart of what I could only call divine love flowing toward me.

All this took time, much more than I approved of. Meanwhile I thought the pain would never end. A turning point in my struggles came when I began to question the true source of my torments. One day, in one of those flashes, I intuited that the obvious villain—the person who had hurt me so grievously—had been but an instrument in the hands of an unseen destiny. I realized the peace I needed to make was not with my errant partner, but with my own heart, my fate, my God. The insight came and went, but the truth had touched my core.

While each story of love's betrayal is unique, as are the individuals involved, betrayal is an archetypal experience. It is an event that we each carry in our collective memory, from the moment of being born into this world. Because of its archetypal core, the study of betrayal's dynamics and impact has something to teach us all. If, however, you have been spared the trial of an intimate betrayal, what I describe may not make much sense to you. It may seem extreme, exaggerated, even melodramatic. That would have been the case for me before I passed through this ordeal. I would not have had the slightest interest in a book such as this one. I had no idea.

For this reason, I offer this book primarily, and believe it will be most helpful, for those who have been betrayed, now or in the past, by someone they loved and trusted; and for those wishing to help another navigate these waters. I offer my story and my perspective, along with the results of my research, not as an authority, but as a fellow traveler. I offer companionship, validation, and solace if you are going through this harrowing time. I admit right now that in the extended darkness, I despaired of ever trusting or caring enough to engage life again. While I hoped against hope that the proverbial "pearl of great price" was waiting to be found in the ruins of my torn-up heart, my doubts were grave. I chronicle many of those doubts here.

I can report that finally the *miracle of saying yes* to what I wanted least in my life did take root in my soul. To my surprise, the shattering of my world had magnetized a grace that was teaching me how and what to trust. As I write now, nearly five years later, recovering myself is a work in progress. But I have learned the greatest lesson in my life to date. Deep suffering invites us into mystery: The pain speaks a message we need and long to hear. The rage and yearning are prayers for truth, for love. At the point of utmost brokenness, I did indeed find a golden pearl—the longing cry of my own heart for a love that endures, a greater, divine love that cannot and does not die.

Please let my words resonate with your own experience where and how they will. I know I cannot speak for what anyone else is going through. But I trust that the universal core of this journey into and through the heart broken in love will ring true for many. I wish for you, too, to find your gold.

*   *   *   *   *

This book is divided into four parts, some of which may only be of interest to certain readers. Part I revolves around the shock and shattering of intimate betrayal. In terms of a rite of passage, this section deals primarily with the radical separation from one's past life a traumatic betrayal initiates. Included in this section is the overall narrative of "my story" (chapters 1 and 2) and of my early efforts to cope with the trauma and make sense of what happened. Some may be inclined to skip the story segments. Starting with chapter 3, I discuss the psychological dynamics of betrayal and introduce a number of themes, such as recognizing and coping with the ego-shattering trauma, and the spiritual perspective that will be developed more fully later in the book.

Part II shifts the focus to the mystery of relationship itself. I explore the impact on the subtle body of intimate relationship through the lens both of my husband's death and of the abandonment that impelled me to write this book. This is a section that I imagine will be most accessible to other women. Sexual bonding, wounds to the etheric body, adultery, the role of psychological projection in intimate relating are all considered. This section also includes a discussion of the cultural blindness to betrayal.

Part III focuses directly on the dark night or threshold phase of initiation: the shock and suffering. I begin with an in-depth discussion of the trauma and dive into the details of the dark night passage, including the opening up of earlier trauma, infantile and existential, the unloading of the unconscious, a travelogue through isolation, fear, shame, rage, helplessness, meaninglessness, and more. The spiritual perspective emerges as acceptance of pain becomes a prayer of the heart.

By Part IV the book moves more directly into the shift to the awakening heart that is taking place. I chronicle the grief that pours forth as the deep heart opens, explore the role of conscience, and grapple more fully with forgiveness. The desperation of the dark time leads gradually to surrender, to prayer, to the acceptance of grace and love, and finally I discuss the challenges of the return to ordinary life coming back from the descent. If you are interested in the narrative, read the book from the beginning. Otherwise, please just dip into topics of interest to you.

*   *   *   *   *

Because I write from personal experience, I speak from the perspective of a woman betrayed by a man. I am, of course, aware that women play out this same dynamic with men and other women, and that men betray other men. I have chosen the orientation of a woman speaking to other heterosexual women for the sake of consistency, and because it best reflects what I have lived. I believe that our common humanity transcends gender, and that the descriptions of betrayal as an often unwitting abuse of power on the psychological level, as well as an initiation into the mysteries of heart on the spiritual, will also resonate for those in same-sex relationships and for men betrayed by a woman. That said, please forgive whatever gender bias has slipped into the telling.

I ask your forgiveness also for whatever blame, harshness, or hurt may still accompany my tone with regard to "the betrayer." I have tried my best to restrain the impulse to character assassination, and, I think, have at least partially succeeded: but I have plenty of blind spots, I am sure. Opening to the compassionate heart that can hold it all in love is a work in progress, the work of a lifetime.

Please be forewarned that I often use the word *God* in this writing. I use God to refer to the unknowable mystery that animates our world. Other terms that point to the same indescribable source of life include: Spirit, creator, Christ or Buddha nature, the Divine, Atman, Allah, Holy Spirit, source, Higher Power, Divine Mother, the Tao, the mystery, love, truth, silence, stillness. Maybe these words should all be capitalized to indicate a compelling, alive presence, both independent and yet part of us. Some people by temperament experience this reality as a presence or a being, others as a place, or a state of mind. My inclination is toward the personal. In this writing, they are all pointers—to the living love that surrounds us, the creative source of all that is.

PART I

The Shattering

CHAPTER I

On the Way to the Altar

There are only two or three human stories, and they go on repeating themselves
as fiercely as if they had never happened before.
—Willa Cather

WHEN MY HUSBAND OF twelve years was dying of lymphoma at the age of forty-nine, I stood by his side in sadness and awe. He declined slowly and passed on peacefully. That April morning in our sun-drenched living room, with lucid clarity Dennis left his body.[1] His death changed me in ways I could not have imagined. The first year after losing him, I gave myself over to grieving, as the ache slowly subsided. Still, it took six years before I was ready to move from our country house in a quiet part of Northern California closer to town with our daughter, Rachael, who by then was sixteen.

Through the alchemy of grieving, Dennis became a part of me that I carried forward into my life. Mourning his passing, grief taught me about relationship; grieving taught me about love. His early death parted a curtain to my interior heart and my subtle senses, extending my vision into invisible realms in new ways. I had always intuited the sacredness of marriage, but it took his death to teach me how two souls can intertwine to create something new in the spiritual as well as the physical world. Losing him increased my reverence for marriage as a path to mystery. I was sobered by how much I had taken these sacred ties for granted and how little I had appreciated the inviolability, as well as the vast reach, of "I and Thou."

With time passing, I began to feel stirrings that a new partner might yet come into my life to continue on the path forged with Dennis. Though I missed him, I relished connection and sensed that partnership was central to my purpose. In my heart, I felt his consent, even encouragement, should the right person appear, to engage more fully the call of intimacy. During my years on my own with Rachael, I spent time with a number of men; but I was only ready for companions and friends, not a life partner. I knew more than ever that marriage could not be taken lightly. Even so, I felt ready, excited actually, as my heart began to open to the possibility of a new love, if it was meant to be.

I had been involved in individual and couples inner work for decades. I am a psychologist, an avid researcher of the link between psychological and spiritual life. I have been a seeker after truth and love as far back as I can recall. I dedicated myself to a Gurdjieff-oriented[2] inner work community, starting in my early twenties, where I became a teacher. I have since been a spiritual director, a meditation instructor, a group leader, a nonprofit development director, and a college psychology professor. I wrote my dissertation that became my first book, *Embrace of the Daimon,* about psychological shadow dynamics, and have led various workshops, such as: "Eros and Chaos," "Healing Early Wounds through Relationship," "Partnership and the Mirror of Self." With this background, it seemed natural, and I looked forward to engaging again with an attuned partner as committed as I to the deepening that can come from uniting your life with another's.

I gave myself a year to meet as many men as I could. No euphemism here. I wanted to get to know these people, and sound them out. I was not interested in dating, but was curious to see if anyone would show up in my expanded world that shared my values and seemed to be my match. So I put myself out there, attending gatherings, dances, classes, and workshops. With this openness, I met dozens of men. It was fun to meet new people, but no one appeared with whom I sensed the mutual resonance and shared values that would urge me to commit, deepen, and go forward.

I was only open to someone who shared my intention of life partnership. I knew only too well the profound implications of intimacy. Loving tied you in unfathomable ways to the other person, to their "karma," to their body, heart, and soul. Some people balked at this definitive approach, but for me, after losing Dennis, it made sense.

About six months into my renewed social life, I met Rob at a concert at our local Center for Spiritual Living. We recognized each other from a workshop some years before and decided to meet for tea. The first time we sat down together, about midway in our conversation, tiny bells of resonance rang, and my heart sang a little song, as if she had spotted a long-lost companion from childhood or beyond. It turned out we had a lot in common, and I wondered even then if we might be meant to go forward together. My mind, however, preferred to be reasonable. I still had six months to go in my project to meet new people, so I soldiered on. Within the next couple months, however, it became clear that it made no sense to continue to meet other men while Rob was on the scene. I admitted to myself that, not only had he already captured a special spot in my heart, but we also shared similar interests and the values that were important to me.

We started slowly while he was getting over a short-term relationship that had recently ended, and I was still open to meeting other men. Once we decided to go forward together, however, his pursuit became intense and ardent. Rob was a psychologically attuned man, comfortable with the language of feelings. He attracted me with his insight and frankness about his "wounds" and issues. He exuded a nurturing care, a sensitivity, and an intense interest in me and in building a lasting relationship that reinforced my budding sense that we were meant to be life companions.

Never before had I felt so valued, seen, and understood by another person, nor had I been so capable of appreciating someone else. Sometimes I worried that he was idealizing me, treating me like such a wise, wonderful woman. He could not seem to get enough of me and spent every spare minute at my place. When introducing me to his family and friends, he radiated warmth and poured out superlatives. He was anxious to become "a couple" as quickly as possible, often referring to me as his partner before I was quite ready to take that step.

During the eight months we were seeing each other before we became sexually involved, I often hesitated and trembled before the prospect of being with him. Deepening emotionally and sexually would be a forever step I would only take once I was sure about him. I could not fathom any other way to enter into a relationship at this point in my life. And, he assured me, the same was true for him.

It continually amazed me: The more I got to know Rob, the more we discovered we had in common. We were in sync on so many important matters—or so it seemed. He shared my intentions, interests, and values uncannily often. We both had built our lives around psychological and spiritual work. We both wanted a "conscious relationship," at least, as an ideal: a partnership as a path through which we could uncover and heal our shadow sides and grow more deeply into love. Besides the physical chemistry and emotional resonance, these threads of commonality drew us together. Or so I believed.

We even wrote up detailed agreements articulating our values and intentions. We treated psychological explorations almost like a hobby, a shared interest we enjoyed, like others might play bridge or chess, ride horses, go to concerts, or perfect photography. Our vacations were spent at relationship workshops and retreats: "Love and Intimacy," "Passionate Marriage," "Undefended Love," "The Practice of Honesty," and "Overcoming Anger and Shame," to name a few that come to mind. From nearly the beginning of our time together, we attended couples counseling sessions as a routine part of our lives.

As the relationship grew as the container for our lives, I came to trust Rob more and more. He became my family, my helpmate, and my love, and the surrogate father to my teenage daughter. With my heart's tenderness exposed and softened by Dennis's death, knowing I would be with Rob until one of us died stirred a new depth in me. Eventually, I allowed him into the most receptive, tender, and also the most wounded, places in my psyche, places I had previously shared with no one. Not even with Dennis. In our coming together, I knew I was entering into a great mystery bigger than us both; and our depth of communion proved that true.

From the start of what was to be our frequent and soulful sexual intimacy, Rob spent nearly every night at my home; but it was not until a year or so later that he officially moved in. Since we had spoken so often about how ours was a lifelong partnership, I assumed we would officially marry before he made that move. But Rob demurred. He explained that he wanted to surprise me, "to wait for just the right, special moment" to propose. I admit I was taken aback and could not believe he wanted to propose formally.

I recall being quietly disappointed, but willing to do it his way if going through the old-fashioned motions was that important to him. By this time, we agreed that we were already married in the most important sense. Also, I reasoned that at this stage in life—we were both in our fifties—the legalities did not matter all that much.

When Rob finally did propose, we had been together nearly three years. At that point, I did not see how a legal paper could add to what we already had with each other. With Rob's continued encouragement, we finally agreed to legally marry a year later. I expected we would go down to the courthouse and find a justice of the peace, but Rob insisted that we must have a "real wedding." He wanted the ceremony witnessed by friends. Again, I protested. At this stage of life, after this much time together, did we really need a communal display of our commitment to each other? But he was emphatic. His men's group, in particular, was becoming such an important part of his life that any ceremony would not be meaningful without them.

With some reluctance, I finally gave in and agreed to a public ceremony that would include our circle of family and friends. And that is how we found ourselves in the archetypal vortex of the engaged.

I always harbored a quiet terror and disdain for public displays of such private feelings. Dennis and I had married in a small ceremony at the home of a friend. Even the thought of being the center of attention in such a clichéd yet intimate ritual made my heart pound and my stomach tighten. To make matters worse, somehow our plans escalated until we were lost in hundreds of details of a big destination wedding set nine months out. For two introverts, we were in over our heads from the start.

I fought against nervousness every step of the way. Expressing my love publicly, even sending out a save-the-date note, made me so shaky and vulnerable that I was sometimes scarcely able to talk about it. But, fortunately, Rob took the lead with many details—the photographer, musician, minister, cake tasting and menu selections, the invitations—and that helped calm me down. He bought me an antique engagement ring that I loved. We chartered a dinner cruise on San Francisco Bay, shopped for my dress and his suit and ring, drafted the ceremony, planned the logistics for out-of-town guests, and, finally, agreed on Kauai for a honeymoon.

Despite my barely veiled panic, which came in fits and starts, as we lived our lives in the atmosphere of the engaged, I gradually warmed to the program. I found myself more and more swept up in these details of dress and rings, food and drink, place and time. I noticed how each step I took in making these plans deepened my love and my bond with Rob. Maybe that was one reason it was so scary. When I did something as simple as buy a fancy pair of shoes, I was not just purchasing shoes; I was making a statement of devotion to him, beyond what I knew was even possible.

In spite of my former cynicism, I began to sense a connection to the ancient rite of marriage. I had to admit something bigger than life, something mythic and meaningful surrounding these preparations was drawing me in. Maybe Rob had been right, after all. Making all the arrangements was opening my heart and deepening our connection. Reaching out and inviting my family and closest friends to participate in such a profound ritual of private feelings made me vulnerable in soft, new ways.

As I recognized that we were being drawn into new realms of intimacy, both my tenderness and trepidation grew.

Our wedding had been set for mid-October. In early September, Rob had a surprise for me.

He walked in after work one day with the big news.

"I am *finished with you*," he announced.... He was leaving.

*   *   *   *   *

Seriously?! I did not believe him. It did not add up. I could not imagine that this man who held my heart in his hands, who pledged his life to me in conscious relationship, would walk out on me. With no discussion, no consideration, no apparent concern about me at all? The Rob I knew would never do something like this. I simply could not believe it.

To say I was blindsided is an understatement. During the weeks and months leading up to his exit, our relationship had seemed normal to me, if somewhat strained by all the planning details. The weekend before he walked out, we had traveled to San Francisco to finalize the wedding arrangements. We felt the time away would be good for us. The week before had been tense, the emotional tenor vacillating between playful, intimate connection and strained, hurt feelings brought on by petty conflicts. Just the pressures of the wedding and the growing intimacy taking their toll, I thought off-handedly. Primarily, I was tuned into the growing closeness I felt taking root between us.

I recall a scene at dinner that first night in the city. Rob took my hands across the table and, somewhat uncharacteristically, thanked me for my consideration of his "special needs."

"Sweetie, it means so much to me that you have accommodated to the way I am. I know how difficult it can be because of my sensitivities."

I was touched that he acknowledged me directly for adapting, however imperfectly, to his numerous health concerns. Rob was so endearing on this point that, when he excused himself after this exchange, the woman at the next table leaned over and said, "That was the sweetest thing I've ever heard!" It gave her hope about relationships, she confided. Then she asked how long we had been married, wondering if ours was a new relationship. It made me smile to realize that our mutual caring had reached someone who did not even know us.

Rob and I made our way back to the hotel after dinner and spent the next two hours making love: wild, crazy, tender sex I described in my journal as "the graced, radical drinking in of each other that changes you forever."

"I'm amazed," he whispered to me as we held each other, wrapped in the afterglow. "How can it be possible? I feel closer to you now than I ever have." I felt the same delicious closeness, and fell asleep grateful, held in his protective embrace, my heart full with a rich, warm honey.

The next morning when I emerged from the bathroom, however, I no longer recognized my lover of the night before. Instead, I discovered a scowling Rob, who bore no trace to that tender man, glaring at me.

"What's wrong, honey?"

"Did you use hairspray?" he accused.

"You know I use hairspray every day," I sighed.

"My throat and ears are tickling. I'm starting to get a headache, too, because of your hairspray."

"Are you sure that's the problem? I had the door closed, and it's been at least ten minutes since I used it, only a tiny amount, as usual."

"Look how large that crack is under the door. The spray must have seeped out from there," he said, as his faced darkened into a deeper scowl.

"Hey, give me a break.... My hairspray didn't bother you the entire week we were in Santa Fe, and I was using it in the same room with you every morning."

"I don't believe you are so insensitive to me, Sandy. Don't you even care that I'm having these symptoms, and you caused them?"

Still feeling the connecting glow from the night before, I smiled and said, "I'm sorry you are feeling bad, honey, I really am, but it is *not* my fault."

By this time, I had grown accustomed to Rob's concerns about his health, especially his numerous food and chemical sensitivities. To me he seemed remarkably healthy, so it took a while sometimes to suspend disbelief and to accept his concerns. I rarely saw any outward sign of his allergies, but Rob felt differently. He took at least seventy-five supplements a day to address his worries and routinely scrutinized menus and the labels on most everything for possible offending substances. Anytime he thought a headache, earache, or sniffles were coming on, he became alarmed, searching for the cause, sometimes to the point of near panic. It was not unusual for some behavior of mine to be the suspected culprit.

I had adjusted my cooking and changed my personal and household products, doing my best to avoid the ever-growing list of things Rob had deemed potentially unsafe (once I made a list of more than seventy). Every day for years, as in this instance, I had been using an approved-by-him miniscule amount of hairspray (organic, unscented, no aerosol, hypoallergenic). After a lot of soul searching at the beginning about his anxious preoccupations, I concluded I loved him enough to commit to him. His better qualities made up for all the hassle. But now if a spritz of my hairspray used behind a closed door could threaten to ruin our weekend, as his moodiness about his health often did, I wondered.

It did not bother me much, however; it was still easy to shift my attention back to the intimacy of the night before and recall our warmth and devotion. Considering how close we had been, this hairspray argument seemed silly to me, something I thought would pass away when his mood shifted. But he did not let the incident go, and it made him prone to episodes of sullen withdrawal the rest of the weekend.

Leaving San Francisco, we made a side trip to Los Gatos for an elegant dinner with my parents. By this time, Rob was in good spirits. He laughed and reviewed wedding plans, joking about dancing with my mother. On the drive home, we spent a few hours listening to old songs and selecting music for the wedding. "This is really fun, we should do it more often," he said as we sang along to "Give Yourself to Love," our song, and "Your Song," the one he had chosen for his proposal. By this time, I imagined we were back in sync, that all was well in our world. I still had no sense that he wanted anything but to spend the rest of his life with me. I was obliviously happy just being with him, relieved we were that much closer to pulling off this monumental event.

But two days later, the issue of the hairspray came up again in one of our regular counseling sessions. Rob was unhappy with my "lack of sensitivity," and accused me of not believing how serious his health problems were. Then, testily, he surprised me by demanding: "Do you think I am a hypochondriac?"

This was difficult territory to navigate. From the beginning of our relationship, even with our commitment to openness, his allergies had been a virtually taboo topic of discussion. I thought of it as the black hole in our communication, and did not know what to say that would not upset him. Normally, I walked on eggshells around this topic. Nervous, but encouraged now that he had asked, I hesitated, but finally replied. I shared that often I did question the timing of his worries, and at times felt controlled and blamed for his symptoms. An impatient exchange followed.

His acid tone was so alarming that I asked, "What are you saying? Are you implying you would want to end the relationship over this?" This was the first inkling I had that such a thing could even have been on his mind.

Rob looked me right in the eye and said, "No! I am *not* going anywhere."

Later that evening, however, he came into the bedroom, and with a satisfied smile—as if he had finally solved a perplexing puzzle—delivered this ultimatum. "You have to promise never to use hairspray in a hotel room again, or I won't go through with this wedding."

"What? What are you saying?"

I felt hurt, frustrated…and angry to be put in this double bind. How do you respond to an ultimatum like that and maintain your dignity? You do not. And, how much of this bait-and-switch was I supposed to take?

"Okay then. I give up," I said, throwing up my hands. "Fine with me, if that is what you want, okay, let's cancel the ceremony."

At that moment, I did not want to deal with this craziness anymore. I suppose I was already in shock, in denial, about the situation, still oblivious to what was happening.

"No. No—you have to think about this," Rob snapped. And he stalked out of the room.

The next morning as he readied for work, the storm seemed to have passed. We emailed later about a few details of the hotel and gift list that still needed tending. I calmed down after speaking with a friend, and was still so clueless, I spent eight hours that day on wedding plans. That evening, though, as soon as he walked in the door after work, I could tell he was in a huff. He said sternly, "We need to talk," and directed me into the living room.

He sat down with his arms spread on the back of our beige floral sofa, and with his head cocked peered down at me. Through a set jaw and tight lips, he asked, "Have you decided anything about the hairspray?"

The hairspray? But before I could even open my mouth to reply, Rob morphed into someone I had never seen before. My supposed heart's companion leaned forward with tightly knitted brows and hissed, "I am dissatisfied with you!" In a tone twisted by contempt, he continued, "You are arrogant and have no empathy."

I drew back, and could barely speak. Stunned by his demeanor and caustic pitch more than his words, all I could think was, *who IS this man?*

"You do not meet my needs at all," this stranger-with-Rob's-face went on. "This has been a joyless, conflict-ridden relationship from the start.... I want a divorce from this 'marriage.'"

Still, no words came. I could not stop staring at him curiously.

He could not be serious. All this over some hairspray? I could not believe what I was hearing. Mostly, I was *frightened* by the appearance in my living room of this alien I did not know, impersonating Rob.

Leaning back on the couch, his arms still stretched across the top, he continued, "I have been doing a lot of soul searching." He paused, and then added as if sharing a secret, "Actually, I've been thinking it over for a long time, and I could not come up with a single reason I want to marry you. Except, possibly," his face distorted in a sneer, "personal growth, and that doesn't really matter all that much." He paused, "Besides, my intuition told me you are *bad for my health.*"

I registered that something serious was happening, but his words barely made sense. "Okay...okay," I said, still chirping along, as if we were talking about fixing the car. "We can cancel the wedding, if you want. I was thinking maybe we can just have a party, since so many are coming from far away and have their airline tickets, and we've already paid big deposits everywhere. We can put the whole public, legal marriage question on hold until we sort this out."

"No." Rob was standing now with his hands on his hips, and swirled around to face me directly. "This relationship isn't working for me. *I am finished with you.* I want *out.*"

He had finally hit his mark, stealing my breath away with this precision strike to the heart. Time stopped dead, and the world began to reel. The lamp, paintings, fireplace irons, shelves of books, floor-to-ceiling drapes all swirled around me, like Alice falling down the rabbit hole. Was this really happening?

"But—it was you who wanted this wedding," I stammered, the room still spinning around me. "Don't do this. What about…our life together…?"

"It was all a colossal mistake," said my beloved icily. "It's over."

He turned to walk out of the living room, and then called over his shoulder, "I will be moving out at the end of the month."

I followed him into the bedroom. "Are you kidding? That's a month from now. Please, you can't stay here—not after this!"

He spun around, eyebrows knit again, his voice dripping disdain, "That's my plan. If you don't like it, evict me."

But he backed off. The next day, he was gone.

CHAPTER 2

Entering the Land of Betrayal

So this was betrayal. It was like being left alone in the desert at dusk without
water or warmth. It left your mouth dry and will broken.
It sapped your tears and made you hollow.
—Anna Godbersen, Rumors

I T STILL ASTONISHES ME, even with the benefit of nearly five years of
recovery, that my heart did not stop from the sheer intensity of the shock of
this turnabout. I did not get it for a long time. My circuits jammed whenever
I thought of what happened, which was about every waking minute. I could
not recall ever hurting so much. It was as if a shard of glass was embedded in
my chest. I wanted to cry, to scream, to break everything in sight to make it
all stop.

I felt like I just stepped out of the pages of Dr. Jekyll and Mr. Hyde. I
needed to know what happened and why. I kept asking myself—Who is this
man? How could he do this? How could my friend and lover, my protector
and confidant turn on me and become a frightening stranger overnight? What
had I done to be treated this way? Whatever it was, it must have been horrible.
Whenever I got past blaming myself, I could not stop trying to make sense
of the confusing gap between what he was saying and doing now and what
he said and did then. For a long time, I continued to cope with these jarring
discrepancies by simply not believing he was serious.

I could not take in that he had planned, plotted and calculated his way out
of the relationship, nor that he was seriously gone for good. At first, I thought
I just needed to hunker down for a few weeks until the shock wore off, or
until he came to his senses and realized he had panicked. I trusted that with
his caring and his psychological savvy he would soon realize what had happened. Then I would calmly put my life back together, with or without him.
We would work that out once he had recovered himself and we could talk it
through.

In my mind, I was well equipped to handle whatever I had to go through. I even fancied myself something of an expert on the subject of emotions, love, and relationship. I thought I knew about partnership loss, too. I had survived the death of my husband, had I not? When Dennis and I were drawn to each other, I separated from a committed partner, a marriage in all but legal terms; and Dennis was ending his first marriage. The other partings I had been through, though not easy, had been amicable.

But this ending with Rob was different. When someone you have deeply loved and trusted cuts you off and shifts overnight from loving partner to contemptuous stranger, it is traumatic and terrifying. As time went on, the sudden wrenching apart, along with the shock of his continued personality change and his disdain for me, proved that I understood incredibly little about myself, about him, or about what had happened between us.

My New Companion: Bewilderment

Rob never did "come to his senses," as I imagined he would. Instead, he would hardly speak with me, and when he did, he treated me with disrespect and contempt. As the reality set in, after the denial of the first several weeks, my condition got progressively worse. I did not recognize myself. I, the competent, stable, psychologically astute professional, became practically immobile with anxiety and grief. Bewilderment became my new companion. When people asked me what happened or how I was, I did not know what to say.

Flashbacks of his leaving, as well as our last weeks together, intruded on me day and night, and flooded me with conflicting feelings. I dreamed and obsessed constantly about what had happened, variably crying and raging uncontrollably with no warning. I was on guard day and night. Trying to sleep was a nightmare in itself. I managed only three-to-four hours of sleep a night for months, but strangely was never tired. Often I woke in a panic, as if there were a predator in the room. This seemed wildly irrational to me, and it was, but that did not mean the fear was not real.

To make things worse, Rob did not entirely exit my life. Instead of returning to the town where he lived before moving in with my daughter and me, he moved in with new housemates just a few blocks away. That meant I encountered him often around our small town. Each time I saw him, my chest constricted in pain and I panicked, freezing like the clichéd deer in the headlights. It got so I hardly dared venture outside. I never knew when uncontrollable grief would strike. On those occasions when I did leave the house, and the heartache hit, often it took my breath away. I would hurry back to my car or just stand in place clutching my chest, trying to be inconspicuous with what felt like a knife lodged in my heart. At times—standing in the parking lot before returning my wedding dress to Nordstrom's comes to mind—I worried I might be having a heart attack. I now understood how people could literally die of a broken heart.

Alternatively, I raged. I burned photographs, cards, letters, stuffed animals, and the sheets from our bed; smashed gifts of jewelry with a sledge-hammer; gave away everything he had ever given me; threw darts at his picture; wrote angry letters; and pounded the life out of many pillows. I consoled myself that these were natural reactions to abandonment and humiliation that would soon pass. But, instead of improving with time, the panic, rage, and grief only continued to worsen. Primarily, I could not understand what was happening to me. My body was quick, however, to let me know how serious the situation was. Under normal conditions, I would not have been able to lose even five pounds, but now my weight just kept dropping until I lost twenty-four pounds. When my concerned daughter finally took me out to get new jeans, I too was alarmed: I had dropped from size ten to size two.

Soon enough, the situation degenerated even further when Rob began to show up in extreme happiness with a new lover who lived just blocks away. I would see them walking about holding hands, carrying shopping bags, and I would freeze in my tracks. I could not believe my eyes. It was as if I had been cut out and this new woman pasted into my place.

Now I faced triggers for panic everywhere—tall, thin men; teal-colored cars; car top carriers; wavy, gray hair; any couple; references to Hawaii, the list seemed endless. The entire town was full of reminders of our life together, a life that was not what I had imagined it to be. I shriveled up inside when anyone mentioned words such as relationship, wedding, husband, ring, or pronounced his name—that was the worst. Hearing, or even seeing, his name was a direct a stab to my heart. I told my friends and family, "Please don't use his name." And for years, the man whom I had taken into my body, heart, and soul became he-who-will-not-be-named.

All I wanted in this demented state of mind was for the torment to end. And the most humiliating thing was happening. To my stunned, shattered heart, the only way possible for the pain to stop—unbelievably, under the circumstances—was for Rob to return and end this nightmare. In such confusion and pain, I was desperate for safety and home, and he was that home. All my life I had disdained women who pined after men, especially men who had mistreated them. I had imagined myself above what I judged as such pathetic behavior. Now, here I was, gone way beyond pathetic.

I had entered a netherworld of human life previously closed to me. I had no idea a person could feel such extreme pain, or that a person could change so radically, or that one person could destroy another like this. I did not understand how anyone could bear the anguish. Looking back, in my desperation to make the pain stop, it was a miracle that I did not drive off a cliff, walk in front of traffic, or exact violent revenge on Rob. Now I also understood why some people do these things, anything, to try to cope with the pain.

A colleague who fell apart in a similar situation echoed my feelings when she wrote to me: "This level of destruction happens to 'less developed women,' doesn't it? It happens to weak women, to women who are dependent on men, not to sexually and relationally experienced, professional women who have done work on themselves and are confident and grounded in their lives, right?" She, like me, was stunned at how, despite her imagined independence and strength, she unraveled under the weight of deception and abandonment. So much for delusions of strength, independence, and "development"! Betrayal is a great equalizer, an equal opportunity shock.

I strained to understand why I had lost my bearings, and felt ashamed for being in such misery. To my mind, this desertion seemed so trivial, compared with the serious problems some of my friends were facing. One had a child with cerebral palsy. Another's partner had Alzheimer's. There was a suicide, a leg amputation, and cancers of the breast, prostate, and brain to grieve and cope with. What about the burdens of the untold women whose husbands of twenty years or more had left them for other women, leaving them with debts to pay and children to raise? Not to mention, the unspeakable collective tragedies of genocide, starvation, war, rape, and sex trafficking. I kept telling myself that these other people were dealing with "real" suffering.

And here I was, walking about crazed, like Hamlet's Ophelia, by a minor soap-opera loss. I imagined I knew myself, but now, who had I become? Psychiatrist and spiritual director Gerard May wrote, "Ignorance is not knowing that we do not know."[1] Unnerved by my own ignorance, I still could not get over how I had been so clueless about Rob's state of mind, or become so distraught and desperate now.

A Mindfulness Assignment from Hell

It is easy to keep your equanimity in heaven; can you keep it in hell?—Zen story

I soldiered on. What else was there to do? The extreme pain actually forced me into the here and now as the only possible refuge. Meditation had been part of my life for more than thirty years, so I turned inward instinctively. To help manage both the pain and my crazed mind, I spent four or five hours each day sitting, riveting myself to each moment, as much as I knew how. Like never before, it felt urgent that I not miss a breath. A mixture of mindfulness, inquiry, yoga, and listening to Bach became my support and solace for bearing the pain.

I believe that only my moment-to-moment curiosity and studied interest in what was happening kept me from falling completely apart or taking up some addiction to manage the pain. No matter how bad it got, how much I wanted to numb myself or drown my pain, mindfulness to the sights, sounds, feelings, and sensations of the moment became my most essential survival tool. Much of this book grew from my inquiries into this contained suffering.

I had a near-perfect laboratory for undertaking the study of what I was going through. For the first time in my adult life, I had time and no responsibilities. More than a year before, I had retired early as development director of a nonprofit and was no longer teaching graduate psychology courses. My daughter had left home to go to college, and the breakup had pretty much blown my social world apart. So I did not need to function as most people do.

I had been looking forward to moving to a new home, building my life with Rob, traveling, and pursuing my many interests. Now that I had reached this pinnacle of freedom and happiness in my life, I never expected to have to undertake an assignment from hell, but here it was. While attentiveness helped me cope, and I learned a great deal, it did not stop my disintegration. All I could do was sit helplessly, watch myself collapse, and use up scores of boxes of Kleenex. I wished I had stock in the company. The crying would not stop, sometimes for hours each day.

As the chaos continued, the scientist-observer in me held steady, holding up a frail light to help me approach the situation and study it more closely. My personal journal looked like a nurse's progress notes on a patient in intensive care. How much sleep, exercise, food? How many hours of crying, preoccupation, rage? It seemed crucial to track the dimensions of what I only later came to realize was a massive psychological trauma. My notes took a turn toward a form of automatic writing, as if I were channeling a guardian spirit offering me consolation and advice. I also began writing about my meditations. In a way, it was exciting to have so much new to learn. I felt like an investigator hot on the trail of a disease of unknown origin.

Words Are a Raft When the Mind Is at Sea

Meanwhile, my mind went into overdrive. What was it, I wanted to know, about this event that had cast me into such darkness? Recalling what Goethe said, "Words are a raft when the mind is at sea," I thought that if I could figure it out, I would have a life raft to climb on to ride the waves, instead of drowning in this sea of misery.

Naturally, the first thing I tried to do was to figure out how I had missed Mr. Hyde sleeping in my bed. I realized I had once before seen a glimmer of this contemptuous, strange Rob when, shortly before we moved in together, he stormed off for a few days; but I had brushed it aside as an anomaly. Otherwise, although he was prone to anxious ambivalence, health concerns, and moodiness, after we settled in with each other, he had not expressed major unhappiness with our life. Despite his unpredictable withdrawals and moods, his charming, nurturing, qualities would eventually return to put me at ease.

He never seemed to tire of telling me "I love you," in person, on the phone, in emails, right up until the day before he left. And, blithely, I believed him. Why not? I wanted to believe him. He seemed to care about the relationship and was always wanting to have "check-in" times to see how we were each doing. For the first few years we spent together, he was actually afraid that I would leave him. The agreements we wrote up were primarily to help quell his fears. I assured him over and over again, I would not leave him. Short of some glaring problem like substance addiction, cheating, or battering, I had committed all the way to him.

Thinking back now to my state of mind at the time of his exit, I realize how clueless and naive I was that I was in any danger. I knew he had puer, Peter Pan qualities when I met him; that was part of his charm. He even had this insight about himself and wanted "to work on becoming a man." But in all the years we lived together, not once did he suggest, nor did I entertain a thought, that he would walk out. There were others problems, but not that. I had never been anxious in a relationship about my partner leaving. I did not even know anyone who would do something like this. It was a pattern I did not know, something outside my repertoire.

I could imagine my socially conservative friends and family shaking their heads and saying I was entirely lacking in common sense to consider myself married when there was no legal contract. In my "spiritually sophisticated" Northern California world, however, where we put more emphasis on the "real" relationship than the one dictated by church and state, our unorthodox arrangement was not uncommon. Somehow, in my life I had been spared involvement with any flaky, noncommittal men, as suddenly Rob seemed to be. I simply could not get my head around seeing him this way. I will say again, it contradicted everything I thought I knew about him, so I continued to imagine this was a temporary lapse into madness, and that the "real Rob" would reappear.

I was soon to find out how wrong I was. The roots of his dissatisfaction had apparently been growing for some time. After he left, I learned from him and others that for months he had been speaking to a counselor, to some of his men friends, and to his men's group, and who knows whom else, about my "issues," sharing thoughts about leaving. It seemed several people knew of his concerns and intentions, while I remained in the dark. He had given himself a six-week deadline before the wedding to get out, and that is exactly when he left. As the facts seeped in, I gleaned this was no momentary panic, but a cool, premeditated maneuver.

Even more disturbing, once he left, I was stunned to learn what he was telling people about why. He spread the word that he had to leave in order "to save himself." He claimed that marriage had been entirely my agenda, that he had been guilt-induced and "held hostage" in the relationship by an overbearing, critical, borderline personality—that would be me—who did not respect or understand him, or "meet his needs." He went on to describe himself as a long-suffering codependent, depressed, and potentially suicidal, who absorbed my mistreatment and set aside his own needs to take care of mine until he found the courage to leave. He was the victim! Thus, neatly, the burden of the betrayal was shifted to me. Before I had a chance to get over the shock, his version of events became the "official" one with most of the people we knew.

I was speechless. My traumatized condition after he left only added fuel to his version of events. "Poor, Sandy," he said to people, "isn't it a shame that she's taking it so badly," implying he had been putting up with my unstable behavior all along. His new lover, in one of two brief encounters I had with her, rationalized their quick involvement by confiding in me, as his new best friend, that he had "left the relationship long ago," and never really wanted to marry me in the first place.

He justified one extended conversation he had with me by telling her (and later my daughter) that I was threatening suicide, and he had to calm me down. My jaw dropped when I heard these things. I also learned around this time that he had been in a number of relationships before ours that he had conveniently left off his official relationship resume history. I was slowly discovering he was an actor of uncommon talent, but I did not realize he was such an inventive scriptwriter. Despite all this evidence, I still could not believe what I was hearing. This was not the Rob I knew. Juggling these discrepancies, I was splitting into two personalities myself.

Certainly, we had both been working on our "issues" and relationship challenges. I knew I could be impatient, superior, touchy, stubborn, opinionated, and more. Beneath those traits hid a scared little girl. I was no saint. Although I admit I did think I was pretty cool because I was at least aware of my weaknesses, unlike all those other unconscious people. Oh, well. Who else had I explored my grandiosity and dejection, my faults and craziness, so openly with? Who knew my weaknesses and vulnerabilities as well as he? No one. Only he had that privileged knowledge. Now that he was using it against me, I felt the dagger embedded in my heart turn more deeply.

And what about his supposed commitment to emotional honesty and openness? Why had I not heard about his concerns and unhappiness during our regular check-ins, "honesty" exchanges, or weekly group? Or how about in weekend intensive psychological "processing" workshops, or our weekly counseling sessions devoted to discussing difficulties arising between us? What could possibly account for the huge gap between his actions and words when we were together, even in these settings designed to encourage transparency, and what I was hearing now? Who was the real Rob—the one I thought knew or the one I saw now?

I considered myself to be sensitive, empathic, and intuitive, especially with him. Now his statements to the contrary, as well as this revelation of his true feelings, not only broke my heart, they decimated my dignity, self-confidence, and self-respect. It was as if he had taken perfect aim at both my special gifts and my most vulnerable self that only he knew how to reach.

His abandonment, in one swoop, dealt a lethal blow to my sense of self; it obliterated my past and darkened my future. Yet it forced me into the here and now as the only possible refuge. Being forced to focus on my present experience to survive psychologically gave me a key to the potential soul-releasing powers of the suffering that I will be exploring in depth later as we move along in the book.

In the face of the immediate shock, the inexplicable inconsistencies in Rob's words and behavior, and little or no community support or understanding—no one else had a clue what I was going through—I was down for the count. I trusted and believed in him. In a real way, he was part of me, and I did not want to believe he cared so little or that he could be this calculating or cruel. I could not just abandon the faith I had in him. Clearly, one of us had been living in a make-believe world. I felt more and more like the legendary stranger in a strange land catapulted into an alternative reality where I could barely breathe the alien air. That is, when I was not waiting, expecting any day Rob would come to, recover himself, and return to beg my forgiveness.

WITNESS FOR THE PROSECUTION

Why shouldn't I hate him. He did the worst thing to me that
anyone can do to anyone else. Let them believe they're
loved and wanted and then show them it is all a sham.
—adapted from Agatha Christie

For most of this book, I will be exploring how betrayal can crack a person open to profound healing, spiritual growth, and uncharted depths of heart. But first, to find my voice and establish my ground, I must pay due respect to the personal damage it has done along the way. I do my best, at least in these early chapters, to express how it feels to have been on the elevated side of the seesaw when a committed partner decides to jump off without notice, walks away, and never even glances back to see how you are faring.

Because I had no say in this reality-bending, life-altering event, it is likely that at times in this writing I sound like a witness for the prosecution against Rob, but mostly against what he did. As much as I would like to be a fair witness, reporting only the facts about betrayal, I admit the obvious: I am prejudiced. From the standpoint of human decency, regardless of its potential for psychological and spiritual growth, I believe most betrayal harms and dehumanizes both people involved. It tramples the heart and desecrates the soul. Regardless of the growth that may come from the experience, when deception is involved, as it often is, it knits degradation and despair into the fabric of your being. It assaults your faith in the goodness of life.

Those who betray may believe they have claimed the high ground, saving themselves, getting off with a little guilt and regret and a lot of self-confidence and freedom. But the lingering effects of inflicting so much pain, however unconsciously, must lodge deep in a soul. At the very least, the violence weakens a person's character, encourages self-deception, and reinforces tendencies to abuse power. Meanwhile, those betrayed are abruptly shaken out of their delusions and denial. They, of course, carry the unmistakable load of the suffering—the trauma and shame falls most obviously on them. Ultimately, both suffer.

Moreover, rather than separating two people, as it intends to do, betrayal ironically creates an invisible, corrosive tie between betrayed and betrayer that only wholehearted remorse on one side, and forgiveness on the other, can dissolve. In the atmosphere of denial, resentment, and distrust that betrayal engenders, both these healing ingredients are hard to come by. The lingering impact of unresolved betrayal between two people can infect them both for a very long time and often spreads its poison out to further degrade the social fabric of family, friends, and community. It is like a plague in our culture that has normalized divorce, infidelity, and casual sex.

There is little worse than being turned on cruelly by the one you love and thought loved you. It is deeply traumatic. Suddenly, the world becomes a barren desert; and you feel like a homeless refugee; or like the little match girl in the Hans Christian Andersen tale who is left alone in the cold to freeze to death; or like Persephone, when the ground opened beneath her, and she was abducted into the underworld. You pass beyond the veil that protected you from the terrible terrain of the traumatized soul. Now, you inhabit a parallel universe, where you no longer speak the language of those you knew and no longer understand who or what to rely on to guide you.

Trauma silences a person. It shatters your identity, and along with it, much of what you thought you knew. You tend to be tongue-tied. You do not know what to say about what has happened. The temptation looms to keep silent, to push away the truth, even from yourself. You pray—please, let it not be true. And for a long while, you may not believe it yourself.

In voicing my point of view from the plummeting side of the seesaw, I hope that it helps you recognize and speak your truth. When we are involved in a betrayal, we face a cultural climate that dismisses and downplays our experience. As a betrayed woman, you are already under an unspoken gag order. Anything you say about what has happened, apart from gracious acceptance, is immediately suspect as coming from a "woman scorned," whose sole motive is vengeance for being rejected. If is difficult not to internalize this message and deny your own reality.

But, as any trauma specialist will tell you, facing the facts, claiming your truth, and telling your story is crucial self-care. Not only is it important for one's own recovery, but also to help others find their voice and come out from behind the cultural shackles that silence victims of such emotional abuse with shame. We can help others reclaim themselves, too, by accepting and naming the trauma and pain in ourselves.

Award-winning novelist Jeanette Winterson writes about how important it is after trauma to tell your story and not to remain powerless and silenced by the trauma itself or the offender's denial of what happened: "All of us, when in deep trauma, find we hesitate, we stammer; there are long pauses in our speech. The thing is stuck. We get our language back through the language of others." She affirms when we face what has happened and share our stories, we raise awareness, come out of the fog of denial, not just for ourselves, but for the collective human soul.[2]

> There are so many things we can't say, because they are too painful…Stories are compensatory. The world is unfair, unjust, unknowable, out of control. When we tell a story we exercise control, but in such a way as to leave a gap, an opening. It is a version, but never the final one. And perhaps we hope that the silences will be heard by someone else, and the story can continue, can be retold.[3]

Our stories offer a structure to hang onto, but leave a gap that both betrayed and betrayer can fill with their own experiences. It is my hope that bringing more light to the hidden trauma of betrayal will perhaps help us to less nonchalantly betray and be betrayed. And perhaps, just perhaps, our hearts will more readily open to forgive ourselves our pain, to forgive the betrayer this trespass against our shared humanity, and to forgive the universe for allowing this to happen.

REASSESSING THE LOSS

What I was learning about the effects of betrayal trauma, how it upends a life, was a far cry from what I, and my family and friends, believed was a regretful but minor event, one to be put behind me as quickly as possible with positive attitudes, visualizing happy-times to come, or writing forgiveness letters you never send. Slowly, I recognized that the degree of my distress did not necessarily correlate with the culture's accepted judgments of my circumstances. After much initial self-doubt and blame, I now know that no one else can determine the severity of emotional pain or the impact an event has on us.

They say those who administer torture know the truth that "anyone can be broken" under the right circumstances. No one is immune to psychological shattering and the powerlessness that goes with it. None of us can know what it takes to threaten a person's psychological integrity, to traumatize and break us or anyone else down, although those who know us best intuitively hold these keys to our undoing. How we have learned to rate outer events, regardless of conventional beliefs about their severity, counts far less than the inner experience.

I first encountered this wisdom in a book by Jerry Sittser, a professor of religion who suffered one of the gravest losses imaginable: His mother, wife, and daughter were killed in an automobile accident that he survived. In *A Grace Disguised* he shares how completely he came apart trying to cope with their deaths.[4] After reading scores of books and finding little that helped me,

I finally recognized my desolation in his heart-rending accounts, and knew I was not alone in my pain. Here was a deeply religious man whose faith was thoroughly shaken. My loss seemed incredibly insignificant compared to his, and I did not understand why his story spoke so directly to me, but I will always be grateful to him for sharing the extreme suffering he went through to come to terms with what happened to him.

The despair Sittser endured caused him to make a study of how people handle loss. He pointed out our tendency to mentally calculate "whose loss is worse?" We tend to rate suffering based on the perceived degree of difficulty of the circumstances which is in turn determined by our cultural values. Death or terminal illness of a child or spouse or family member (murder or suicide add to the gravity), life-threatening disease, mental illness, severe accidents, violent crimes, physical or sexual assault are considered some of the worst misfortunes. When we undergo what we commonly consider a severe loss, we are much more likely to acknowledge the grief and despair, forgive ourselves our misery, and receive support from others to cope with the loss.

Everyone perceived Sittser's irreversible losses as catastrophic and devastating. As you might expect, he reports receiving a tremendous amount of encouragement during the darkest days after this tragedy. When my husband died, people consoled me, too: I received cards and letters, phone calls and casseroles, invitations to dinner, flowers and visitors, understanding from coworkers, clerks, even from AT&T customer service. But those to whom Sittser had spoken who had undergone what were considered minor or less-significant losses experienced the opposite; that is, they received little, if any, acknowledgment or support for their pain. He found, however, that the effects of so-called "minor" loss can be equally or even more traumatizing and difficult than those of a conventionally perceived major loss.

Many minor losses, he found, are catastrophic and irrevocable, in the sense that their impact is incalculable and cumulative. In these cases, a person's helplessness and despair intensify because others marginalize the loss and do not understand how seriously it affects them. Losses considered less severe include financial, home, or job losses; unemployment or retirement; crushing disappointments; chronic, low-grade physical or mental illnesses such as fibromyalgia, allergies, eating disorders, life-threatening diagnoses, depression, and addictions; seemingly minor insignificant automobile accidents; and domestic violence, divorce, adultery, abandonment, and betrayal.

His conclusions about minor loss also fit my experience. After I was deserted so publicly, I received only one note of condolence—from Rob's mother, of all people, who commiserated and understood my pain, as she herself had been there with Rob's father. Bless Rachael, my intuitive daughter, also, for insisting, against my protests, on coming home from Chicago to be with me during the worst time. Her loving presence soothed me, and with her help, I got rid of most of my things and moved out of the now psychically toxic place I had shared with Rob. I was also fortunate in having a few friends who stood by me as I came undone; but most people were embarrassed by the situation and quickly changed the subject if it came up. I certainly did not receive any flowers or casseroles!

CHAPTER 3

When Trust Shatters

I, or any mortal at any time, may be utterly mistaken
as to the situation he is really in.
—C. S. Lewis

LOVE AND THE POSSIBILITY OF BETRAYAL go hand in hand. When we entrust someone with our normally guarded, unprotected essence, we grant him or her access to our defenselessness. We lay our heart open when we love someone. We give this part of ourselves only to that person and to no one else, along with a diagram of how to cut most agonizingly into us. You could say, when we love, we give another the power to destroy us...and we trust them not to.

The more we love, the more we trust and let someone into our world, the more we can be hurt by their betrayal. Thus the psychic damage is likely to be greatest where trust is greatest. In the words of James Hillman, Jungian analyst and founder of archetypal psychology, "The greater the love and loyalty, the involvement and commitment, the greater the betrayal."[1] If we have been led step by step into opening up our vulnerabilities and deepening trust, when our partner has been deceiving us about his activities or been insincere about his affections or intentions, we are at high risk for a traumatic shattering of trust.

Betrayal wounds by decimating basic trust. In his book *Love & Betrayal*, couples therapist John Amodeo describes betrayal as the "sudden tearing of the delicate fabric of trust" that has united us with another.[2] The breach of the trust we developed in childhood sets betrayal apart from other major relationship losses such as death or mutual parting. When close personal trauma shatters this foundation of trust upon which we have built our strategies for living, it affects every aspect of life, causing what one researcher called "multilayered, bio-psychosocial distress."[3] Once basic trust shatters, it shakes the foundation of your world with the intensity of an 8.0 magnitude earthquake. Until basic trust is shattered, we do not realize how much we depend upon it or how bereft and disorienting it can feel to be without it.

The shock goes beyond any physical threat and can trigger an ontological crisis; a crisis of being that has far-reaching consequences. You no longer know who you are or why you are here. You think, this cannot be happening to me. Suddenly, you do not know what is important to you or how to live. Trust keeps us wanting to get up in the morning and face the day. When trust curls up and dies, joy and meaning depart, too. Primarily, we lose faith in ourselves. If the one you were most sure cared for you misled you so easily, how can you trust or rely on yourself again, or on anyone else? You feel embarrassed, castigate yourself for not suspecting, and castigate others who knew for not telling you what was going on.

Having your trust shattered alters the quality of your life. It causes the focus on instinctual safety to become exaggerated to protect against further pain. The splintering of core trust is a traumatic make-or-break event, after which we are not the same. This selection from George Eliot's novel *Romola* describes the deterioration of soul life that comes from what she calls the "sinking of high human trust":

> No one who has ever known what it is to lose faith in a fellow man whom he has profoundly loved and reverenced will lightly say that the shock can leave the faith in Invisible Goodness unshaken. With the sinking of high human trust, the dignity of life sinks too; we cease to believe in our own better self, since that also is part of the common nature which is degraded in our thought; and all the finer impulses of the soul are dulled.[4]

"All the finer impulses of the soul are dulled" meant for me that the capacities for joy, faith, compassion, and other qualities that make life worth living take leave of the traumatized soul.

PLUNGED INTO POWERLESSNESS

Where love rules, there is no will to power, and where power predominates,
love is lacking. The one is the shadow of the other.
—C. G. Jung

After Rob left there was one feeling I could not shake: I felt utterly powerless and out of control of my life, like I was falling into a black hole with no bottom. No matter how I tried, and I tried about everything imaginable, I could not escape this sense of helplessness. That my perspective, thoughts, and feelings in response to a situation so important to my life did not matter to him and had zero influence on the outcome left me more debilitated than the abandonment itself. At the time, I thought powerlessness must be my deepest dread—it was excruciating.

As far as I was concerned, for reasons I did not and probably never would understand, Rob had taken all the power in what I had believed was a relationship of mutuality and equal responsibility. He had worked it all out. He knew what he was doing. He weighed his options, considered his future, had his version of events worked out, and made his decisions in light of his desires. On the other hand, his disclosure had upended my reality, erased my past, and brought on a tumultuous crisis with far-reaching damage to my trust in myself and in life. It left me floundering on my own, trying to piece together the puzzling discrepancies.

All the attitude adjustments and healing techniques I tried to change my attitude about this perspective were no match for the anxious helplessness that became the ground of my daily life. I kept wondering why this terrible thing had happened to me. What must I have done to bring it on? As I began to grasp the extent of my brokenness, I also wondered why one person might be unaffected, even strengthened, and another destroyed by such a trial. I found no solutions, but I could not stop asking the questions, looking for an answer, any port in this perfect storm that was dismantling my reality.

The most honest explanation I came up with was that *no one really knows why things happen to us.* I unearthed an abundance of theories—a cornucopia of karma, grace, mercy, evil, the devil, sin, infantile or generational trauma, accident, collective redemption, attachment, projection, repetition compulsion, possession by spirits, to name a few. But they only revealed the confusion we face when trying to understand the apparent randomness of painful events and misfortunes. This randomness, I concluded, applies not only to the inexplicable sorrows of good and bad people alike, but also to whether we are eventually renewed, reduced, or ruined by such experiences. In the larger scheme of things, the scary truth we do not want to admit is: We simply *do not know.*

The other questions I could not help asking revolved around Rob's behavior. Who was this unrecognizable man I had been in close relationship with? Why did he do this? What had I done to him to deserve this cruelty? As I continued to feel like an inhabitant of an alternate universe, I kept struggling to understand how, despite all my effort and caring, I could have missed his abject misery and so utterly misread and misunderstood both him and the relationship we had been living. I believed in blind spots, but this one of mine, I reasoned, must have been legendary in proportions.

The revelation of betrayal I was learning may be slow, stealthy, silent and indirect; or it may dramatically blow you apart. In my case, the discovery was both insidious and dramatic. In retrospect, I realized many self-doubts had already been stirred by the adaptations I had made for him, particularly my efforts to avert blame for his unpredictable allergies, moods and other sensitivities. My discernment and self-respect had been seriously undermined as I tried in vain to meet his ever-increasing requirements to conform myself and our environment to his needs.

Mine was like the story of the live frog dropped in boiling water. If you drop a frog into boiling water, it jumps out right away. However, if you put a frog in a pot of room-temperature water, it feels warm and cozy to him. If you then bring the water very slowly to a boil, the frog will stay in the pot until it dies. The gradual deterioration of a seemingly cozy situation prevented me from realizing the danger. I became more and more willing to go along with my own undoing. Rob's departure with virtually no warning or discussion was the coup de grace of an ongoing betrayal, like his finally deciding to cover the pot of simmering water trapping me inside

Hypocrisy and the Imbalance of Power

One is easily fooled by that which one loves.— Moliere

Thinking it might shed some light on my fall from paradise into this obsessive hell, one evening I picked up Milton's *Paradise Lost*. As I read along, I stopped at the following simple lines, illuminated as if I had been struck by lightning: "*Neither man nor angel can discern / Hypocrisy, the only evil that walks / Invisible.*" In that moment, it began to sink in: Rob's lack of openness, his duplicity with me had been—and continued to be—a profound betrayal.

We betray when we fail to keep our promises and agreements, this was clear. I had done that; I knew how bad it felt to be unable to keep one's word and to hurt another person as a result. What was less obvious and more insidious was how we betray when we act as if we are someone we are not, pretend to feel a way we do not, or play out commitment and loyalty when we are not committed or loyal. In little ways, we all do these things to manage our interactions with others; we are all hypocritical in certain situations, but the stakes skyrocket when that hypocrisy infiltrates love and loyalty.

The situation I had been living with was slowly becoming clear to me, although I still did not want to believe it. I even looked up the word *hypocrite* and found it comes from the Greek for *playacting, coward,* or *dissembling.* Hypocrisy means feigning high principles, and putting on a false show of virtues or beliefs you do not actually accept. Or it can mean a Janus (i.e., two-face), a person who pretends one set of feelings while acting under the influence of another. I realized I had behaved this way in my life at times to get along or try to impress people. Now that I was on the receiving end of this manipulation, I was strongly motivated to bring more awareness to this terrible tendency and to understand what had made me susceptible to its allure. I did not take long to realize that when *someone is telling you what you want to hear*, we are particularly susceptible to believing them, regardless of the facts.

I was coming to appreciate the way meditation teacher Susan Piver described betrayal. She said we are betrayed when promises, overtly spoken or implied by actions, have been broken—without our participation or even knowing a decision was being considered.[6] When the person you trust withholds the truth after having promised to honestly share their thoughts and feelings with you, they create two worlds: theirs—in which they are aware of their opinions, judgments, and struggles concerning you and the relationship—and yours, in which you are not. Letting someone believe something that is not true produces the same result as saying something false: It is the passive version of lying. While this is obvious now, at the time, seeing hypocrisy in action was a revelation to me.

Typically, when we are aware of our dishonesty, we make up various reasons to justify withholding information and deceiving our partner: The truth would hurt them; it would only confuse them and make matters worse; they would not understand; it is not their concern; they do not really care anyway; they might think poorly of us. Or distorting the truth may simply be second nature, a part of our personality that operates almost unconsciously—something we hardly notice, an automatic survival strategy we have learned to uphold our self-images, to get what we want, or to appease or manage others.

If we are aware of our deceptions, it is perhaps most common to imagine that withholding the truth protects the other person from harm, such as when parents conceal adult matters from children. But in every one of these situations there is an implicit imbalance of power and an undermining of trust. If the deception comes to light before its necessity can be explained, the emotional damage to the other person can be extensive, not to mention the way it corrodes one's own integrity. In some cases, the distortions amount to gaslighting, a studied manipulation of the facts that causes the other person to question their sanity.

When I was faced with Rob's fictions, half-truths, and outright denial of what had happened, I began to seriously doubt myself—my memories, perceptions, and emotional stability were suddenly on shaky ground. I was coming to understand that whatever the conscious or unconscious motivation, in realms of intimacy, routine deception, especially when cloaked in the hypocrisy that all is well, hurts everyone involved. In the worst cases, the emotional abuse can destabilize your mind and poison your soul.

It took a while for me to realize how profoundly the power dynamics had already shifted for us before Rob left. His sudden departure only demonstrated the extent of my blindness to what had been going on all along. As the truth became apparent of how much hypocrisy had been woven into the partnership, I began to see that betrayal besets you with powerlessness because so often betrayal is an *abuse of power*.

Hillman offered an explanation that confirmed my conclusions. In making the distinction between conscious and unconscious betrayal, he speaks of "the sage" and "the brute" in each person.

> Certainly a part of love is responsibility; so too is concern, involvement, identification—but perhaps a surer way of telling whether one is closer to the brute or the sage is by looking for love's opposite: power. If betrayal is perpetuated mainly for personal advantage (to get out of a tight spot, to hurt or use, to save one's skin, to gain pleasure, to still a desire or slake a need, to take care of Number One), then one can be sure that love had less the upper hand than did the brute, power.[7]

When we betray "mainly for personal advantage," we use the power to touch into naked vulnerabilities granted to us by our partners, to hurt or otherwise undermine them. Whatever our capacity for empathy, for putting ourselves in the other's shoes, in those moments, it fails us, and we trample something precious in the other. Suddenly, their personhood does not matter anymore. Their thoughts, feelings, wishes, and needs have been discounted, if they have been considered at all, in favor of the needs and wishes of the one who betrays. When the betrayer delivers the blow, it stuns the trusting partner into powerlessness as effectively as hitting them with a two-by-four. There is no defense against this guerrilla attack, little we can say or do, except stagger away before we crumple from the shock.

We all have mad slivers of brutality in our psyche. Mostly we resist acting them out. The temptation to seize power in relationship arises most often in times of unusual stress—unless one is extremely narcissistic or sociopathic. Since narcissism is often involved in betrayal, you may want to take the time to learn more about whether it was a factor in your relationship. I have chosen not to focus on it, but offer suggestions for further study in the endnotes.[8]

For most of us, when we feel threatened or powerless ourselves, grasping for power lurks as an attractive option to manage our distress. Power acts like an addictive drug. It casts a compelling, narcotic spell against our own insecurities. Power gives a jolt of adrenaline that can restore a faltering sense of self and offers an immediate sense of superiority, control, safety, and relief. There are many small ways to overtly or subtly grab power in a relationship:

by demeaning, withholding, ignoring, seducing, triangulating, dominating, playing the victim, criticizing, or withdrawing.

Exercising power over someone else can feel pretty good. When we transfer our own insecurities to the other person and undermine them, we stand a little taller, feel a little more confident and secure. Additionally, by projecting our pain onto our partner, we cause them to feel what we are feeling, and thereby we repress or split off our own distress. In a close relationship, emotional bombs dropped on another's privately revealed vulnerabilities cause intense pain. The other person's pain provides additional proof, a surge of potency, that we are somebody able to make an impact.

We are all subject to temporary empathy collapses and power surges when our primitive instincts (such as lust, fear, rage, hunger, or fatigue) press on us.[9] Normally, our moral compass or conscience alerts us eventually to what has happened, and we try to repair the harm we have done. But with a big betrayal, the offender makes an all-out push to complete an end run around some of the most unbearable feelings a human being can experience, and may not be able to face their pain and what they have done for a long time, if ever.

While both people are hurt in betrayal, for the betrayer, the exercise of power acts like a buzzing steroid drug to mask its corrosiveness. Although abusive power hardens the heart, in the midst of the exhilaration that comes, it can be very hard to recognize the consequences. We do well to pay close attention before we execute the lethal blow of betraying our commitments.

THE DEEPEST RING OF HELL

In the near-paralysis during the first few weeks after Rob left, denial kindly softened the blow and kept the demons at bay. I downplayed the loss as I tried to be upbeat, cover my hurt and humiliation, and carry on, as everyone seemed to expect me to do. I did not realize it at the time, but the shock not only caused me to dissociate, it also opened me to numinous energies that acted like a steroid drug to further mask the pain. People even remarked on how calm I seemed, how well I was doing, taking it all in stride. This temporary enlightened calm I will be discussing later is a common reaction to traumatic loss.

My mother—who barely trusted Rob anyway—came through, consoling me with her usual sense of humor. She asked me for Rob's address so she could "send him a thank-you note" for leaving. But then she paused and added, "You can't let this destroy you." She was onto something, although it took a while before I fully appreciated her warning. Under my gauzy denial, I already suspected this was not a trivial loss that I would get over with a little time and a positive attitude.

The impact was to be far-reaching. I lived with a pain in my chest that ached like an abscessed tooth for eighteen months; waves of uncontrollable grief went on nearly every day for two years; and posttraumatic hypervigilance and obsessiveness plagued me for nearly four years before my nervous system began to calm down. My distress only began to make sense when I started to grasp the extent of the trauma I had undergone.

As I dug further into my research, I was surprised, as well as consoled and validated, by what I learned. I was relieved to learn that the desolation I felt was neither exaggerated nor unique. Others who had been betrayed in love also resorted to extreme statements to describe what they experienced. They characterized betrayal variously as "the most difficult of all woundings," "the most deviant form of attack,"[10] "a wound beyond words,"[11] "an irreparable devaluation,"[12] and "the most underrated traumatic experience."[13] So thoroughly could betrayal destroy a person's life that some went so far as to call betrayal "the greatest evil."[14]

Dante's famous inscription on the gates of hell in *The Inferno* reads, "Abandon hope all ye who enter here." The brokenness and hopelessness that sets in after betrayal can creep up on us for many reasons. The Latin root of the words *betrayal* and *traitor* is *trader,* which means to *hand over, place in the hands of, deliver.* Its derivation helps to understand what happens to the betrayed soul. In this sense, to betray is to "deliver into the hands of an enemy by treachery or fraud in violation of trust." Who is the enemy in an intimate betrayal? We might believe the answer is obvious—the abandoning villain who now harrows and haunts us, of course. But beyond the lover-turned-assailant, betrayal delivers us to a more substantial enemy—an enemy within that lies beneath and beyond our brokenness.

Soon enough we discover that our powerlessness over the betrayal extends beyond our external life to what is happening inside. Trauma shatters our defenses and causes us to lose control of our minds. The reasoning neocortex goes offline, co-opted by the early survival brain, and an influx of unconscious images, feelings, and states of mind come pouring in. That is a highbrow way of saying at times we morph, alternately, into Lizzie Borden, accused axe murderer; Ophelia, who goes mad in *Hamlet*; or Chucky, the evil infant strangler doll. To our civilized personality, these primitive shadow energies—the most reviled and rejected parts of our psyches—feel understandably like *enemies*.

With our more sophisticated defenses crushed, we regress into the most primitive survival strategies. The well-locked basement of the personal, and likely ancestral and collective psyche, blasts open and overruns our conscious intentions. Overwhelming, punishing regions of the psyche—those associated with highly charged feelings of rage and terror—flood our systems and can be deeply distressing. Even though our organism is only trying to protect us from what it perceives as a life-threatening situation, we do not realize this, and cannot believe who we have become. Temporary insanity is not an exaggeration of how this feels. If you have a standard psychological diagnostic manual at hand, you may suddenly believe you are exhibiting symptoms of a wide range of disorders: hysterical, dependent, borderline, schizoid, paranoid, narcissistic, antisocial, obsessive-compulsive, even psychotic. In these states of mind, you believe you now understand why he left you: It is obvious—you are a basket case.

Perhaps this unmitigated distress was what prompted Dante to place betrayal, which he portrayed as fraudulent acts between those who share special bonds of love and trust, in the deepest ring of hell, below even murder. He depicts the betrayers trapped in a frozen sea where they suffer the ultimate pain of hell: isolation from all light, life, and warmth. When I read this, I thought he was describing how it feels *to be betrayed,* then realized, in some profound way, betrayer and betrayed must undergo similar experiences, only the betrayed more readily feels the cold alienation.

While the infliction of this psychological trauma leaves no physical evidence or injury on those who've been betrayed—they may not die, they live on—their faith in living has been so jeopardized they live wishing they could die. Suicide is as much a state of mind as an action. If the pain is great enough, something in you decides that dying is a better fate than enduring the torments of betrayal and you shut down inside. You make yourself sick or fall into addictions or other self-destructive behaviors, or simply resign yourself to go on living like one of the walking dead. Betrayal is no trivial matter, and needs our attention and care to avoid falling prey to its corrosive impact on the soul.

"Two Sides to Every Story"

Not surprisingly, Rob balked when I told him I felt betrayed. He let me know this interpretation was strictly my problem. He saw my professed pain as high drama designed to make him feel guilty. He did not then, and has not since, seen his departure as anything but his right—a wholly conscious choice, a soulful, inspired decision on his part to save himself and escape a dangerous, oppressive situation. He liked to call himself "the initiator." He accused me of exaggerating my pain and of not accepting responsibility for provoking him. He said, "Everyone knows that all breakups are 50/50."

Rob was a New Age "sensitive man" who specialized in intricate, feeling-laced psychological explanations for his behavior. For a woman like myself, this style of relating is one of the most compelling covers for control and manipulation you can imagine. Rob liked to gaze into my eyes and put his hand on his heart, as if deeply moved by things I said or did. These qualities of emotional sensitivity and openness that had attracted me as unusual strengths in a man, turned out to be disarming acting devices in a considerable arsenal he may not have even realized (I like to believe) he was using to manage me.

In a rare conversation some weeks after he left, he told me that it took a "strong man with big shoulders" (tapping his shoulders) to leave. He confessed that during the entire relationship he had been "behaving as a boy" out of guilt due to his "mother wound." Only now was he "grounded" and "being a man" by standing up to me and following his intuition of what was best for him. As you can imagine, I had trouble accepting his explanations. A strong man would never inflict such humiliation and hurt on the woman he professed days before to love and partner for the rest of his life—except in a moment of panic and rage, right?

Nursing my heartache, I still made an effort to follow Rob's line of reasoning, but the pieces did not fit together. I agreed that a higher soul calling could, at times, lead to a betrayal of one's commitments. A partnership or marriage may conceivably need to break apart. Dissolving such a union would most always be harrowing and difficult, but a "conscious relationship" would not end in a one-sided, off-handed way like this, would it? We were not teenagers anymore and knew better than to make big decisions based on momentary feelings, did we not? Early on, Rob and I had explicitly agreed in our written commitments that neither of us would blindside the other this way. I had not been abandoned before, but he had been, and he wanted assurances it would not happen again.

That agreement added to my disbelief that his leaving was for real. But when I asked him about it, he emailed a reply: "Sorry I couldn't keep the agreement." He went on to explain that it was a mistake to have made the agreement in the first place. Rob had a habit of basing his decisions on the opinions of authority figures. True to form, he shared that his counselor had assured him that such an agreement was unrealistic and could never have worked anyway, since in her experience couples almost never agree to separate. I thought to myself, "At least not those who show up in her office!"[15] He said it was just another way I had guilt-tripped and entrapped him. Interpreting this as betrayal was, unfortunately, my problem, and there was nothing he could do about that.

I will admit I was like a pit bull with regard to this commitment to mutuality. For a long time, finding reciprocal ground in the decision to part was the one thing for which I held out hope against the abyss of bewilderment and powerlessness I felt. While I knew I needed to find a way to recover myself no matter what he said or did, I could not let go of the idea that it was a "missed step" in what had happened between us. Communication was the cornerstone of everything we stood for. Not only did I want to understand his perspective, I was confident we could negotiate an agreement we would both accept if we were willing to pause and step back from our positions—his to leave and mine to weigh the other options. For a long time, I could see no other way to reconcile myself with the abrupt one-sidedness that made no sense to me, given our values and who I believed we were.

In the early weeks, and even years after we separated, I several times asked Rob to enter into this conversation. If we could at least share our perspectives with each other, I imagined it would help restore a shred of personal dignity and clear the painful field of resentment and indifference between us. Nevertheless, after he eliminated me from his life, it was not something he was ever willing to do, except for show or in sound bites. He claimed he was too busy or that it was "too hard" to revisit what happened; he had other priorities now.

After he walked out, I set myself up for a one-two punch every time I tried to interact with him. I longed for reconciliation or closure and felt like Odysseus tied to the mast to resist the Siren's song, but 99 percent of the time I restrained myself from interacting with him. The other 1 percent, maybe five or six times in five years that I gave in and had an exchange with him, I was retraumatized, and it took me weeks to recover. One time the anxiety from his crazy-making words and actions resulted in four days of intermittent vomiting to get the poison out of my system. I understood the advice to have no contact with someone who leaves you in this way. If you can do it, you will save yourself a lot of disrespect and additional heartache. But I also understand how very difficult it is without their help to make the massive shift in your reality required to: 1) assimilate who they have become, 2) realize the lies you have been living, and 3) rebuild your shattered identity.

As much as his sudden manner of leaving dismayed me, the way he cut me off and treated me afterward with contempt and indifference broke me most of all. It showed me how much of a sham our friendship and "conscious relationship" had been. As much as I did not want to believe it, it showed me I had given my heart to someone polished and practiced in award-level performances as best romantic lead who now could no longer be bothered to keep up the act. Except for hit-and-run contacts between his series of new lovers, he hardly had the time of day for me, and avoided me if we did encounter each other. For years, I struggled with the trauma, frustration, and powerlessness of being summarily dismissed by the person to whom I had given my love and who I believed was equally devoted to me. I was left on my own to wonder what I had done and what had happened to the man to whom I had pledged my life.

CHAPTER 4

Falling Apart

*Trauma changes you. It's like a veil is lifted from your eyes
whereby you see the world differently*
—Deanna Doss Shrodes

FOR A LONG TIME, I could not figure out why, against my best efforts,
images of Rob's departure scene unnerved me day and night. I kept hearing his voice saturated with contempt, "I am dissatisfied with you,"..."I want a divorce,"..."bad for my health,"..."colossal mistake." I kept seeing his arms stretched along the back of the sofa. I kept wincing at the memory of the slight smile on his face as he nonchalantly delivered the blow. Each replay threw my system into turmoil, like a nightmare that dogged me everywhere I went. It was also as if I had been struck down suddenly with a debilitating disease of unknown origin—the voices in my head, the constant anxiety, the ache in my chest, the dizziness and disorientation. No matter what I did, and I tried many things, I could not stop this horror story from playing over and over in my mind. Later, I found out how the neurophysiology of shock contributes to these intrusive replays, but for the longest time I asked myself, "Why can't I shake this?"

I also experienced unprecedented loneliness. As a Type-A personality, loneliness was new territory for me. I had always been busy with friends and family, plans and projects; lucky me, never before in my life had I faced feeling either lonely or despairing. I was the oldest of three sisters, all close in age; I went from family to college to a spiritual community, then to marriage and my own family. Loneliness? What was loneliness? Who knew I had lived such a charmed and easy life? (Or that I was so well defended?)

It was not that I had not experienced trauma before. I had bounced back from muggings in New York City, a knife-bearing intruder in my bedroom, a miscarriage, two serious car accidents, violence in my family, betrayal by a spiritual teacher, the deaths of my grandparents, and, of course, losing my husband—but nothing was like this. I had engaged these losses over the years through regular somatic healing work and experienced few residual symptoms. Believing I was one of those resilient people who faces the pain and picks themselves up from loss, I could not understand why I felt trapped now in a torture chamber of obsession, pain, and loneliness I could hardly endure over the ridiculous loss of a man.

I finally had to admit to myself I was in new territory. Far from certain that I could live through this and emerge intact, I recall the moment, sitting in my living room staring blankly at the maidenhair fern in the window, when it hit me—*so this is what it is like to fall apart.*

The first order of business after betrayal is to recognize and to treat what is likely the most severe trauma of your life. We cannot take care of ourselves without a proper diagnosis. Normally, we reserve the term "trauma" for what we believe are more severe, life-threatening experiences than betrayal or abandonment. Everyone will agree being "dumped" is humiliating, disappointing, enraging, and heartbreaking, yes. We are expected, however, to pick ourselves up after a few weeks or months at the most, brush ourselves off, and get going again. Thankfully, in the past twenty years, with the help of neuroscience, we are beginning to crack through the cultural denial of the emotional pain and psychological trauma involved in such a serious breach of trust.

Human beings are delicate creatures. We become traumatized when we feel that our life is under threat—physically, psychologically, or both. The terror and helplessness overwhelm our survival instincts.[1] Any situation that violates our sense of safety and justice, any experience that we feel overcome by, that leaves us helpless and powerless to go on as before—in short, any experience that makes us unable to bear reality—qualifies as a trauma.[2] An injury to our psychological integrity can threaten and traumatize us as much, if not more, than damage to the physical body. Most often, an egregious betrayal is traumatizing. In many cases, it is emotionally violent. The life of your soul, if not your body, is at risk. Betrayal trauma is serious business that can *radically change the quality of your life*, especially if the damage goes unrecognized.

When a person is traumatized, they vacillate between the extremes of arousal, panic, and rage; and numbness, exhaustion, and passivity. They do not ever feel relaxed or at ease. Their body seems to have turned against them and can make them feel completely out of control. With the sense of safety and agency gone, they tend to isolate themselves for protection and inhabit a world of agitation, loneliness, insecurity, and unpredictability. If you are caught in this cycle, you cannot help asking, "What is wrong with me?" when the more appropriate question is "What happened to me?"

While trauma is ultimately a subjective experience—the same event can traumatize one person and not another—certain stressors increase the chance of trauma for anyone.[3] According to Judith Herman, MD, in her classic study of trauma victims, *Trauma and Recovery,* the most complicated and chronic traumas occur when someone you trust and on whom you depend deliberately hurts you. "The damage to the survivor's faith and sense of community is particularly severe when the traumatic events themselves involve the betrayal of important relationships."[4] Interpersonal traumas cut to the core. She goes on to explain how when events are sudden, unpredictable, emotionally or physically violent, or rupture close attachments, they increase the risk of trauma exponentially.[5]

We know the emotional pain of betrayal is indescribable and far-reaching. But, I, like most people, was not previously aware that the brain does not differentiate between physical and emotional or psychic, pain. With the help of MRI studies, we now know that heartbreak and rejection register in the brain as life-threatening dangers. A broken heart lights up the *same brain centers as physical pain* and produces similar sensations.

In response to the perceived ongoing danger, the instinctual brain hijacks consciousness, overruns higher brain functions, and compromises your capacity for intimacy of any kind. The nervous system, in an overzealous effort to protect us from this hurt ever happening again, goes on twenty-four-hour alert, and we start to scan every person and situation for possible danger. "Traumatized people feel utterly abandoned, utterly alone, cast out of the human and divine systems of care and protection that sustain life. Thereafter, a sense of alienation, of disconnection, pervades every relationship, from the most intimate familial bonds to the most abstract affiliations of community and religion. When trust is lost, traumatized people feel that they belong more to the dead than to the living."[6] Now at least I understood how the isolation and loneliness had set in.

Intimate betrayal adds a complicating factor to the broken heart of any attachment loss. In addition to the pain regions of the brain, rejection stimulates another area of the brain, this one associated with addictive compulsions. Can you believe it? So important is attachment to our survival, our neurophysiology generates a visceral craving for your former mate.[7] Thus betrayal tosses you into a crossfire of love and fear, longing and rage. The disparate messages of these two brain centers whip up a biochemical torrent with their conflicting impulses and emotions that throws the nervous system into pandemonium.

As we shall see, unrecognized interpersonal trauma plays a big role in the dynamics of betrayal. I devote an entire chapter (11) to the subject. For now,

I will say, the more I learned, the more I appreciated the suffering invisible trauma can create. When our love attachment, trust, and former identity are crushed by shock, and the brain interprets the loss as a threat to survival, it causes unbelievable distress. In the words of analyst Diane Courineau Brutsche, "One should not underestimate the courage it takes to heal from a human betrayal. Betrayal invariably affects the psyche to its deepest roots. When it is made conscious, it is experienced as a threat to one's own being, and the path toward healing is paved with pain."[8]

With all I was experiencing and learning in my research and talking with other people, I was coming to some harsh conclusions. I was coming to consider betrayal, however unintentional, a *moral violation of another's humanity*—akin to torture. While characterizing betrayal as a moral crime similar to torture may sound biased and extreme, the description not only captures the subjective experience, it corresponds to what happens to you biochemically. Ginette Paris, a psychotherapist and professor of psychology specializing in neurobiology, used similar language in her study of heartbreak. "The psychic pain of mourning and heartbreak is truly unbearable, with all the neurobiological evidence of a stress similar to being submitted to torture."[9] If you are reeling from a senseless betrayal, you do not need science to tell you about the anguish, the crazed desperation you feel for it to stop, but it helped me to know, at least, it was not "all in my head."

Time Freezes at the Great Divide

The most poignant complaint of the trauma victim is the loss of the sense of "who I was," and "who I am now."
—Robert Scaer, MD

Traumatic events change you. They stop the flow of your life. Trauma stops time from moving forward and shrinks your world to the size of a postage stamp. To better recognize what has happened to you, think of the instant you realize you are going to be in a serious car crash. Your brain wakes from its usual state of being lost in thought and becomes hyper-alert. Suddenly, you are catapulted into "the now." You enter into Matrix-like slow-motion time, and the event imprints every detail on your nervous system with uncommon accuracy and intensity. This extremely heightened incident becomes the centerpiece of the psyche, and you lose your ability to take in whatever else is happening to you in ordinary consciousness. Until it is treated, and you realize the danger has passed, the nervous system keeps replaying the scenes of the shock.[10] It is as if time stops; life goes on hold right there, freezing at the moment of the trauma. *And the event becomes the great divide in your life.*[11]

Freezing at the moment of trauma is the natural response to the helplessness we feel when we cannot fight off or flee from danger. The shock imprints deeply in memory what you felt at that moment, and your identity solidifies around the scene. The event becomes an *idée fixe*; that is, you become fixated on the circumstances, and the trauma plays over and over, as if the shock is occurring again in present time. Your nervous system goes into a state of constant arousal, as if you are in continual danger.

In the case of a recognized, one-time trauma, the immediate shock reaction tends to lessen with time. Ordinarily, the reasoning brain comes back online and determines that the danger has passed, in which case a person eventually returns to normal functioning. Whenever a traumatic event goes unrecognized and untreated, however, as commonly happens with betrayal or abandonment, posttraumatic stress disorder (PTSD) is likely to set in—weeks, months, even years later.

PTSD is a mental/emotional/spiritual syndrome, a severe anxiety disorder that involves structural changes in the brain. Trauma turns on the body's alarm systems, and if it is not treated, they never really turn off. To never be able to relax, to live in constant arousal is a highly aversive, tormenting state. The damage interferes with memory and emotions and the ability to assess danger accurately. The upshot is an inability to concentrate, think clearly, or function normally. Besides the physical and emotional distress, PTSD is also a moral injury that disrupts spiritual life. The loss of faith and anger at God the pain brings on drains the meaning and joy from life.

If you feel like you are losing your bearings after betrayal, it is because, in a way, you are. In this condition, regardless of what the rational mind says, there is no resolution, no return to normal. You are no longer who you were. Suffering with unrecognized PTSD, a person can spend months, years, even a lifetime fixated on the traumatic event or harmful person. Much of this book grew out of my attempts to live with and recover from the multi-layered impact of PTSD.

In my research, I encountered a number of people who were still ruminating on a betrayal from ten, twenty, even thirty years before. I recall one particular woman whose husband had left her thirty years earlier and who had disappeared completely from her life. When she realized what I had been through, she shyly admitted that she has continued to think of him and what happened every single day since he left. For myself, when the betrayal scenes were triggered, even years later, I could morph from being a friendly, functioning adult into a shaky, panicked victim in an instant.

People who have not experienced the insidious results of shattered trust shake their heads and have no way to explain what looks like your volatility, withdrawal, and apparent loss of contact with reality. The primary defense to the lack of understanding is either to shut down inside or to hide your symptoms from everyone. Because our culture does not acknowledge betrayal as a trauma, it will be up to you to recognize if you are living with PTSD symptoms. Do not let our ignorance about the trauma, or your own shame, discourage you from persevering in taking care of yourself. What looks like "moving on" after betrayal is often closing down. We are at much higher risk of not fully recovering our lives if we sweep the symptoms under the rug.

The Risks of Falling Back

Betrayal immerses a person in such isolation and suffering, if we do not get the help we need, the chance of not recovering is high. In grappling with the trauma, we stand the risk of falling back, of giving up, of having the capacity to trust permanently injured, and shrinking into a smaller life. There is no guarantee that we will not stay stuck in the defensive bitterness, resentment, frustrated longing, or go into denial; and there is no timetable for how long it takes to grieve and recover from the wounds.

As I talked to others, I learned that many people never get beyond a serious betrayal. Their lives are scarred by the wound; their hearts permanently closed down. The price of intimacy is too high. Some withdraw from relationships altogether; others survive by hiding their pain and moving into new relationships—only to be left again. Or they inflate defensively with a power drive and become abusers and abandoners themselves, unwittingly perpetuating the cycle of violence. Others develop compulsions, addictions, eating disorders, allergies, migraines or other chronic illness; some engage in other risky, self-destructive behaviors, such as gambling or unsafe sex. In extreme cases, a person may succumb to despair, actually dying of a broken heart or a health crisis initiated by the betrayal; some commit suicide. Even with the best outcome, the betrayed must endure many trials to cope with this underrated trauma.

Realizing how deeply you have been traumatized can help you to be on the alert for the symptoms, better understand what is causing the distress, and motivate you to get the help you need. It will require the best attention and support you can find to recover and to turn the traumatic aftermath of betrayal to your advantage. For working through trauma, it helps tremendously to have the company of another person you can trust. One needs support to face the vulnerability, heightened defenses, and, especially, the pain. Monitor your symptoms, and if it feels right, seek professional help to get your mind and body back. On that calmer ground, the deep healing your soul is calling for can begin. It takes a lot of support and courage to recognize and to recover from a serious betrayal in a culture that downplays and dismisses what has happened to you.

CULTURAL DENIAL: SECONDARY TRAUMA

The psychological trauma of betrayal takes place in the world of private, interpersonal interactions. In the eyes of family and friends, such betrayals are difficult to assess, as they pit the word of one person against that of another, much like domestic violence, or date or marital rape. As a betrayed woman, you are up against several prejudices and stereotypes that can amount to a secondary trauma that I will address in more detail later.

As much as we do not like to admit it, in this culture we are still steeped in patriarchal values of power and control. Our society dismisses emotional pain; at the same time it enables, colludes with, and rewards the powerful while devaluing the powerless victim. It makes us uneasy when it looks as if someone lacks control over their destiny, as victims of betrayal or any trauma do. We cast about for explanations to reassure ourselves it could never happen to us. We find reasons the victim must have had a hand in the situation: "You must have seen it coming," "You chose him, after all," "It always takes two," "How did you provoke him?" "You must be reliving a childhood trauma to be so upset"—come to mind as common responses.

To counter these prejudices and preconceptions, I de-emphasize individual "susceptibility" to trauma as a factor in this discussion of the impact of betrayal. Additionally, according to Herman, "The most powerful determinant of psychological harm is the character of the traumatic event itself. Individual characteristics count for little in the face of overwhelming events."[12] With our culture's tendency to revere power, disregard emotional abuse, and blame its victims, you will be told otherwise.

After being asked by concerned friends how I was doing, I cannot tell you how many times I heard from these well-meaning people the conversation stopping, "There are two sides to every story, you know." Most commonly, others are likely to explain away your intense reactions by pointing to your personality weaknesses, upbringing, wrong attitudes and beliefs, or traumatic past history. What has happened to you is quietly brushed aside, and you become the problem.

Due to the tendency to unconsciously blame the victim of any misfortune, one of the most important things to keep telling yourself when you have been betrayed is that it is not your fault. You will also be working against powerful inner forces telling you otherwise. Rejection by the one who knew you best is virtually guaranteed to cause you to feel unloved and unworthy, and to blame yourself for what happened—especially if you already harbor doubts about your value as a person. And who does not? The mind needs to make sense of the situation, and the first line of defense is often to believe you must have done something terribly wrong, or that there is something intrinsically wrong with you to be treated this way.

There is something wrong: You have been traumatized and are likely experiencing post-traumatic stress, a debilitating anxiety disorder! I want to underline that the madness and brokenness you feel now is a direct result of how you were treated. Yes, you have your issues and problems, and a trauma history—we all do. Yes, this shattering will excavate and expose your inner life like little else ever has, and your past pain will play a role in the arc of your recovery. But you did not cause this to happen. Any beliefs that tell you that you did will not serve you at this time. This is not the time to apply the New Age idea that "you create your own reality" or that it is your interpretation or attachment to suffering that is causing your pain. Nor is it the time to blame yourself with the heavy concepts of karma or sin. Now is the time to anchor your dissociated soul with down-to-earth facts.

When someone plants love in your heart, lures you into trusting them with your deepest vulnerabilities, and sexually and emotionally bonds with you, then walks away as if you do not exist, it inflicts a massive psycho-spiritual trauma. It sets up a biochemical torture chamber that puts you on the rack between longing and terror, eats you alive inside, and paralyzes your soul. You will be tempted to believe these reactions are because your betrayer is so special, or because you are so unstable and disturbed. However, the truth is that the trauma is a biological, instinctual reaction to having a deep attachment torn apart in a way that reveals your reality was a sham.

You have every right to feel like a wreck. Discovering that you have been living a lie shatters your life the way a hammer shatters glass. To have no one validate that truth isolates and further destabilizes you. If you step back and look at the situation, past the natural denial that comes to protect you from the pain, you will see. The person who holds the deepest emotional significance in your past, present, and future; the one you so recently lived with, slept with, had sex with; the man with whom you shared your most intimate secrets, your finances, your family, your world, has turned suddenly against you for reasons unknown to you, and into someone you no longer recognize.

No wonder we look away, accuse ourselves, and do not want to accept the facts of what has happened. We are hardwired to deny the unbearable truths of betrayal until we have the strength to tolerate them. Once we are ready, however, facing the facts is what will bring on forces of regeneration and renewal we hardly knew existed. That is what working through trauma is all about.

"My Soul Went With Him"

I do not need to tell you that betrayal stirs deep forces in your soul. By soul I mean the invisible aspect of Spirit, the animating, creative force that inhabits all things, including our physical bodies, and expresses our specific essence. Soul links the body with the Spirit. It also connects us with one another through the medium of the subtle energetic senses I explore in part II.

One way to understand growth in soul life is the drive to *individuate*. Individuation is a Jungian term that describes becoming more authentic, whole, or who we are meant to be. We individuate by incarnating our potential; that is, we bring our individual spark or soul into the body through living fully our unique set of life experiences. An acorn has the potential to become an oak tree, but not every acorn will grow into a tree. From this perspective, the more we individuate, the more we realize our purpose, the more authentic we become, and the closer we grow to the mystery at the heart of our existence.

Trauma, you might say, causes the acorn shell to crack open. The fragmenting may lead to germination and growth or not. That is one reason I consider betrayal to be a make-or-break event. The shattering causes parts of the incarnating soul to go underground and become inaccessible to us. In other words, *trauma causes soul loss.* When we are overwhelmed, we split off from the hurt and dissociate. Some traditions, such as shamanism and, more recently, depth psychology, describe dissociation as soul loss. Shamanic healer Sandra Ingerman explains that "whenever we experience trauma, a part of our vital essence (or soul) separates from us in order to survive the experience by escaping the full impact of the pain."[13]

In the indigenous worldview, we need to take the steep path down into the subtle body realities of the traumatized psyche to recover more of our lost soul. We are all dissociated to some extent from the start, due to early traumas and frustrations, and possibly simply as part of the human condition. Once the wounded self goes into protective hiding, it is highly resistant to coming back into life. If we do not recognize the danger and take steps to recover our soul forces, betrayal threatens us with a diminished, constricted life. But betrayal also invites us to enter into the mystery of the wound to discover new depths of heart and soul.

Another way to understand facing and working through trauma is that we are coaxing lost pieces of our soul back to life. For this, we will likely need help. Christa Mackinnon, in her much-needed work *Shamanism and Spirituality in Therapeutic Practice*, discusses soul loss as a spiritual illness and encourages the incorporation of shamanic practices into psychotherapy. Work like hers demonstrates that more therapists are recognizing the crucial importance of a spiritual container for healing significant trauma, making it easier to find someone who can understand and help you.[14]

Shamanic traditions also speak of *soul theft* as another way we may experience the loss of our finer soul qualities after close personal trauma. Soul theft occurs when one person takes soul force or power from another. In the altered state brought on by shock, subtle energy transfers between mates readily occur. We may inadvertently hold on to parts of our abandoning partner to help soothe the loss before we find the strength to resolve the trauma. Due to the unequal power dynamics involved in betrayal, the betrayer has more than likely taken aspects of his partner's soul with him.

This subtle body dynamic reveals one of the darker potentialities of intimate attachment rupture that can radically influence your well-being. Common descriptions—"He ripped my heart out" and "My soul went with him"—suggest this. One woman said to me, "He took my strength and left me with his emptiness," and I knew so well what she meant. In a serious betrayal, the sense of being depleted of the very substance your former mate now exudes suggests an ongoing link between the two of you that begs for an explanation. I explore some possibilities when I discuss projection in chapter 10.

Whether we consider the soul to be dissociated, lost, or stolen, betrayal changes us—for far better or worse. It creates a great divide in our lives after which there is no going back. I know I cannot help but think of my life now as separated into two segments: before and after the bombshell of that September evening.

Ego-Shattering and Injured Innocence

For a long time I was in denial about the extent of the trauma. At first I tried to bypass the rage and pain and get over the shock as quickly as possible; I even imagined I was on my way to the Mother Teresa award for my enlightened handling of the situation.

For instance, the day after Rob left, I was in the back garden phoning friends and family to inform them that the wedding was off, as though I were giving a weather report on a fine summer day. I sounded so cheerful that a number of them were certain that I was the one who had called the whole thing off. The denial may have loosened my grip on reality, but it was helping me survive and protecting me from more pain than I could handle at the time.

The initial dissociation also opened me to dimensions of spiritual life that were inaccessible to me before my heart was broken open.

Betrayal shatters not only the heart, but our crafty, well-hidden and well-groomed ego defenses that protect the heart and form the basis of our false self. Despite the physical, emotional, and mental distress it brings, betrayal uncovers frightening truths that are hard to bear about the human condition. Betrayal is ultimately a spiritual crisis. It is a cry of the heart to deepen into the mysteries of suffering. Trauma disrupts our connection to the world of spirit that is crucial for our well-being. Yet, the emptiness, pain, and powerlessness we feel reveal a profound truth: We are alienated from our true selves. We have the potential to fly free in the world of spirit, but normally we plod along burdened by identification with our body-bound reality. Our spark of spirit lies hidden in a little cocoon of ego or "I"—self-images and beliefs from the past that imprison and weigh us down.

Until the constricting shell of our usual ego sense of self is crushed, we barely notice our misplaced identification. In the comfort zone of daily life we each carve out to survive, we lack the motivation to go beyond the trance of self-involved separateness. We work our spiritual practices, offer service to others, and engage creatively to chip away at the trance. But, unfortunately for us, it often takes trauma to jolt us awake. Otherwise, the forces of consensual reality, habit, and heredity are too great for us to break through to deeper truth.

When traumatic circumstances bring us to our knees, flattering life-long illusions we have lived by are forced into the open to die. We can no longer so easily maintain the fiction that we are patient, kind, competent, compassionate, wise, "together," basically nice people, in charge of our lives.

Beloved Buddhist teacher Pema Chodron teaches that any calamity can potentially wake us up from the limiting self-images and self-involved trance we all share. Her classic *When Things Fall Apart* was my bible early in this crisis. It was the first book I was able to read, and an inspiration to tell my story to help others. Her warm-hearted, yet tough, advice for surviving difficult times (she was left suddenly by her husband for another woman) gave me hope and made me smile through my tears. Pema explains how frightening life-shattering events are for us, and how important it is for recovery to understand how the fearful ego operates so we can face the fear. "When the barriers come down, we don't know what to do. We need a bit more warning about what it feels like when the walls start tumbling down....Finding the courage to go to the places that scare us cannot happen without compassionate inquiry into the workings of ego."[15]

What is the ego? In psychological terms, it is the reasoning, executive branch of the personality we need to function well in life. In Eastern spirituality, the ego is the delusional sense we have of being an autonomous, separate "I" in control of our lives. From the Buddhist perspective, our experience comes about outside our control, through "causes and conditions"; there is no separate self; and our true nature is boundless love. Transpersonal psychology combines both these psychological and spiritual perspectives—and this is the sense in which I primarily use the term "ego" in this writing.[16]

There is nothing inherently bad or wrong about the ego itself. While we need our executive capacities to function in the world, our spiritual growth involves shifting the center of gravity of earlier life from the ego mind to a more interior sense of connection and love grounded in the heart. Developing ego identity is an important accomplishment, but if we do not grow beyond it, the cost of this feat to our soul's longing for love is great.

Consider this: *The root cause of all suffering* is said to come from clinging to the ego, believing too much in its false power and importance. You might say that every ego has a secret "God complex"; that is, we each imagine that "I alone" am in charge of my life. Yet, deep down under our separateness we are lonely and yearn for something more. We long for communion with our higher selves, with spirit, with God. Plus, under our masks of control and confidence, a nagging suspicion that we might not be in charge as much as we imagine makes us feel insecure.

As long as things are going our way, we hardly notice how we cling to this imaginary control. Only when things do not go according to our plans and expectations, do we get to see our soul sickness, how isolated and powerless we are, and how painful that helpless alienation can be.

In Buddhist thinking, the best possible time to reveal the shaky roots of the ego and break out of the belief in the false self is when we are in a state of injured innocence. Little injures our innocence like a serious betrayal. Betrayal trounces the vulnerable, trusting heart. It brings so much pain, so much that we do not want. Yet betrayal offers medicine for what ails us; by overwhelming our carefully constructed defenses, the shock reveals what lies beneath.

When the raw kernel of our usually hidden self is struck, it virtually glows in the dark. No more hiding! Our anxieties and deficiencies are revealed. The struggles of our well-disguised, smooth-functioning "I" come into full focus, and the crushed, outraged ego stands exposed. Under layers of sophisticated personality defenses, we fall suddenly into the long-repressed pain of our earliest trauma. The unbearable pain of our earliest abandonment wounds pours into awareness, and we see the truth of who we have taken ourselves to be.

The trauma blasts open a rare window of opportunity for self-knowledge and freedom before the forces of habit and consensual trance close back over us.

UNCOVERING THE PRIMITIVE AGONIES

The wound is a prayer to God. —Stephen R. Schwartz

Before psychology developed, religion and myth had other ways of describing the frightening, soul-constricting forces that trauma stirs. Evil, demon, devil, Mara, sin, and karma are a few that come to mind. With my background, I found the term *primitive agonies*, coined by British child psychologist D. W. Winnicott, the most illuminating and helpful for navigating this terrain.

Primitive or primal agonies describe the severe distress we experience as infants when our instinctual needs go unmet, most often in situations of perceived abandonment. Winnicott explained these feelings as the original "unthinkable state of affairs that underlies the defense organization" of the personality.[17] Due to their overwhelming nature, these feelings have been repressed and buried in the body, and rarely rise into awareness. Faced with a current trauma, however, we regress, and the early grief and anguish pour into consciousness.

Early abandonment threats lay down nervous-system pathways that make us excruciatingly sensitive to rejection, especially in intimate relationships. These early fears carve deep grooves in the nervous system and are believed to register in the infant brain as "there's something wrong with me," a belief that we commonly associate with feelings of shame. We are painfully, subliminally, attached to these feelings as fundamental to who we take ourselves to be.

Touching into the ego core, we feel an aching gap—a black hole, a chasm, an abyss—in the deepest recesses of the psyche. It feels like something vital that every cell in the body craves is missing. No words can capture the texture of these primal agonies. We experience them as amalgams of competing sensations: powerlessness, terror, torment, longing, despair, emptiness, grief, shame, envy, and rage. Because these states of identification with early pain are preverbal, they are more somatic than conceptual. They are built into our bodily sense of self, unlike later self-images that form once we develop rational thinking. I believe these states may even be pre-personal, existential, part of our hardwiring.

This is why cognitive approaches to rewiring our painful early imprints, as popular as they have become, can help but used alone are insufficient for the deepest healing. Affirmations and positive thinking easily reinforce the hubris at the core of the pain—the belief that "I" can solve the mystery of the suffering built into my humanity. For these reasons, we cannot *think* our way out of these states, but, rather, we have to *feel* our way through. Whatever the source, these early somatic identifications form the roots of the cocoon of illusion, familiarity, and safety in which we live our lives.

This is the dark secret the shattered ego self reveals. Betrayal reactivates the primal agonies like little else. The loss of trust and companionship deprives us of so many basic needs—security, love, and safety. It is as if we have been living our lives with an underground rivulet of pain and shame that, after the flash flood of betrayal, becomes a raging torrent. That torrent holds unanticipated riches we are called to find.

Our identity is deeply entwined with this underground suffering in ways we barely perceive. These terrible feelings signal, *"I exist"*—even if "I" am abandoned, afraid, unseen, and exiled from what I most need and want. We do not know what it means to let these intense energies flow through us without our primitive interpretations and self-assessments. These sensations carry deep, limiting beliefs about who we think we are.

Sometimes we can detect these roots of "I" as a premonition of an underlying "basic flaw" or fault—an underlying sense of core defectiveness, of unease, shame, or dissatisfaction in our own skin. At times, when it comes more vividly to awareness, we may feel unwanted, unloved, worthless, invisible, inadequate, or full of fear. These deep beliefs, not necessarily expressed in words, arise concurrent with the sensations of pain and perpetuate our suffering.

Psychiatrist and meditation teacher Mark Epstein in *Thoughts Without a Thinker,* points out the crucial importance to the soul's growth of having the ego core uncovered.[18] He talks about how all our practices and prayers have been to prepare for this moment. The evasive, manicured self has finally been revealed in its humiliation and outrage at being hurt and mistreated. This may sound like great news to the spiritual seekers among us. Here we are "advancing along the path!" But it takes a lot of courage, compassion, and grace to go through the grief and pain of the deconstruction of the reality we have held dear.

Death by Embarrassment

A serious betrayal is the ultimate disrespect of the dignity of our existence.
—John Amodeo, *Love & Betrayal*

To suddenly have what feels like the reprehensible core of who we are exposed terrifies us. It is mortifying to encounter the "defective self" we have worked so hard to keep hidden. It is crushing to have others see us laid bare in this way. The humiliation alone after a public betrayal can feel as if you are dying a slow death. You might call it "death by embarrassment." Being cast aside or replaced by a loved one devalues a person, no matter how much you "know" it says more about the rejecting person than about you, that you are a precious child of God, etc., etc.

Betrayal inflicts a massive narcissistic wound. I use *narcissistic* here to refer to our natural self-love and self-interest as a unique individual. A healthy ego needs a dose of narcissism or pride. Hillman suggests that normally we keep ourselves vital by the ego's self-love, its pride, dignity, and honor, while humiliation shatters and defeats our vital forces.[19] Betrayal exposes the ego at its early narcissistic core. Narcissistic injury occurs in varying degrees to all of us when our early needs for mirroring and affection go unmet, and that pain makes up part of the primal agonies that underlie our surface personalities.

Betrayal torments perhaps most severely if we have been drawn into trusting directly through our narcissism—our sense of specialness or uniqueness. A successful seduction zeros in on the place of childlike hopefulness that finally our dreams are coming true: someone values, loves, and cares for us; we are special to them, seen and cherished for who we are. It is at this tender source of dignity and pride where we feel most traumatized, mortified, and humiliated when we discover we have been manipulated and are discarded or replaced.

Humiliation and pride go hand in hand. Under any conditions, it is traumatizing to have your pride and dignity assailed. The ego thrives on pride and self-absorption. By the time we are adults, we have worked hard to craft a self-image; learning to operate in this world is no small accomplishment. The instinct to hold on to our dignity and pride arises from our need for the ego to navigate in this world. We guard this accomplishment carefully to ensure our survival and our place in the community.

Humiliation and shame hurt so profoundly that normally we do whatever we can to avoid the embarrassment they bring when exposed. We defend ourselves against this nameless dread of these early feelings with all our might. Betrayal overrides these defenses as it merrily tramples our dignity and pulverizes our pride. The temptation is enormous to deny these shameful feelings and to find a way as quickly as possible to patch up our self-images. "Good riddance. I am so over him. What a jerk." Or in my spiritually correct environment, "I am equally to blame. It wasn't meant to be. I only want him to be happy" are the more likely bromides to cover mortified pride and a broken heart.

If we find a way to be honest about our feelings, however, we must admit being deceived, rejected, and rendered powerless are *deeply painful insults*. The pangs of betrayal hurt terribly, yet they can motivate us to investigate the pain, to nurture and tend our wounds, and to discover who we really are beyond our pain, powerlessness, and shattered pride.

In short, betrayal brings unheard-of opportunity to work through our own narcissistic injuries. If you are like me, whatever tendency you have to veer between believing you are God's gift to humanity on one day and a toxic dump site on the next will come into clear light and get a strenuous working over. I had plenty of grandiose tendencies to see, regret, and admire. The more public the humiliation, the more crushed we feel, the greater the opportunity to wake up to the delusions.

I had been proud of my relationship with Rob, proud of our commitment to partnership as a spiritual path; proud of our ability to converse and to negotiate conflict; proud of our mutual caring, soulful sex life, and heart resonance; proud that we were about to pull off this wedding we had poured ourselves into; proud that our family and friends were coming from far and wide. And that was not all: Personally, I was proud of my intuition, empathy, and sensitivity with Rob; proud of my inner work and self-awareness in facing my own shortcomings; proud of how I cultivated gratitude for my life; and proud of my love and devotion to Rob. Needless to say, having every one of these ego accomplishments revealed as delusion and blown apart so publicly and so close to the wedding date—every person in my circle of friends and family knew I had been deserted—was deeply humiliating. My pride and dignity were decimated. Any cover I had for my hidden vile nature was effectively blown. And I had to face these terrible feelings of worthlessness and deficiency. No wonder I withdrew from the eyes of the world to lick my wounds.

Learning to be with our suffering is what rising from the ashes of betrayal is all about. We are invited into the mystery of consciously suffering the pain at the very core of our being. With help, the trials of the darkness that falls become an initiating rite of passage into the depths of the heart I will discuss in the next chapter. The humiliation, isolation, and heartache take us on a path beyond the threshold of trauma to the caring, healing spirit that lives in and around us.[20] The path winds through some of the most difficult and most mystical terrain of human nature.

CHAPTER 5

A Spiritual Crisis

*Prayer and love are learned in the hour when prayer becomes impossible
and the heart has turned to stone.*
—Thomas Merton

WE NEED TO GIVE OURSELVES CREDIT if we have been living with a broken heart. To be touched to the quick by betrayal, we had to have taken the risk of caring, to have opened our heart to cherish, trust, and depend on another. We had to have shown up enough in our tenderness and vulnerability so that losing that love would crack us open in every way. In other words, we had already signaled our willingness to be changed by the alchemy of love. Opening the heart in intimate relationship goes against the grain of our protective shells—it takes guts. By some grace, we must have found the courage to trust before we could love...and before we could be betrayed.

A broken heart testifies that we have taken the first steps on the pilgrimage to the mysteries of the heart, to a greater, enduring love, beyond any partnership. Throughout the months and years of grieving this loss, I gradually reframed loving Rob as an act of bravery and faith, not naïveté and delusion, as I had believed. Loving him was a necessary step in awakening to a love independent of his actions. It brought me back to the question that had hovered nearby most of my life: *What is love?* What is love when you are angry and hurt and feel like life is not worth living?

Opening my heart to love had set off a monumental battle between fear and love, between the past and the present, in my soul. The longer I struggled with my splintered heart and wrestled with the many barriers to love that crashed down around me after Rob left, the more astonished I was to learn how fiercely I normally resist love and how many masks that fear can hide behind. Fear can even appear disguised as love itself, a clinging, dependent, possessive, or manipulative love. In the long work of rebuilding trust, I saw plainly that pain and hardship were not the biggest blocks to my heart.

Rather, the greatest barrier was my fear of love. And this crisis was testing my faith that love was even possible in this world.

When we open our hearts in love with another person, we stand naked, not just before one another, but before divine forces ready to refashion us for their purposes. Loving takes us beyond ordinary hopes and fears to the borders of spiritual life. When love stirs the heart, it threatens us. The fundamentally fragile ego reacts by flashing a red alert, "Danger! Danger!" We long for union, yet fear we will disappear if the substance of love trickles or, God forbid, pours into us. At the first flush of that divine nourishment, our hearts snap shut and harden against the possibility of pain. In fear, we may grasp at or push away the person who has carried that love, as if they are the source of the love or the pain.

Our longing for love and connection conflicts with another drive: the drive for the freedom to discover who we are without having to adapt ourselves to the requirements of another human being. While we long for intimacy, we fear being engulfed or tied down. Usually, both forces are at work in us, though we likely identify with one more than the other. Both are strategies of the ego to stay in charge. We are afraid of losing control; yet when we open ourselves to the alchemy of love, we must be willing to release our grip to be led we know not where.

The soul needs love like the body needs water. Since the love we fear is the very thing we need to satisfy our heart's deepest longing, we live our lives in conflict. We are made for love and suffer terribly without it. We need love to dissolve the barriers to the holy presence that dwells within us and does not depend on outer circumstances. And yet the closer love—human or divine—comes, the faster we run away or shut down in fear.

How poignant it was to realize that I most feared what I needed and wanted more than anything. While I did not know what love is, I was starting to recognize this tricky fear. The fear of love, I was convinced, was not just about my personal limitations, it was a dilemma built into human nature. It must have something to do with why we are here in the first place, to engage this conflict with conscious awareness.

AN ARCHETYPAL INITIATION

No matter how much I railed against it, I had to admit, betrayal plays an integral part in the ongoing drama of human life. The shock catapults you into the land of myth and story, the land of the archetypes. Although arising from our personal history, intimate betrayal has its roots in collective, universal experience. Themes of betrayal inspire and vivify religion, myth, literature, and music, not to mention popular entertainment. From *Anna Karenina* and *Samson and Delilah* to the *Twilight Saga* series, many literary plots turn on the centrality of betrayal; and hardly a tragic opera exists, from *Carmen* to *Norma* to *Tristan and Isolde* that does not revolve around betrayal.

Enduring stories, myths, and symbols are the language of the soul that carry the condensed content of human experience and wisdom over the ages. There must be a reason that many religions have myths of betrayal embedded in their founding stories. Senior disciples attempt to assassinate the Buddha; Cain kills Abel in the Old Testament; in the Sufi tradition, Rumi's beloved teacher Shams is killed by jealous followers; in the central mythos of Judeo-Christian culture, the Passion turns on the betrayal of Christ.

Myths and stories can help us appreciate the deeper meaning of what we are going through as we grapple with our own situation. Stories, including our own, show how betrayal takes us beyond our personal pain to engage evolutionary forces at work in the soul. We bring our individual filters, but the core feelings, thoughts, and reactions are universal and predictable.

Regardless of gender, age, social status, education, intelligence, spiritual maturity, or any other personal characteristic, when a person is betrayed we know they are highly likely to fall apart, panic, rage, yearn for their lost love, and feel helpless, alone, and powerless. In other classic responses to numb the sorrow and pain, they may strike out against the betrayer or themselves, shut down, turn to distractions, or fall prey to addictions.

Betrayal inducts us into a secret society of those who know the swirling dark waters of brokenness and it can humanize us in entirely unanticipated ways. Untold numbers of people are experiencing the same ordeal even as I write. And how many others through history have been initiated and altered by the chaos that intimate betrayal brings? Hearing these stories, we are inspired and sustained by the aspirations of those countless souls who have gone before and those who struggle now through the same trials. I found holding the larger, archetypal context in mind during the long nights of betrayed love brought quiet support—like a distant light you see on the horizon while trekking a barren desert.

Along with Buddhist and Sufi stories, the myths and symbols of Christian mysticism became important to me during my darkest days. When I left town to try to escape the trauma triggers, at my friend's house in Chicago where I was staying I picked up a bible one quiet afternoon. Randomly, I opened, of course, to the story of Job, and was immediately drawn into the details of Job's unfair trials and inexplicable suffering. The story came alive for me and spoke directly to my pain as little else had. It drew me into the Psalms, where again I saw my rage and anguish expressed on almost every page. I knew I had tapped into a vein of ancient human suffering, handed down through the centuries to resonate with us and offer meaning even now.

It turned out that on the pilgrimage to my deeper self that betrayal initiated, the paradox of the Christian Passion—of love won through intense, unwanted psychic and spiritual pain—also spoke loudly to me. The enduring image of betrayal with a kiss pointed to the universality of shattered trust between intimates. Even Christ pleaded against his fate at Gethsemane. His cry to the Father on the cross, "Why hast thou forsaken me?" expressed the despair of abandonment and what feels like meaningless suffering, while the resurrection demonstrated the promise of new life that could not be imagined on the cross or inside the tomb.

Stories of initiation, of rites of passage from indigenous cultures also helped me frame this experience. I understood how, taken as a purifying ordeal, betrayal initiates us into a new stage of spiritual life. A traditional rite of passage includes three stages: severing, threshold or transition, and reentry or incorporation.[2] Initiation always starts with a severing or shattering, a dying to the life that is. Betrayal forces a traumatic rupturing from the past. It splinters our reality, tearing away what we have most valued and challenging our familiar stability.

After the severing, we enter into the second phase—*threshold*—the actual transition or dying to the past. This is an extraordinary time of liminality and strangeness, and of great stress. Much of this writing emerged from the experiences of the transitional threshold phase, which can also be described as a dark night of the soul or a night sea journey.

The final stage is *reentry* or incorporation. We return to everyday life after the descent with the gifts and lessons of the journey. Like all rites of passage, betrayal presents trials to test our readiness for truths about ourselves, about human nature, and about the nature of existence itself.

In these and other symbols and images, I saw portrayed the mystery of the heart's growth into love through suffering. I was coming to understand betrayal as an *initiation of the heart*, the trials as a dark night of the soul, and the impossibility of mutuality or reconciliation as the cross I needed to learn to bear without understanding why. Even the trauma itself I gradually came to see as a call of the heart, an event orchestrated by forces beyond Rob or me to open to new depths of soul.

Unseen hands seemed to have crafted this dangerous passage to the far edges of my nature, this place of torment where *no one wants to go*. Who wants to go through an ordeal, to be publicly humiliated or destroyed, or to be tortured, or to have been so frightfully wrong about themselves and the people they love? Who wants to lose what has brought comfort and happiness and given life meaning? Nevertheless, precisely here, in this unwanted place, stripped of what is most important, in the muck of meaninglessness and despair, the mystery of divine love most readily enters the heart. The myths and stories said it all.

TRUSTING THE PAIN AND POWERLESSNESS

A significant betrayal places us in the throes of a humanly cruel, but spiritually rich, collective vortex that could befall anyone. But when it is our reality that has been blown apart, it asks a lot to remember the archetypal nature of what we are going through. In fact, until the traumatized nervous system calms down and the pain lets up, it is next to impossible.

The soul takes flight to escape the situation. It is terrifying to feel so powerless, to realize *how little control we have over what happens to us.* All the enemies of our conscious personality stampede on stage to grapple for control, while the wounds keep shouting, *something is wrong!* All this time, we did not realize we had arranged our lives to avoid this pain, and now with our world shattered, there is nowhere to hide.

Before we can stop believing that the anguish at our core is *who we are*, we need to let ourselves feel the painful truth of *who we think we are* that we have kept hidden for so long. Betrayal trauma shoots a sharp arrow through our defenses aimed directly at our earliest wounds. The arrow lodges in our hearts, and the bleeding shows how full we are of ancient grief, longing, despair, and so many other feelings we interpret as painful but do not really understand. The strange, compelling sensations that scare us arise from the deepest caverns of our being. That is where we find the most potent medicine for the soul.

The time has come to stop pushing our pain away and to listen to our suffering. We can learn to listen, to befriend our distress, to love our "enemies." For nothing less is being asked of us than, against all instinct, that we trust the pain and powerlessness. By bringing the magic of friendliness to these places that terrify and control us, the darkness itself will school us in how to survive.

But first we must make a radical turn, a turn against our natural distaste of suffering. Wisdom traditions say that it marks a distinct stage in the growth of spirit when we make the turn toward consciously accepting suffering (I devote chapter 13 to the subject). The dark gift of trauma may bring the grace we need to move *contra natura*. When we begin to surrender, to *accept fully* the humiliation and hurt, we take a step away from our more mammalian drives for security and safety toward another impulse of our nature, an impulse toward our spiritual essence, toward our true home. Fortunately, there are helping hands to guide the way.

SPIRIT MESSENGERS AND THE HANDS OF LIGHT

Be helpless and dumbfounded, unable to say yes or no.
Then a stretcher from grace will come to gather us up.
— Jalaluddin Rumi

Being cracked open not only reveals the depth of our suffering, it also allows spiritual realities to penetrate the heart that otherwise have difficulty reaching us. At the moment of shock, when the soul takes off for other worlds, many people report some version of an out-of-body experience, including a slowing down or stopping of time. In my case, Rob's disappearing act catapulted me into an altered state in which I felt as if I were living in a dreamscape. Life did not seem real, as if I were watching someone else in a movie going through my days.

While I could not read much at the time—words had become nothing but meaningless squiggles on a page—music consoled me. Music that spoke to my sadness and pain helped get me out of my possessed mind and hear wordless messages of guidance and care. Sometime during the first weeks, I happened one afternoon to listen to Bach's "Art of the Fugue." The music was so sustaining that I listened to it for an hour nearly every day during the first year. With its calming counterpoint, it transported me into a state of bliss in which I felt as though the voices of angels were speaking directly to my hurting heart through the notes. This was just one example of the other-worldly support I felt come to me in the early months on my own.

Traumatic shock jolts you into a gap between the worlds of spirit and matter. In this liminal land, we meet semi-spiritual, archetypal, or *daimonic* energies. In ancient Greece, daimons were considered soul messengers that connect the world of spirit with the world of matter.

A daimon can feel like an invisible being or presence has come into our lives; at times it appears as a helpful spirit, at other times, a malevolent demon. In the aftermath of betrayal, depending on our temperament, we may sense a daimonic presence as an obsession, possession, or difficult emotion; or as an inspiration, insight, welling of love, or as creative power. Daimons may materialize in the psyche as a predator, demon lover, or tormenter; or conversely, as a muse, guardian angel, inner guide, or teacher.

These little recognized, and mostly feared or idolized, forces are transformative agents that pour into the traumatized psyche and have the potential to radically change us if we are willing to develop a relationship, and not be overwhelmed by or identify with them. These archetypal energies saturate the drama of betrayal with otherworldly intensity and give the feelings unleashed in response to the shock their abnormal, high-octane quality.

The supercharged fuel they carry can swamp and frighten us but can also be used for plumbing the deep seas and reaching for the stars within. In the dark night, these intense energies initiate the dissolution of the sense of "me" that makes it feel like we are dying. They also, surprisingly, provide a sense of being held and cared for as we go through this difficult time.

While we can describe the demonic difficulties with relative ease, the "hands of light" that reach in to carry us through the darkest of times are difficult to portray. These experiences are more the province of artists, musicians, and poets. I can only say that the touch of what I sensed as helping hands soothed and encouraged me. During this graced time, one reason I spent hours each day "just sitting" attentively was that I could more readily feel their invisible presence supporting me through the chaos.

I noticed another marvel about being broken open I hardly understood at the time. At times when I most felt my torn heart, I was intensely aware of my connection with Rob. Paradoxically, in the midst of those painful sensations, I felt him as a warming light that was more authentic to me than anything he had done or said that had hurt me. The place in my heart where I had fallen in love with him reemerged with a conviction that melted and relieved my brokenness. Through the heart wound, I had entered the divine center that sourced that relationship. At times, I expanded through this love for him to touch a holy light shining at the heart of the world.

People say that we tend to idealize a lost lover, but what I experienced was not about idealizing Rob. If anything, when he left, his character weaknesses stood out in higher relief than I could have imagined. He was not the man he professed to be; that was clear. This was about the truth of my own heart, and the truth of my love for the light of his soul, despite the underhandedness and other failings of his personality. That love, which was there all along, but normally tucked away in a secret corner of my unconscious, now lay exposed as an integral part of my raw, exposed heart, and could not be denied.

I spoke with others who shared similar experiences. In one example, a man whose partner of five years left him suddenly for someone else when they, too, were planning a wedding wrote this explanation, "The residual shock, anger and sadness I've been left with for these past few weeks have opened my mind and heart to the deepest and most raw sense of love I've ever experienced. I can't adequately explain it just yet, but underneath all of the anguish is a very true sense of love that has nothing to do with romance or feelings or concepts. It isn't a feel-good kind of state, nor is it necessarily a painful one when I'm brave enough to be with it directly. But I do feel as if I get these amazing glimpses into the truest and deepest sense of love imaginable, even though I'm sure this makes no logical sense at all."

Betrayal not only wounds and tears open the heart, it also reveals forces of love and light hidden in our pain that have secretly informed our life all along. Previously, we have been too busy hiding from our suffering with surface distractions. The hands of light that reach in to soothe the aching heart, especially in the early weeks or months following a shock, come as a prelude, a reassurance that we are not alone going through this unfolding ordeal. These quiet forces keep us pointed toward the love, the prayer, and the promise in the pain. They will show us through the darkness how to rebuild our trust and faith in life.

Taking the descent into the suffering that lives at the core of our humanity is not for everyone. Who can say why this downward path calls one person and not another? We do not know. If you feel called, no matter how long ago the betrayal may have taken place, it is not too late to acknowledge what has happened, unlock the trauma, and "march into hell for a heavenly cause." If you are reading this book, it is likely that you or someone important to you is responding to an urgent call to open up a pained past or dive into the swirling seas of a currently upended life.

The suffering of betrayed love calls us deep within toward an unknown mystery. I recall a song from Rob's fiftieth birthday celebration, the year after we got together, when the glow of being "in love" was still in the air. I dedicated a song by Jami Lula to him that expressed how I felt about being with him. The refrain was, "Something's calling me a little bit deeper than I've ever been before." Only now do I realize how prophetic those lines were.

The pain and powerlessness at our core resides at an underworld threshold between spiritual reality and the world of form. As long as we resist and repress these terrible feelings, we shut tight the door to Spirit. The hurt—if we allow it—opens a passageway to the softened, sad heart that can melt these antique lies we tell ourselves, and bring more love and communion with life than we have previously known.

Writing this reminded me of the story of the Buddha sitting under the Bo Tree, where he committed not to move until he awakened fully. In response to his pledge, the forces of Maya or illusion attacked him mercilessly with arrows of craving, hatred, and delusion. Using the strength of his mindfulness, the Buddha turned the arrows into flowers as they struck him. Even as the trials of betrayal torment us into engaging our demons, we may notice little sprouts of hidden life budding—some ancient yearning for the angels of our better nature, our lost soul, breaking through.

I would not wish the torments of betrayal on anyone. You have heard me rail against it. However, if you have been betrayed and are compelled to take the plunge into the icy waters, you must be ready to engage the mysteries of powerlessness and pain. In being taken down into the turbulent depths, though you are likely to feel abandoned by all for a time, I believe you are in good hands. With determination, kindness, and the hands of grace, you will eventually rise from your knees and, with new eyes, see a holiness at work beneath the rubble of your former life. The mystery of betrayal invites us to enter a realm most of us could not have conceived of before the fracturing of our world. Onward.

PART II

The Mystery of Relationship

CHAPTER 6

The Subtle-Body Connection

When two people relate to each other authentically and humanly, God is the
electricity that surges between them.
—Martin Buber

BEFORE GOING MORE DEEPLY into the personal truths that betrayal reveals, we need to make a slight detour. Betrayal is, after all an interpersonal event. Betrayal always happens in the context of a relationship. With no relationship, with no love, trust, and commitment, there is no ground for betrayal. Jung said when two personalities meet—if there is any reaction at all—it is like the contact of two chemical substances; both are transformed. Love and betrayal change you.

Before Rob's exit, my most powerful lessons about relationship transformations came when my husband died after his long struggle with lymphoma. I did not know losing your mate could be such a mighty teacher. Loss of my partner through death and the loss through betrayal had certain similarities. But the impact of Rob's leaving was fundamentally different from losing Dennis. I believe what I learned through my husband's death offers keys to the subtle inner realities we face when an intimate relationship has been severed, not only by death, but by divorce, betrayal, or abandonment.

Even when we are expecting it, the death of a beloved is a shock. Death so rudely reminds you of its power when it shows up at your side. Because my husband's death was not sudden—he had been diagnosed four years earlier, and was at home under hospice care for his final three weeks—I was somewhat prepared. But, if we could fully prepare for such a shock, it would not be one.

When Dennis died, he was conscious and aware until the very end. I sat with him that Wednesday morning in our sunny living room, holding his hand, as I had been throughout the night. Minutes before he died, he said to me, "I am going now," took three very long breaths and passed away. When his last breath left his body, it took my breath away. At that moment, I "saw" him leaving his body, and simultaneously felt myself cut in two down the middle of my body, as if part of me went with him.

The severing of our attachment stunned me into a period of dissociation before the grieving proper began. As the weeks and months passed, I experienced grieving as a call of nature that took me into the unknown. Waves of sadness moved through me frequently, often when least expected. Throughout the first year, the muscular demands of grief astonished me; but what most surprised me was the mix of sorrow and pain with joy.

During these grief episodes, I discerned a strange alchemy, as if my constituent parts were being agitated and rearranged by each aching wave. It was as if Dennis's essence was mingling with mine, the molecules of his subtle body interpenetrating my own, in a way I could swear was changing the signature of my soul. In these moments, even as I was absorbing the loss of his physical presence, the illusion of "me" and "he" dissolved in the depths of my body—far more completely than it ever did in our intimacy while he was alive.

I had no idea that grieving would, or even could, be anything but painful and sad. Who knew that this joyful, even blissful, alchemical blending would be part of coming to terms with this loss? Each outpouring of tears altered the flavor of my being and opened me to richer communion with him and with a larger life. The paradox of grief was confounding: Despite the hurt at losing him, I felt closer to him in death than I had in life. I began to understand the biblical phrase "Love is stronger than death."

Marriage, I learned, ties you in inexplicable ways to the death of your partner. Simultaneous with the infusion of Dennis' essence into my own, I felt that a part of me was dying, gone with him behind the veil between worlds. Through my connection to him, I, too, entered the realm of the dead. In a very real sense, I was given a foretaste of my own death. Grieving a lost partner can make you homesick for that unknown land beyond this life. You travel with your love to an evocative realm where you taste death's vast emptiness.

As I surrendered to the sovereignty of grieving in those days, the dying led me to a horizon where I met his soul in the dark nothingness and longed to follow him there. For a time, Dennis was everywhere, and I was with him: in the evening star, in the robin in the mimosa tree in the morning, in the breeze at midday.

The sweet anguish of this surgical mystery—parts of me sheared away into death, parts of him entering my soul—astonished me. I struggled to find the words to describe this. *Grief* seemed inadequate. Was the pain of loss mixed with the joy of his soul joining mine bittersweet? Tender? Overwhelming? Sublime? Dreadful? Terrifying? Ravaging? It was all of these, but, yes, *ravaging* best described this ineffable phenomenon. Grief takes you over like a ravaging lover.

Most important for the discussion here, through these experiences, I came to realize that in marrying another, *two become one.* Death served as the catalyst for the etheric or subtle body presence that had grown between us, that we had taken for granted, to come sharply alive. With death, Dennis's essence locked into my own with a permanence only hinted at in the most soulful lovemaking. I felt the "one body" of the relationship take final, quasi-material form and settle inside as part of me.

With time, mourning soothed the sharp hurt of the loss, leaving a delicate, clean scar of otherworldly and tender memories, an inlet to another world. Psychologist Robert Romanyshyn wrote when he lost his wife, that grief "is a wound which leaves a scar, and that scar is forever etched in the fabric of the soul."[1] As I went forward with my life, I felt forever changed, carrying Dennis's essential signature blended into what and who I was.

LOSS IN DEATH AND BETRAYAL CONTRASTED

We are never so defenseless against suffering as when we love, never so helplessly unhappy as when we have lost our loved object or its love.
—Sigmund Freud

I did not realize it at the time, but during this period of intense sorrow, I was quietly learning about the magnitude and mystery of intimate relationship. The traditional marriage vow "until death do us part" became meaningful to me in a new way. I saw how death brought a definitive end to a bond I did not even realize existed. At the same time, death revealed the depth of the connection and confirmed marriage for me as a *vehicle for a divine mystery* to permeate human life.

I began to understand why people consider marriage a sacrament. A sacrament is a place on Earth where the grace of the Holy Spirit, can manifest in the material world. As the relationship grows in the container of married sanctity, a door opens to grace. The partnership becomes a medium in which Spirit penetrates and refines the souls of the two individuals involved, into one body of love. Such a union comes into being as a divine gift whose purpose we cannot know, but which, as willing participants in its mystery, we can only honor and revere.

I thought I knew devastation after losing Dennis but was soon to learn the limitations of my experience. Grieving his loss stretched my heart and increased my capacity to love in ways I could not have imagined until I opened again to a new partner. As integral philosopher Ken Wilber put it: "Real love hurts; real love makes you totally vulnerable and open; real love will take you far beyond yourself; and therefore real love will devastate you."[2] I thought I was aware of the cost of love's vulnerability, but I was wrong. I had no idea how much more traumatizing betrayal could be than losing a love to death.

In the gloom that descended after Rob's departure, I grieved the loss, not only of my mate, but also of my soul. I felt as if some essential quality that made life worth living had deserted me to go in search of my lost love. When I was finally able to let myself penetrate the grief of losing Rob, a keening echoed inside me like the cry of the seabird in Walt Whitman's poem, "Out of the Cradle Endlessly Rocking." In those verses Whitman recounts his experience as a young boy of watching a seabird pair nest for many days in a row. When one of the birds does not return to the nest, the he-bird calls for her all through the night, into the next day, and even longer. The bird's plaintive call pierced the heart of the young poet, and he conveyed it with these words: *Whichever way I turn, O you could give me my mate back again if only you would;/ For I am almost sure I see her dimly whichever way I look.*[3] The poem ends with a poignant reverie on grieving and on the beauty and inevitability of death.

I imagined the seabird must have been one that mated for life. His cries of despair as described by Whitman articulated for me both my losses. In each case, it felt like an essential part of me had disappeared.[4] I recognized this expectant mourning as the atmosphere in which I spent my days and nights after Rob left. I experienced shades of these same phenomena the first few months after Dennis died, but *he was gone*. His death was imbued with a quiet mystery and wonder, as well as the sense of completion, not the insistent ache, loneliness, and longing interlaced with bouts of panic and despair I was to experience for years to come after Rob left.

In my grief after Rob left, some primal part of me not only kept searching for him, but also *expected his return*. Against all rational thought, I routinely expected Rob to turn up at the door, or to crawl into bed beside me at night, or to walk in nonchalantly to tell me about the day's events. Each time the phone rang, or emails chimed, or a letter came in the mail, I imagined it must be Rob reaching out to return. Until the trauma subsided and my nervous system reorganized sufficiently to register that he was really gone (it took more than three years), I imagined I saw him almost everywhere I went, even in the most unlikely places (two thousand miles away, for instance). I found this hallucinatory seeking beyond distressing but was helpless to stop it.

As I had with Dennis, I realized what I most missed was a fragrance, an atmosphere, a Rob-ness, the irreplaceable essence, or music, of his unique being that had resonated with my soul and occupied a huge place in my heart.

What confounded me was that the music did not grow ever fainter, as it did in the year after Dennis' death, nor did it stop. Rob's music continued to play on and on, only with the lyric lines broken by cacophony, static, and stuck phrases, like a scratchy loud record caught in a groove, like a tune you cannot get out of your head.

I discovered that betrayal, too, wrenches the tissues of attachment, but not with a sharp, clean cut as death does. Instead, betrayal leaves you with a jagged open wound that grieving does not heal completely. Nor does separation through betrayal cut or assimilate the etheric bonds. Grieving Rob's absence did not dissolve, but inflamed the bond. The torn etheric ties lived on, exposed like raw nerves to the movements of my "other half" who was still walking around the planet.

Learning to live with an unresolved betrayal is like learning to live with a chronic illness. It feels as if a *part of your own being has turned against you*, like an autoimmune disease, and your work becomes learning to manage the pain. And in a real way, when a bonded partner walks away a living part of you has turned against you.

THE HAUNTING PRESENCE

If every event which occurred could be given a name,
there would be no need for stories.
—John Berger, *Once in Europa*

The ongoing bonds left me susceptible to Rob in eerie ways that fueled my heart's longings but also continued to insult and aggravate the hurt. Within days of his leaving, besides the pain and disorientation, whenever I relaxed and turned my focus inward, I noticed something strange happening. Unbidden surges of his presence poured through my body. Rob's facial expressions and body postures, his touch, his warmth of heart, and more—everything that comprised his essential signature lived on vividly in me. I felt imprinted with the rhythm of his breath, the beat of his heart, his characteristic gestures and, above all, his fragrance. It was if he were still living in my cells, my bones, the very fibers of my being. He felt fresh, alive-right-now, as if he was with me, here now. This uncanny experience came frequently and filled me with startling force. It—"he"—could appear anytime, anyplace. Despite my desire and efforts to cut off all memory of him, I would be overcome by these surges of his presence, both evocative and painful.

What was this unsolicited presence alive in me, breathing as part of my own breath? For a while, I thought it must be body memories. We made love often in the weeks and days before his leaving. Could these be somatic memories of those out-of-time moments brought to awareness by the sudden cutoff? I often felt I carried him with me after we had been particularly close. No, this uncanny presence did not feel like a memory, although memories intruded on me often enough. I wondered if the haunting could be a by-product of sudden loss, another type of hallucination, like the seabird imagining its mate everywhere, or me imagining I spotted Rob whenever I went out.[5]

Perhaps my mind was creating a somatic fantasy in its desperation to have his companionship, or to hang onto my identity in relation to him? Could this merely be a vivid romantic fantasy, my belief in lasting love taking form in my subtle body? Or, maybe it was a sign of incipient psychosis. Was I losing touch with reality? Was I running my own version of *A Beautiful Mind* with him as the imaginary companion?

Whatever it was, I felt bedeviled by his haunting and could not see how to make it stop. When I brought it up with others, primarily therapists and other professionals—I would say, "He's here. What is this?"—no one could really explain. I began to feel ashamed to tell anyone, imagining they must be rolling their eyes when I turned away. This presence confounded my intention to "let go" and be free of Rob and the hurt he represented. I wanted to banish him entirely from my world…but I could not. No matter what method I tried, the haunting persisted.

Even more than wanting to squash this phantasm, I wanted to explore the truth of this experience. I did my best to drop my futile, frantic attempts to figure out what was happening. I recommitted myself to simply keeping my attention focused on what I was feeling and sensing. In this way, I was drawn further into an exploration of uncharted realms of relatedness, realms that seemed unimportant, even unreal, to my rational mind but now begged for my attention.

With Betrayal, He Is *Not* Dead

For a long time, I believed the intensity of the grieving would eventually assimilate and sever our ties, as it had with Dennis' death. To speed the process, I visualized and repeated over and over to myself, "Rob is dead to me… *He is dead to me.*" While my rational mind accepted that he was gone, my limbic and reptilian brains, along with my heart and my physical and subtle bodies, roared in protest. They knew it was a lie. The "soft animal of the body" sensed he was still living.[6] The early brain registered his energetic presence at a distance, and lamented this loss in an entirely different way than it did when death separated me from my mate.

My soul was unable to make someone dead who was not dead. As much as I tried to convince myself that these hauntings and the ongoing preoccupation and anticipation of return were symptoms of PTSD, an ego-fixation, a romantic fantasy, or a sign of extreme emotional instability, it was to no avail. Even when all rational thought continued to insist, "He is dead. I will never speak to him again, never!" the facts were: He existed still; his actions reverberated within me. I intuited his whereabouts. And at any moment, the phone could ring, or he could appear at the door and walk through it back into my life. I could neither stamp out these channels of connection nor deny them. Yet the relationship was over, and soon enough he was with someone else. It made no sense to me.

The length of time Rob's presence lingered (it went on for years), the unbidden nature of its arising, and the fact that my awareness was often more, not less, crisp and alert when it arose, were all factors I weighed as I sought to discern what was happening. I concluded that a partnership or marriage does not necessarily end energetically because one person walks away.

More and more, as the evidence gathered, I came to believe that his leaving had jolted into awareness the substance of the relationship we had formed together, the subtle-body "third" I discuss in the next chapter. I deduced that this blended being that formed in the course of our life together lived on as a part of me at subtle soul levels. I even believed there must be a counterpart of my energetic body alive in him, although I had no way to be certain.

For these reasons and more, I came to believe that betrayal serves a different purpose and requires a different type of mourning than death. The betrayed relationship does not die but goes into limbo. Betrayal is less about healing or completing the relationship to your mate than it is about the relation to your self. The grief work of betrayal does not end by blending the qualities of the beloved into your being. The mourning of betrayal requires and performs a different kind of surgery, a surgery that aims to restore not our relation to the other, but our relation to depths of our own soul—to love itself. Through betrayal, we learn to "go deeper than love," in D. H. Lawrence's terms, to touch into a reality vast enough to contain even the subtle realm of what may be unbreakable bonds.

Subtle-Body Realms

I kept wondering what it would take for the connection with Rob to diminish, or if it ever would. The tenacity of the haunting made me want to know more about the durability of subtle attachment. Might humans not come hardwired with a propensity to form enduring bonds? I wondered if lifelong partnerships and marriages were not only a result of willed commitment or romantic dreaming, but also a quasi-physical manifestation? Perhaps these attachments reflect a kind of biochemical bonding between two people that is not under our control.

How similar are our blueprints to that of the seabird, the albatross, the swan, the wolf, or the prairie vole, all of which mate for life? Can the blending of the essences of two people, once accomplished, be undone? What if two people naturally form indissoluble bonds that can be severed only by death? We are part of the physical world, after all, where once you mix the ingredients for a cake, for example, you can never get the flour and egg back again. What happens to the mixture of two into one when one person walks away, or they mutually separate, while both still live, as is so common now? Questions like this, I found, cannot be answered solely with the rational mind. To explore relationship connections and separations, we must be willing to enter realms that are not accessible to reason.

We need to plunge more deeply into the sphere where the processes of relational union take place. We need to explore the "inner body"—also known as the subtle, etheric, or light body.[7] While still viewed as science fiction in the mainstream, many people, especially women, are aware of the subtle, energetic body in and around the physical body as one of the unspoken realities of inner life.[8] We know it, for instance, as the field of connectivity between our loved ones and us. When we tune into the subtle senses, we can feel how we are part of a transformative medium that dissolves boundaries and links us with the surrounding world.

Within the field of the subtle body, we connect, merge, and commune with one another, and intuit fundamental information about the world. Because the subtle body houses the heart of compassion and wisdom, it is in this realm that we feel the joy and misery of other beings and taste the wonder of being part of the creation. Subtle-body awareness forms a mediating bridge between our physical and spiritual realities, where "things divine are joined with lowest things."[9] French Islamic mystic and scholar Henry Corbin called the subtle body an organ of perception, an instrument of knowledge, as real as intellectual intuition.[10] Jung described it as "semi-spiritual in nature,"[11] neither mind nor matter, but existing in an intermediate realm.

The existence and importance of the subtle body have long also been recognized in the worlds of religious mysticism, philosophy, medieval alchemy, and, most recently, archetypal and analytic psychology. The subtle body is also referred to as the incarnate mind, the body of resurrection, the subjective or dream body, and the somatic unconscious. Mystics call it soul, and religious philosophers refer to its faculties as the spiritual senses. It is a liminal place where Eros rules: a cauldron where opposites come together in a series of unions and separations, births and deaths. The subtle is the bodily base of intuition, a sixth sense that helps guide us through the invisible realms of life. It is the imaginal realm of the daimons, where spirit incarnates and word becomes flesh. However we name it, we intuit the subtle body as the borderland between form and formlessness, body and mind, reason and unreason. If you have not noticed it previously, betrayal trauma will catapult you into subtle-body realms for a crash course.

Quiet and attention are necessary to bring awareness to this delicate inner realm where Spirit meets form. In times of meditation, prayer, openheartedness, crisis, or suffering, the inner body can more readily be felt as a layer of refined aliveness, reaching out into the world around us with filaments of sensitive receptivity. As occurs with the physical body, we often take the subtle world within for granted until we are hurt or injured. Who pays attention to his or her foot unless someone steps on it? A wound to the soul calls this preconscious layer of our existence to our attention. When Dennis died, my subtle-body senses came vividly into awareness. Later, in the wake of Rob's desertion, they virtually screamed out their paradoxical messages of haunting, torn connection, and mourning.

Many of the most confusing, painful times after Rob left me—especially when he took up with someone new—began to make sense and resolve only when I dropped in and considered subtle-body realities.

FEMININE MYSTERIES

We live in a culture that ignores subtle-body, relational realities, and for good reason. These states of union mediated by the body represent *the fundamental mystery of the archetypal feminine principle*, just as individuality does the masculine.[12] If the mystery of relationship were to be valued equally with the importance we place on individuality, a serious realigning of our existing priorities would need to take place.

Cultural historian Richard Tarnas eloquently discusses how our rational Western mind set sacrificed the values of the feminine mysteries in order to establish its dominance:

> The evolution of the Western mind has been founded on the repression of the feminine—on the repression of undifferentiated unitary consciousness, of the *participation mystique* with nature; a progressive denial of the *anima mundi*, of the soul of the world, of the community of being, of the all-pervading, of mystery and ambiguity, of imagination, emotion, instinct, body, nature, woman.[13]

In the modern Western world, relational feminine experiences, such as communion, attachment, dependence, family, and community, are perceived in stark contrast to the accepted masculine icons of the collective—freedom, winning, aggression, domination, and individualism. It is easy to forget that, until the 1960s, gender inequality itself was a pervasive and well-protected ideology.[14] In the self-centered ideologies that dominate our culture, crucial human relationships are considered replaceable, unimportant, and extraneous. We prize an autonomy that devalues both nuclear and extended families, assigning a lower status to preserving and honoring enduring bonds than pursuing one's own agenda. With the needs of relatedness degraded, the social fabric that holds us together has shredded and worn thin, leaving many as lonely little fragments in a disjointed world.

Not only do we tend to underestimate the importance of subtle-body experiences, such as sexual bonding and other relational realities, we do not even know how to identify them. We not only lack the words, but we risk ridicule or marginalization if we try to speak of them. Unfortunately, what goes unnamed can be treated as if it does not exist.[15] Despite our denial of its importance, this world of relational mystery and wonder remains our birthright. As we tune in and refine our awareness to the subtle senses, we find another dimension of existence in and around us. This attunement promises to deliver us from the isolation and madness of a surface life cut off from the authenticity and richness of the depths. When we dive deep, deeper than the love of the broken heart, we find a greater love burning in our soul. D.H. Lawrence adds a poet's touch to this idea:

> *Go deeper than love, for the soul has greater depths,*
> *love is like the grass, but the heart is deep wild rock*
> *molten, yet dense and permanent.*
> *Go down to your deep old heart, and lose sight of yourself.*
> *And lose sight of me, the me whom you turbulently loved.*
> *Let us lose sight of ourselves, and break the mirrors.*
> *For the fierce curve of our lives is moving again to the depths*
> *out of sight, in the deep living heart.*

CHAPTER 7

Sex & Erotic Entanglement

It isn't possible to love and part. You will wish it was.
—E. M. Forster

I HAVE ALWAYS BEEN PASSIONATELY ATTRACTED to the opposite sex and, at the same time, felt a reverence for the mystery and weightiness of sexuality. When Eros touches our lives and we fall in love, it pulls us into a turbocharged world in ways we can hardly fathom in our ordinary state of mind. In the hormonal bath of two new chemistries, we feel inebriated with delicious sensations as we revel in the beauty of the other. It is as if we are on a drug high; and science tells us the endorphin surges of romance make that analogy close to the truth. If the relationship deepens into mutual commitment, we travel beyond the excitement of the early days of intrigue and attraction to even more profound territory.

The continuing electrical infusion from the mutual exchange of sensuality, caring, and openhearted vulnerability leads into a world of mystery, surrender, and sweetness—and to potential terror and chaos as well. As the easy endorphins of novel sex give way to oxytocin-infused communion, a delicate intimacy encourages bonding and creates safety for the emergence of our core vulnerabilities, the wounds from our infancy and childhood. At this juncture, it takes more than passion; it takes courage to follow the path of love downward into our early selves. In the words of poet Rainier Rilke, "For beauty is the beginning of terror we can barely endure, and we admire it so because it calmly disdains to destroy us."[1]

It is understandable how people can get addicted to the early pleasures of romance, attraction, and mating—and frightened as the stakes grow larger and intimacy grows. Even while coming of age in the 1960s, when sexual experimentation was considered to be a sign of a woman's liberation and wisdom, intuitively, I sensed the power of mingling myself so intimately with another human being and proceeded with caution. To have sex for fun and pleasure; sex as a haven from loneliness; sex to forget; sex to feel wanted; sex to fill the emptiness, to satisfy the yearning; sex to dominate or be dominated—I recognized all were possibilities.

Though I tried in my day to give it a go, still, temperamentally, it was never a fit. In my sexual nature, I feel like a cross between Carmen and Teresa of Avila. The concept of casual sex always eluded me, but I have a wild, curious sexual nature that readily connects to my religious instincts. After I married, most often sex was like a prayer for me, a Dionysian, ecstatic, exhilarating prayer where I lost myself in the mysteries of two becoming one. I am sure now I was inflated by the many transcendent sexual experiences I have had in my life. I even fancied myself some kind of *daikini*, a kind of spiritual muse who introduces others to these mysteries. My experience with Rob demolished that delusion rather thoroughly, needless to say.

So, fair warning, I have my temperamental prejudices and perspective on this subject. I am not certain that sex of any sort does not attach you to your partner.[2] In my experience, no matter how detached or casual you try to be about it, the binding quality of sexual energy acts something like super glue.

When you glue together two sheets of paper with a strong adhesive and attempt to pull them apart, both sheets end up being torn. Pieces of each sheet remain attached to the other (a fitting metaphor for ripped attachments). From this point of view, some aspect of your sexual partner's energetic essence stays with you; and part of you goes with them. You may not even remember the name of your hook-up or hot date, but the impression of that sexual meeting remains with you, binding some piece of you to that person.

We imagine it is all behind us. But if sexual memories break unexpectedly into your mind, or you make the effort to recall, you can see how they stick and bind your energies through guilt, shame, triumph, regret, or craving. In this way, we leave little bits of ourselves with our sexual partners and may have less and less to offer the next person as a result.

The idea that we drag around torn pieces of our former lovers that impinge on our ability to bond with another person is not exactly at the top of the charts in terms of popularity. In fact, outside of the evangelical Christian world, it is wildly unfashionable, even ridiculed as an anachronism or throwback to less enlightened times. Yet, current freewheeling attitudes toward sex deny the potential strength of sexual attachment. With the alluring possibilities of open relationships and serial partners suggested by sexual liberation, who wants to give up the pleasures, or face the lasting consequences, implied by the suggestion that sex creates enduring ties? Acknowledging that we may be forming energetic bonds to our sexual partner that will stay with us long after they are gone puts a crimp in the concept of sexual freedom and "trial relationships."

We are wise to honor and respect the power of sex to transform us in ways we cannot anticipate, but must be willing to serve. Sex is a potent mystery. Sexual energy coupled with a tender heart opens us to spiritual depths; and, when it is misused, potential dissipation or devastation.

The Sacredness of Bonded Love

A soul connection is a resonance between two people who respond to the essential beauty of each other's individual natures...
—John Welwood

The merging of body and soul in loving relationship marks for many the point of greatest intensity and meaning in their lives. For some of us, myself included, it is the place where they most readily touch the Divine. As we learn to surrender to each other in good times and bad, we are, in effect, surrendering to a power greater than ourselves. When we are in touch with the subtle world, we begin to recognize the sacredness of bonded love. The partner becomes our earthly representative of the Divine, and the relationship serves more and more as a vessel for Spirit incarnating.

We discover that when we marry another, it is not just symbolically or legally, but *actually*. In the erotic container of the relationship, most often in lovemaking, but also in simple moments of everyday intimacy, the energetic signatures of the partners come together to be profoundly changed.

In the field of the subtle body, the Holy Spirit enters to spark an alchemical blending of individual essences and to create the new life of the relationship itself. This potential to bring the Divine into the physical, to spiritualize the connection, is why married love is considered a sacrament in the Christian tradition. Sexuality, as an expression of love and surrender, can provide a vehicle for expanding consciousness and shearing away the separated self of both people. In such transformative moments, lovemaking becomes a prayer or active meditation. From this perspective, lovers invite the alchemy of a holy communion to touch upon their fragile vulnerabilities and ignite the fire hidden there to burn away the obstacles to love.

Contemplative prayer retreat leader Cynthia Bourgeault calls sexuality in the context of committed union *Eucharistic sex*, a sacrament of profound receptivity.[3] "It is the daily experience of 'this is my body given for you,' lived out in the myriad opportunities for self-surrender and forgiveness, that gradually fashions a sacrament out of our human sexual passion."[4] In the container of conscious relationship, each partner becomes a more permeable channel for divine love.⁵ I had been intensely aware of this gift, and grieved most for this sacred mystery.

SEXUALITY AND LA PETITE MORT

The orgasm has replaced the cross as the focus of longing
and the image of fulfillment.
—Malcolm Muggeridge

In the language of the subtle world, the energetic presence that grows between two people is sometimes referred to as the *relationship body*, the *spirit child*, the *wedding garment*, or simply, the *"third."* This field of energetic presence defies our usual relational categories, but sometimes we can perceive it when we tune into the subtle senses, especially the heart center. Notice how bonded partners seem to become increasingly like each other as they spend more time together, even as they become more distinct in their individualities.⁶ Paradoxically, love both enhances their uniqueness and nourishes the spirit child between them. The field of energetic warmth growing between them appears to both encompass and be rooted in each partner, like a blooming energy plant with two taproots.

How does a living field of interconnectedness, a spirit child or third, come into being? At our current level of awareness, no one can explain it, but by examining our experiences, we can make some revealing observations about this mystical fact.

It is perhaps easiest to grasp in the context of sexuality. If you have had deeply satisfying sexual experience with your partner, recall the moments of your most profound love, surrender, and mystery. These moments will be most accessible when you are in an "out of time" altered state of consciousness of appreciation and caring, in nature, with a loved one, or in meditation or prayer.

In the course of your relationship, you and your partner may have experienced many hundreds of orgasms, scores of mutual cascades of intense pleasurable release with each other. In openhearted sexuality those little ego deaths of surrendered delight make an indelible imprint on your soul. The electric moment of mutual surrender—*la petite mort*—as the French call it, when you dissolve into each other, melts the two of you into oneness. Even a nanosecond of that dissolving dark bliss can carry you into the realm of the sacred that informs and profoundly nourishes your relationship and your respective souls.

Consider how those moments of connectivity may cohere into a psychic substance, adding each to the next, to create a *shared living field* that links you and your partner in the mystery that drew you together. Once established, this field forms a magnetic field between you that has subtle, enduring qualities.

This is the field I am suggesting may give an inviolable, lasting quality to experiences of union: something created that cannot be undone.

The adhering nature of deep sexual connection is only one factor that contributes to the forming of subtle-body bonds, but it is a powerful one. Bourgeault discusses how sexuality itself has the potential to blend the material and the subtle worlds, and how the physical substances of lovemaking contribute to the alchemy of spiritual union. She describes the third or spirit child as that which forms the love itself in marriage:

> This "sphere of existence" [created from love between two people] is not simply an energy field, but in fact a body—or to put it more accurately, an energy field is a body. There is a subtle substantiality involved here, a kind of "flesh within the flesh" that…is built up not simply by the acts of loving self-surrender between the partners but by the actual commingling of their substances during their physical lovemaking. In other words, it has a real though subtle materiality to it which is equally at home in this realm and the next.[7]

I would add that, as well as blending bodily substances or fluids, shared orgasm introduces a catalyst of electric potency for binding the energetic bodies together in a way that we do not understand but that urges our consideration.

In another iteration of a similar idea, there is a Sanskrit belief that when you allow a man to penetrate you, you take on each other's karma through the orgasm. Through the mixing of bodily fluids, you fill your DNA with the blueprint of the other's karmic memories and carry them forward with you until that karma is resolved. They also believe the interlocking of DNA creates unbreakable cords. As if working through one's own karma were not enough! The path of bonded union is not for the fainthearted.

Evidence for a Lasting "Third"
What we once enjoyed and deeply loved we can never lose,
for all that we love deeply becomes a part of us.
—Helen Keller

The interpenetrating bond of two people in a love relationship has been alluded to for centuries, but we are only now beginning to explore it seriously in the context of our culture's secular, scientific outlook. Starry-eyed romantics such as myself, with our mythic, metaphysical, sentimental, or psychological imaginings, did not invent the notion of an enduring third. That two separate things can be so bound at the energetic level that they form a new entity has also been demonstrated in the world of science.

Quantum physics, for instance, provides at least an evocative metaphor, and likely an actual energetic dynamic, for subtle-body bonding. Physicists use the term *quantum entanglement* to describe the state in which two particles that have been in interaction remain correlated forever. Erwin Shrödinger, a pioneer of quantum mechanics, coined the term *entanglement*, calling it the most characteristic trait of the quantum world. The two formerly connecting particles remain on the same wavelength, able to affect each other, no matter how distant they become in time and space.

If you separate the particles and change even a single characteristic of one of them, the effect is *instantaneously* reflected in the other, without the transfer of any known type of signal. Scientists have verified this trait experimentally and confirmed it as an accepted property of nature at the subatomic level.

Einstein considered this inexplicable, resonant linking "spooky" because it defies the laws of Newtonian physics. In this respect, the two particles act *as if they were one entity*. In a very real sense, quantum entanglement implies that a new creation has been forged—a kind of third entity—that persists indefinitely.

Behavioral scientists are finding similar links and action-at-a-distance dynamics in experiments with human beings. For example, at the Institute of Noetic Sciences in California, in a study IONS called "The Love Study," scientists conducted research to see if they could measure the impact of compassionate intention between couples. Senior scientist Dean Radin explains: "If it is true that entanglement actually persists, by means of which we do not understand, if they are physically entangled, you should be able to separate them, poke one, and see the other one flinch."[8] Researchers were able to demonstrate that an entanglement-like link does, in fact, exist between partners, not only in their emotional and psychological selves, but also in their physical bodies—even when the two people are not in close physical proximity.[9]

In this study, the action was not a poke, but the generation and sending of feelings of compassion and love. Researchers placed husbands and wives in two separate rooms; they shielded the room so that not even electromagnetic waves could penetrate, ensuring that whatever feeling conveyed was not an energy currently known by conventional science. The husband watched a closed-circuit TV on which he could see his wife. At intervals, researchers instructed him to send her loving thoughts. They directed his wife, while connected to monitoring equipment, to just sit comfortably and relax. She had no visual cues to indicate when her husband was sending. Yet her body knew! The monitoring equipment showed that her blood pressure and perspiration rate changed dramatically at precisely those times when her husband was connecting lovingly with her. Similar results were found in a number of double blind, randomized studies at other institutions.

These studies suggest that two emotionally bonded people are entangled at a molecular (or other) level. That is, we become so physiologically aligned with our partners that parts of our nervous systems resonate and respond to one another, at a distance, even without physical contact. These findings point to the existence of the subtle-body third I describe.

Modern depth psychology, another tradition entirely, conceptualizes the mystery of the third through a process called the *coniunctio*: the holy wedding or sacred marriage. Subtle-body coniunctio experiences drive us to individuate, to become more fully who we are meant to be.

Carl Jung conducted extensive research into medieval alchemy that he believed described symbolically and precisely deep processes of the psyche.[10] Jung recovered a series of twenty woodcuts, the *Rosarium Philosophorum*, that depict a king (sun) and queen (moon) joining together in sexual union. These fascinating, psychologically astute images portray graphically and in detail the gradual transformation of the king and queen into *one being*.

In Jungian psychology, these images are believed to illustrate steps in the union of opposites that take place in the medium of the subtle body, both within an individual and between two people. Midway in the transformation, we see an image of a hermaphrodite, in the form of a merged being with two heads, which describes the spirit child who becomes the vehicle for further transformation to the final stage of a Christ-like resurrection into light.

A source more traditional, more familiar, and suspect to many, the Catholic Church, recognized, centuries ago, that a mystical third is created through marriage. Catholicism considers the "one body" of marriage inviolable, a sacred covenant, or sacrament, a visible sign of the invisible mystery of union with God.[11] With our modern secular sensibilities, we tend to discount such notions as "the two shall become one flesh," as marriage is depicted in the Judeo-Christian tradition—not to mention the antediluvian description "The wife hath not power of her own body, but the husband; and likewise also the husband hath not power of his own body, but the wife."

Nevertheless, the subtle-body experiences I discuss here give cause to reexamine these concepts. The implications are that what one spouse does with his or her body necessarily has an impact on the other. As wildly unfashionable as it sounds, what if this dusty notion turned out to be based on a real phenomenon, as the subtle-body evidence suggests? From this point of view, a truly married pair no longer exists simply as two individuals with two different bodies. At the levels of the heart, mind, and spirit, they have "become one." They literally belong to, and are part of each other via the subtle connection between them.

I am not suggesting that the energetic third forms in all relationships, perhaps not even in many. While we can say that sexuality binds us to our partner, many factors, which are only now coming to be understood, determine whether or not we connect with our partner in this sacred, powerful manner. But we need to acknowledge that, even without conscious intention, such connections do form, tying the partners together in an abiding way that is barely understood in contemporary culture, and certainly rarely respected.

This entanglement characterized by the third encompasses and contains a couple in a way that parallels the magnetic field surrounding an individual, which some call an aura. Perhaps most palpable between certain couples who have been together for decades, in heightened states of awareness, this field can be perceived. After my husband's death, in liminal time, with my subtle senses sharpened, I began to notice the energetic fields of others around me. During that time, I could actually discern a person's relationship status. A person in a close-couple relationship had an aura with diffuse boundaries and tendrils of energy extending outward, rather than an aura that contained only his or her body. If I traced these tendrils, I saw they led to the field of the partner—even if he or she was in another room.

These relationship fields had particular qualities or colors, seemingly unique to each couple, which made it possible to track them. They usually felt sweet, warm, lively, and vivid to me, although sometimes the field was jagged and hot; perhaps they were in conflict or under stress, and the field was charged with other characteristics, such as fiery eroticism or gathering storminess.

We can experience this phenomenon ourselves as the marvel of seeing into our partner—especially when we first fall in love and become aware of the potential for creating this vivid field of connectivity together. Normally, once the union begins to form and grows as the foundation for a couple's life together, they tend to take this relationship body for granted—until it is ruptured, that is.

ETHERIC CORDS AND THE SUBTLE-BODY WOUND

Energy healers claim that the tearing of a bonded pair creates gaps in the etheric bodies of both partners. Subjective evidence showed me that when a bonded union is torn apart by betrayal and abandonment, both partners walk around as entangled echoes of each other. Each trails the serrated tendrils of energetic connection that keep their inner bodies *resonating*.

Our culture may pooh-pooh the idea of such relational ties, but the shamanic traditions of indigenous people that recognize the energetic interconnectivity of the world do not. Shamans have a name for harmful intimate ties: *cords*. Cords are described as dense ropes of subtle materiality formed by fear-based relational attachments. Energetic projections run back and forth through these cords between people, often draining the energy of one at the expense of the other. To have a clear picture of betrayal, it helps to understand the concept of cording. I even devoted an entire chapter (10) to exploring psychological projection as the psychological equivalent of cording. It is impossible not to form these attachments in a close relationship. Normally, we just do our best to be aware of them, and work to minimize the damage they can do.

When betrayal shocks you, these cords of connection are especially apt to light up and transfer strong feelings between you and your mate. In shamanic traditions, "cord-cutting" ceremonies are said to help release these dysfunctional energetic ties. I was willing to try anything, so underwent numerous cord-cutting rituals to help undo my remaining, fear-inducing, destructive connections to Rob. The rituals helped raise my awareness of the anger and fear I needed to clear, but I still sensed that something even more fundamental was taking place.

Slowly, I began to differentiate the energetic cords from the spirit child third: Cords were associated with delusions, with afflictive, compulsive emotions. The third, grounded in the spiritual or heart connection, emanated love. We might call the cord an unholy tie, and the spirit child a holy tie. A cord reveals our humanity; the third, our divinity. Both likely exist in a betrayed relationship.

Falling in love, opening our depths, and sexually uniting with a partner impact our inner being like little else. Believing that we can simply terminate this intermingling whenever we decide a relationship has ended defies the physics of intimate engagement. Abandonment and betrayal may jam the circuits of the connection; but despite our conscious intentions, missives holy and unholy keep running back and forth between the two individuals. It is as if we are still in relationship, and on one level, at least, we are.

I am convinced that the psychic resonance between formerly bonded partners continues even at a distance. We can experience this ongoing bond with a former partner in myriad ways: becoming aware of his or her whereabouts and activities without being told; telepathically sensing the other pulling us into their state of mind; "hearing" mental conversations with them; feeling their presence in bizarre dreams or unexplained sexual arousal, and other forms of physical distress, many of which are explored in this book.

Betrayal seems to make an incomplete cut in the bonds we form; it does not entirely sever either the cords or the third. The heart resonance makes you keep loving him, though you hate what he has done; the sexual reverberations keep you yearning for his body, though you are sickened by the idea; the attachment keeps you longing for his return, though you feel disgust and revenge at the thought.

What is most important to understand is that the ongoing tie makes you highly vulnerable to his actions, especially his sexual activities. Energetically, it is as if you are still in the relationship. Meanwhile, he may engage in extremely hurtful behaviors, oblivious to the impact on you, as he will be acting as if no relationship at all exists. And you, too, will not understand and tend to blame yourself for what more and more starts to feel like an obsession you cannot shake.

CHAPTER 8

Desecration

You own everything that happened to you. Tell your stories.
If people wanted you to write warmly about them,
they should have behaved better.
—Anne Lamott

I N THE WEE HOURS one Friday night a few weeks after Rob's departure,
as I was settling into bed, an alarming pain struck my heart. It felt like a
hot poker piercing me. As I grabbed my chest, my belly contracted with the
same sensation, and I let out a little scream. I went dizzy with the pain and was
frightened. This was one of the first times the pain was so purely physical that
I felt I might be dying. These heart contractions went on for nearly an hour
before letting up. I rocked and soothed myself, like a mother holding her child
through the delirium of a fever.

Once the initial intensity abated, a wave of intuition arose. It took the
form of images, more like a communication directly from my subtle body
than from my rational mind: *Rob is with another woman right now.* What I
suspected may seem farfetched, or simply the conjurings of my jealous imagination, but my intuition was confirmed soon enough. Rob had indeed been at
a hot tub scene with a number of women that evening.

I had a rare, ill-advised meeting with him soon after this experience and
tried to explain the distressing impact I believed his foray into opening so soon
to other women was having on my body soul. It seemed important enough for
us both that he would want to know. I felt we needed time for our ties to dissolve and to grieve the relationship. I did not comprehend yet how radically he
had cut me off, or that he already had his sights set on someone else.

He looked at his watch, tapped his foot impatiently, and suggested that I
"get support elsewhere." He accused me of trying to guilt-induce and manipulate him. He had already "completed his grieving" and was ready to "move
on," to make a new life. Any impact on me was my problem. My rational mind

took his side. I told myself, "He has a right to do whatever he wants—the relationship is over." So, I questioned my intuition. How could these pains, arising seemingly from nowhere, be a reverberation with Rob's prowling activities anyway? Surely, it was a coincidence. I must just be hurt and envious that he was with others and fabricating this physical distress with my thoughts. Thoughts create feelings, do they not? At least that was how I had previously related to disturbing emotions.

I knew, and had taught others, how to take responsibility for feelings when we are hurting. I was convinced that how we feel has nothing to do with how someone treats us, and everything to do with how we *choose to react to or interpret* what happens to us. Once I had spent an entire semester teaching an introductory psychology class built around the idea that "attitudes are the wires that connect us to events."

In our relationship, I had wholeheartedly embraced this belief and put it into practice whenever I was upset, doing my best to own my pain, regardless of his words or actions that appeared to be the cause. Surely, all I needed to do now was to change my attitude, drop my interpretation, and these pains would stop.

I tried; I really did try, but my efforts were doomed.

That night I was registering the first signs of a real interpersonal phenomenon. My rational mind was dismissing the truth my body, intuition, and subtle senses were trying to convey. Given our blindness to the nature of deep bonding, I had no context for categorizing what was happening to me; nor did Rob, of course. While I discounted my body's messages and intuition, and concluded I must be wrong—that what he did no longer had anything to do with me—this episode turned out to be the prelude of many more reverberations yet to come.

Within weeks of leaving, Rob had landed my replacement, and I was treated to the visceral agonies of his taking on a new lover. I will never know exactly when it began, but he decided to go public with their liaison on New Year's Eve. When I was on retreat, he emailed to inform me he was "officially dating as of tonight."

The presence of another woman in the still vivid field of my connection with him added animal insult to my broken heart. Being set aside had been bad enough, but being so easily and quickly replaced put the nail in the coffin of my equanimity, dignity, and pride. In the next few months, the torments also opened the Pandora's box of my psyche and let out some of the most horrid feelings imaginable. Rage, envy, jealousy, malice, resentment, vengeance, and hatred came flying into my inner world to show me how evil I could be. I did not like this other woman and I hated him.

Soon I had the unfortunate experience of encountering him with my successor at a small, weekly free-form dance event in town. I have to admit, I went with a visiting friend, even knowing he might be there, curious to see whom he was "dating." Still, I was completely unprepared for what happened. There he was, with her. Although he saw me, that did not faze him. They were all over each other on the dance floor, not five feet in front of me. He gazed at her adoringly as he stroked and played with her. While he behaved as if I did not exist, *I was there.* When I paused and looked him directly in the eye, I started to tremble, and it took everything to keep from walking over and slapping him. Finally, I found the presence of mind to grab my friend's arm and say, "Let's get out of here."

This may sound like a typical "B" movie scene, but its impact took me off the set. As I stumbled toward the car, hundreds of points of light swirled in the blackness above me. I felt like I was hallucinating my way through Van Gogh's *Starry Night*, or Fellini's *Satyricon*, or a surreal painting by Salvador Dali. I tried to laugh it off, as if it were the ending of a bad film.

My friend turned to hug me as we walked out of the building and said, "That was the cruelest thing I have ever seen." I did not quite get it at the time, but it was another instance of psychological trauma that ransacked my reality. I had no way of knowing how much this simple scene had traumatized my body and soul, or how long the repercussions would last.

The next day, as my shocked dissociation wore thin, my belly went into convulsive tremors, and I was sick to my stomach. The sight of my so-recently-doting fiancé enraptured with his new woman, as if I did not exist, had been the equivalent of acid being poured into my insides. It seared me with pains more piercing than the intense contractions I had while in labor transition with Rachael.

Now,I was not only a brokenhearted, scorned lover, but an enraged, grievously wounded creature as well. These pains were real, as were the primal feelings of rage and fear. After this, I was tempted to engage in revenge sex myself, and came close, but stopped myself. I felt how unfair it was to use someone else that way, how angry I would be at myself afterward, and how it would muddy the waters between us even more.

The reverberations did not stop there. Rob continued to go quite public in our small town with his new affair, frequenting other venues we had attended together. Not long after the dance scene, he showed up with her at an annual poetry event we had attended for years. They came in late and finally settled into my row, only five or six seats from me. I could not avoid seeing him rubbing her thigh, nuzzling her neck, stroking her hands, hair, and shoulders. I should have gotten up right then, but the place was full, and I had frozen in my seat when I saw them, as if stunned with a cattle prod. I was attempting to be cool and act like the grown woman I am, but to the animal brain, and to the child in me, these sights were torture. Each stroke of her thigh felt like someone rubbing my insides with sandpaper; yet, still, I did not move away.

Someone said, when I told them what happened, "You must be jealous." Really, was that it? Was this jealousy? Or maybe this was envy, the primary weakness of my supposed personality type? The last time I remembered feeling jealous was in the eighth grade, and it was nothing like this. I admit wanting what I not did not have (envy) was in the mix, as well as feelings of possessiveness (jealousy); but the visceral intensity of the pain, the breath-stopping panic, and the confusion went far beyond what I had known as either jealousy or envy. Later, as I learned more about trauma, I understood how trauma amps survival instincts up to daimonic proportions in a misguided attempt to protect us from further harm.

Shock freezes you in life-threatening situations, like when a rabbit is faced with a coyote. Since there was obviously no physical threat in seeing my so-recent mate seducing another woman, it would never have occurred to me that such a sight would register in my brain as "life threatening." I did not realize then that the brain makes no distinction between a physical and a psychological threat. Even though our relationship was supposedly over weeks before, my body soul did not see it that way. The threat that had me frozen in my seat was a threat to my identity, to my psychological integrity, and to my soul.

What Next?

A nightmare had taken hold of my body.
Lunacy had dug its way inside my mind.
    —Amanda Steele, *The Cliff*

Rob was embedded as my mate in so many parts of my brain, that seeing him with someone else jammed my circuits. My brain could not compute the radical new information with its former templates of reality. But the onslaught was not over. Soon afterward, I began to sense an even more disturbing resonance with his activities.

One night, I woke up in bed with a start in a mild panic. I was uncharacteristically hot with sweat, agitated, and powerfully sexually aroused. A throbbing energy between my legs, penetrating through my genitals into my deep belly, had awakened me from desperately needed sleep. This was not like waking from a dream. No, definitely not a dream. In a highly unusual way, I felt as though I was being sexually assaulted. It felt like—the only word that came to mind was rape—it felt like an energetic rape.

As bizarre as this may sound, it was as if Rob's double was ravaging me, at the same time as he was having sex with the other woman. The sensations of sexual attack had awakened me with panic and passion, nearly to the point of orgasm. Good grief, I thought, what next? Had my hysteria reached into my dreams to do this to me, or what?

Throughout his yearlong liaison with his first new lover, these startling episodes continued, occurring at times when I was simply sitting in my living room, but more frequently they awakened me in the night, mostly on week-ends. When I looked at the clock—several times it was around midnight—I thought, "Ohmygod, they must be having sex now." Just a vivid imagination, you say?—more like the invasion of the body snatchers. I felt literally possessed. I began to wish I had never wakened to my subtle senses. I could not believe it. No one would want to believe or admit it, too icky, but I *knew* somehow I was entangled in a sexual triangle, an unwitting participant in their affair.

I felt like a bit player in someone else's life. Sensitive now to constantly shifting levels of angst and sexual stimulation I associated with being pulled into their romance, I noted lulls and peaks in their contact. I would sense when they were apart on a particular weekend, for example—relief, and then I would find out accidentally that I had been correct. At times, when the onslaught of these humiliating sexual-intrusion experiences would increase in frequency, I cringed and wished they would take a break from each other so I could recover myself. I especially detested when I could sense how my energies were contrib-uting to the intensity of their affair.

Against my conscious will, their twosome was actually a threesome that was costing me plenty. Somehow their relationship was living partly on the fuel of my *shakti*, or sexual essence, a tap that had been fully opened with Rob in the weeks building up to our wedding ceremony. It seemed that they were enjoying an extravagant vacation together financed by my considerable emotional and energetic investment in Rob.

I thought I was coming to understand what the Buddhists meant by the "misuse of sexual energy." Using the energies I had poured into Rob for their enjoyment seemed so wrong. I was angry about it but felt helpless before this realization. I could think of no way, without being considered a nutcase, to communicate this sense of violation.

Are your eyebrows lifting? Mine probably would be if someone had told me this before it happened to me; but I am simply reporting my inner body sensations, along with my interpretation, of course. My mind kept telling me it was not possible to still be "connected" with Rob—much less with his new lover. Yet, in a way I did not understand, this flow of subtle-body substance felt like a two-way street. In deep dives into myself, I did my best to suspend my story, my interpretations, my analysis, and just stay with "don't know" mind, and with the intensely disturbing sensations.

As irrational as it was, I still could not escape the feeling that my energies were implicated in his new love affair. I lectured myself with the litany of other possibilities: My imagination was on overdrive; I must be fantasizing, making up stories, exaggerating my sensations, stirring up my envy and rage, even hallucinating to keep myself company. Or maybe I was punishing myself for being abandoned or conjuring up these torments as a projection of my own rage.

With all this analysis, I vaguely intuited that my mind was busy trying to deliver a rational panacea to paste over the suffering pouring forth from my physical, subtle, and emotional bodies. Beyond my overactive imagination and tendency to label experience, I came to believe a real phenomenon of a torn and desecrated sacred connection throbbed in me with the intensity of an amputated limb.

I longed to communicate, to say, "stop," as you would instinctively, if someone was inadvertently stepping on your toe, for instance. Yet, with no context for understanding this phenomenon, no one would believe me, least of all either of them, lost in the throes of fresh sexual excitement. I had trouble believing what was happening myself. While I felt certain neither of them would choose to be participating in such hurtful "karma," if they only knew, I was at a loss about what to do about it. Everybody did things like this, didn't they, going from one relationship to another, or even carrying on with two partners at the same time? It was so commonplace; yet I had not heard of anyone talking about anything like what I was going through, so I continued to doubt myself.

Haltingly, I tried various methods to heal and protect myself. Finally, I spoke with my therapist about whether I might be hallucinating the whole thing, going a bit psychotic; I worked on withdrawing the projection of my rage; I journeyed with a shaman to do cord-cutting and to cast out this "possession"; I talked with a priest about "exorcism"; and I consulted with more than one psychic to help put up shields to protect me. I was highly motivated to get this pain and torment to stop. Still, I mostly felt powerless against these distressing intrusions that I still believe were entering me through my subtle-body connection with Rob.

I could not escape feeling like a victim. The chaos and pain was register-ing *in my body*, while he was oblivious, pumped up with the gratification of a new lover. I brooded about how bonding with him had given him this key to my undoing, and began to consider it the worst mistake I had ever made. My spiritual attitudes that "everything happens for the best" or "you create your own reality" were absolutely anemic in this situation, and had all but evapo-rated by this time anyway in my efforts to cope with the turmoil.

Eventually, I left town for six months; perhaps, I thought, physical proxim-ity was contributing to my sensitivity. The distance, however, made little dif-ference. In addition to the ongoing sexual intrusions, I started to have dreams that attested to the continuation of the triangle. In one striking instance, two nights in a row, I woke dreaming of Rob on a white-sand Hawaiian beach, with plumeria trees and all. The following day, I got a call from my daughter, who started the conversation with "Guess where Rob is?" Her best friend, who was visiting Maui, had called to say she had seen him at a local store with some woman.

At around the one-year mark of our breakup, I registered a longer lull in the sexual invasions. At first I felt a ray of hope, "Ah, the connection with him is finally dissolving." Then came a renewed flaring of these intrusions for sev-eral weeks, followed by a sudden dying out. It occurred to me that they may have split up. Not long afterward, I learned that, indeed, their relationship had ended. Finally, I had a respite for my energy body to rest and recuperate, especially as I heard he intended to take time off from relationship this time— kind of like going on the wagon.

And a respite it was, until nearly a year later when I began having regular dreams of him with another woman again. Oh, my. Then, for the first time in my life, my lower back went into spasm for nearly six months, diagnosed as piriformis syndrome. The piriformis is a muscle deep in the buttocks. The contraction of the piriformis may be an unconscious neuromuscular protec-tive response to unwanted sexual penetration that gets retriggered by current stress or reminiscent life events.[1] I sensed the "unwanted sexual penetration" was related to Rob, not only from his inauthenticity in our sexual relationship, but from the distressing intrusions I had experienced the prior year.

During this time, I was still struggling with the PTSD symptoms from the breakup. I had no idea what Rob was up to, but in a rare chance encounter, he confirmed that he had indeed been "deepening," his new term for having sex, with another woman the past few months. Perhaps it was again coincidental.

Were my back problems a residue of the sexual violation I felt with him, or from some entirely unrelated event? Or might they too be attributable to a continued resonance—to my subtle body reacting to his renewed sexual activities? I could not be certain but had my suspicions. Coincidence or not, soon after my back problems finally improved, I heard that relationship, too, had ended.

The final incidents I will share with you that attested to a continuing resonance came in the fourth year. I woke in a mild panic from a dream in which I spotted Rob dancing with a very tall woman in a sea of people surrounded by pools of steaming water. Within weeks, I heard he had taken yet another lover; this one was nearly six feet tall; and they frequented dances at a popular hot springs. Soon afterwards I had a series of dreams where he appeared again to be on a tropical island, often on a boat as if touring. I simply sighed when later I heard they, too, had traveled to Hawaii.

ADULTERATION

There's a sort of rage a man feels when he's been deceived
where he most trusted. It compares to no other anger.
—Orson Scott Card, *Treason*

These psychic and subtle-body experiences added up, and each one increased my awe and respect for the lasting impact of sexual bonding. Later, I heard from several others of stories similar to mine that attest to the powerful crosscurrents of relational ties. Be careful to whom you commit yourself to emotionally and sexually! Ignorance of the repercussions does not save us from the results. Many others learned, like I did, the harsh consequences you suffer if you have deeply bonded with someone and they connect with a new lover before your ties dissolve.

If you find out about the betrayal while you are still with them, learning of the faithlessness crushes you; but at least what they have done is obvious. It is easier to see it is their problem, and you know the cause of your distress. If they have already left you, however, how can you possibly fault them? For beyond the original shock of hearing of their new lover, it defies logic that you should continue to be affected. You must either: discount and repress the irrational protests of your subtle body, or question, shame, and blame yourself for your inexplicable reactions. Either way, you are likely to imagine you must be seriously impaired.

When we consider the etheric truth of enduring ties, however, these reactions begin to make sense. Through the bonds of subtle entanglement, in ways that we do not understand or perhaps even recognize, the inundation of the foreign energies of another person into a bonded relationship leave you cooking in a toxic brew. It is a brew that not only feels like adultery, but may well be an actual pollution of a susceptible, torn, highly sensitized connection that *you cannot will away.*

To *adulterate* means to *pollute* or to *contaminate.* The otherwise inexplicable sense of defilement that invades the psyche when you are drawn into a triangle with a current or a former partner, rises, I believe, from this bona fide subtle-body reality. The quasi-physical toxicity of mixed sexual energies infuses the etheric body, and contributes to the multilayered crisis of betrayal. As long as the ties endure, you cannot prevent yourself from resonating with your mate, from feeling sickened, even outright poisoned, any more than you can will yourself not to have food poisoning when you have eaten contaminated meat.

Most women may not even make the connection between the sickness that comes over them and the activities of their current or former mate. The stress of this intrusion into your energetic body can express itself in many forms less direct than those I have shared with you here. It had been my practice for years to delve into my bodily sensations and feelings, so naturally I noticed the disturbance most through those channels.

Each of us has our individual way of coping with these subtle intrusions. For no apparent cause, you may fall ill—develop headaches or allergies, or get depressed, or over or under eat, or indulge in other addictions, or become uncharacteristically angry and irritable, or overwork, or go ahead and start up an ill-advised affair or two of your own.

Although it may be inexplicable until we realize its source, sometimes the connection between our subtle-body intelligence and our physical body becomes too evident to ignore. One woman I spoke with told me of experiencing recurrent gastrointestinal disturbances along with nausea and other flu-like symptoms for a number of months, which her doctor had trouble diagnosing. Finally, she discovered through an errant email that her husband had been sleeping with another woman. After she read the message, she doubled over, ran into the bathroom, and threw up. She finally connected the dots between her physical symptoms and the hidden activities of her mate. Once the affair was out in the open, her symptoms began to clear up.

There are many similar stories, but women are often reluctant to talk about them, lest they be accused of hypochondria and hysteria at best, or mental illness at worst.

In the cultural ignorance about the lasting ramifications of emotional and sexual subtle-body bonding, unfortunately, we normally have no support or framework for understanding what we are going through. That is one of the reasons I am sharing my story. Getting a proper diagnosis goes a long way toward healing. If we can become aware of these subtle realities, by speaking our truth with each other, we can help others to recognize what is happening before they lose their self-respect, dignity, and mental health. We can better garner the resources we need to stand up for ourselves and to weather this suffering as the spiritual trial that it is rather than an indictment of our stability and sanity.

My truth is this: Deep sexual contact imprints powerfully in the most delicate, receptive parts of one's being. The ties that bind are sensitive, mysterious, and resonant with our partner's depths. Depending on the strength of the bonds, they dissolve only over a long period of time. That is, if they ever do. The implications of these facts are that betrayal, adultery, and abandonment can inflict their damage on the soul whether you are consciously aware of it or not—even long after either one of you walks out the door.

THE YIN POINT: A TEMPLE OF THE DIVINE

In my struggle to understand what was happening and to recover myself after Rob left, I engaged in literally dozens of healing modalities. Some I had used for various purposes over the years; others I tried for the first time. Acupuncture I was accustomed to; it was a restorative approach I used regularly. I always felt more balanced after a treatment, and in dealing with PTSD symptoms, going in for a session helped calm my system.

An acupuncturist feels the pulses of the main energetic points of your body to determine where blocks lie and inserts needles or magnets to help balance your subtle-energy body. In one of my monthly sessions, a needle was inserted in my lower belly, into what my acupuncturist told me was the primary yin point in the body. I did not realize it at the time, but this subtle-body point corresponds to that most tender, receptive place in a woman's body—the spot near the opening to the cervix. In the subtle-energy system, this is also the location of the second chakra, one of seven points in the human body considered to be a center of life force. The second chakra is said to be the only energy center where the subtle body, at least in a woman, can be touched by another's physical body.

I usually tolerate acupuncture needles easily, but when this one was inserted, I recoiled as a sharp pain brought tears to my eyes. The so-delicate tissue being energetically stimulated at the entrance to the cervix felt raw and torn. Over the course of the next hour, the fierce sensations spread through my abdomen and lessened only slightly in intensity.

During this time, I was catapulted into what I would call a visionary state of consciousness; or more likely, I was simply more open to the subtle-body field that had been activated strongly within me.

Out from this tender point, Rob's energy body, "the haunting presence," emerged in high resolution, and somatic imprints of our sexual connection poured through me. As if rooted there in a quasi-physical manner, I *saw* that his energetic essence was emanating from the ultra-sensitive yin point.

The merged body living on in me, still apparently connecting me, against my conscious wishes, to this man I had barely spoken to in almost two years, was anchored there. A quiet light surrounded this pain, and I knew the yin point was not only the entrance to the physical womb, but to the spiritual womb as well. In an instant, I grasped I had happened onto the subtle-body site of the "marriage of essences," where the energies of male and female come together in a new creation.

When a woman is with a man, she needs tremendous trust and grace to allow herself to be touched, not only physically, but also energetically, at this place of transformative power. I saw that the yin point most often remains closed to protect the innermost feminine core, that the opening is not mediated by the will, but rather by a woman's surrender.

That surrender develops from a sense of trust, safety, protection, and love in relation to her partner. I could see why this opening happens outside our willed control. The yin point was communicating with an exquisite intelligence, like the heart, with its own logic, values, and reality. When a woman does open herself in this way, her receptivity meets the man's assertive force, and she becomes the containing vessel for a merging love.

It made sense that the tearing of the etheric bonds had registered most profoundly at this point. The broken heart has its counterpoint in the lower body: the womb-heart. As the needle began to unfreeze the numbness and constriction that had been protecting me, fierce pangs of grief around the sexual betrayal poured out. Body memories that had registered as a visceral pillaging of my subtle-body—of Rob penetrating me during the final months as he brooded over his departure, his dismissiveness during the abandonment scene, the queasy intrusions of his new lover—flooded forth.

ENERGETIC AND EMOTIONAL RAPE

come back so i can say yes this time. do it again now that i know
what to call what you did.
—Daphne Gottleib, *Why Things Burn*

It was here, at this most vulnerable place in my body, that the betrayal had imprinted as a physical and energetic rape. I do not know how else to describe this, though I do so with caution out of respect for physical rape victims. I am fortunate never to have been violently forced into sex, so I may not have the right to compare. Nonetheless, my body was telling me that sex, even when freely consented to, that takes place in an atmosphere of manipulation and deceit leaves an indelible imprint and *registers in the subtle body as a sexual assault.* Sex, I realized, can be a form of energetic and emotional rape.

My body recoiled at this sexual violation. But its truth was difficult for my rational mind to accept. Still, when I read about rape victims and spoke to a number of women who had been raped, I was confounded by how resonant my experience seemed to be with theirs.

There are many ways to manipulate and misuse sexual love. Even if your partner is a skilled lover who aims to satisfy you, if a man uses lovemaking primarily to support his self-image as a great lover, or purely for his own sensual gratification, or as a means of power, control, or conquest, not connection and appreciation of you—*your body knows.*

Your conscious mind may be oblivious, but your body is not. If your partner has sex with you, professing to be committed and to love you when he is not and does not—not to mention while planning his exit or being involved with another woman—you are likely carrying a sense of *inexplicable sexual violation* deep within.

Until that moment in the acupuncture office, I had not had the strength to let the full traumatic imprint of this sexual deception into awareness. Although I had done hours of trauma-unwinding therapy, the pain of Rob's duplicity as it extended to our most intimate sexual relating had remained buried. For whatever reason, Rob had gained my trust—with his professions of love and loyalty; his eye-gazing, impassioned sexuality; his nurturing touch—and my body had opened to receive him with utmost receptivity. Perhaps he even deluded himself for a time, at least as long as he was excited and turned on.

I will say again, I am not suggesting that he knew what he was doing, though he may have had an inkling, any more than I did. We were proceeding together in an atmosphere that condones a man's entitlement, seduction, and hypocrisy in relationships and a woman's collusion. I prefer to believe we were functioning in mutual denial, born of collective blindness to both the sensitivity of the subtle body and the lasting impact of sexual bonding.

I am setting aside for now the issue of personality disorders, such as narcissism, where an individual routinely idealizes, uses up, and devalues their intimate partners as a way of life. Even though now it seems he did not care whether he hurt me, I give Rob the benefit of the doubt. I would rather believe he was oblivious to the harm he was sowing in dishonoring the trust involved in our friendship and our sexual love. The alternative, that he intentionally manipulated me, taking pleasure from exercising his power over me and causing me pain, is too horrible for me to assimilate.

The harm that was done, as I was soon to discover, extended far beyond the dyad that had been Sandy and Rob. As my low belly released the spirals of constriction I had been holding back, a river of sadness welled up in me, a river with tributaries flowing from time long past. I felt the betrayals of my mother-line, those of my own mother, grandmother, and great-grandmother, and how they had suffered the abuse of their men in silence.

The experience went beyond my personal lineage: I heard the keening groans of ages of women who had endured a similar slaying of their trust and love. The deeper we go into our suffering, the more we touch into collective images and memories. Hearing these sounds of ancient grief told me it is the womb-heart of women that carries the pain of the desecration of what we hold most dear.

GUARDIAN OF THE MYSTERIES

Tell the truth as you understand it. If you're a writer you have a moral obligation to do this. And it is a revolutionary act—truth is always subversive.
—Anne Lamott

For me, the cervix had become the physical correlate of a spiritual altar for the reviled and repressed aspect of the feminine, symbolized by the dark goddess. The dark goddess archetype oversees the feminine mysteries, the intimate processes of sexuality, birth, and dying. She presides at the altar as the guardian of the womb, of the sacred nest from which we all emerge. Women themselves are the guardians of the mysteries of physical and subtle union, and of sexuality as the most holy ground of those mysteries. Some men intuit the same.

When a woman opens this tender inlet deep in her body to a man, she initiates him through the grace of spirit to the secrets of Eros and of bonded love. In her sensuality and sexuality, the woman carries a sacred charge, access to a temple of the Divine. She may not even recognize this gift for what it is in a culture that commercializes and trivializes sexuality. Yet, under the right conditions she may open these sacred depths to herself and her lover. To magnetize the deep feminine core that allows both partners to taste the goddess mysteries, a woman must show up in her utmost receptivity and vulnerability. I remember how often I quaked and trembled before the ritual surrender in making love. She must trust enough to be willing to put herself completely in her partner's hands as the emissary of Spirit.

Sex is one thing, but generally, men are only granted a more profound level of surrender and trust once they have demonstrated their devotion and respect. Explicitly or implicitly, they promise cherishing, faithfulness, protection, and companionship, which they prove through repeated acts of caring, mutuality, and love.

It makes sense that men want access to this portal of relational potency and mystery. Some will do what they must to convince you that they deserve entry simply out of curiosity, craving, or desire for conquest. Thus enters the temptation of male seduction and the whisper of empty acts and assurances of love and fidelity. These behaviors build the trust necessary to taste the mysteries that can emerge when a woman surrenders to Spirit with the right man.

Speaking for myself and many others I have spoken with, when a woman who has trusted this deeply learns that her man has betrayed her with another woman, she is pained and outraged to the core. If she learns he has been willing to manipulate and seduce her by feigning love and fidelity in order to taste these secrets with her, the Furies stir within her. When she learns he does not truly care for her or intend to honor his word, her outrage goes beyond her personal pain and humiliation into the impersonal, collective realms.

Archetypal, dark-goddess powers arise in protest along with her own. When the woman's gifts, offered in the seeming mutuality of love, turn out to have been taken under false pretenses, the man not only betrays her trust, he dishonors the sacred forces she has unfolded with him. When a man who carries the substantial psychic fruits of union with a woman cavalierly walks away from such a connection, it is not just her body and soul that recoil. So, too, do the collective body and soul of other women who have been harmed this way.

If he uses the evocative powers of his partner's *shakti*—her life force conferred on him—to pursue and claim another, the clamor of the buried communal pain and protest rises to a deafening pitch, crying for atonement and retribution. Once we can recognize the scope of what we are experiencing, it adds dignity and purpose to the pain of being betrayed. The work we do to stand up for and transform these hurts goes beyond our personal healing to the desecrated feminine powers of the collective.

These were the truths of the womb-heart spoken to me that even a mountain of logic could not override. In our time, the wounds from the denial and defilement of these relational sacraments are coming to awareness, asking to be healed and restored. The violence of rape, incest, prostitution, pornography, genital mutilation are only the most obvious abuses. Divorce, abandonment, adultery, betrayal, the commercializing and trivialization of sex also cause untold human misery. I am only one voice among many who are waking to the sacredness of relationship, the inviolability of bonded love, and the damage done through our ignorance that tramples these gifts of the gods.

Again, I do not want to suggest that this level of connection and communion happens in all marriages or partnerships, perhaps not even in many. In a culture that has lost respect for the sacredness of connection, it may be rare, or awareness of this subtle body gift may simply be dulled by our secular beliefs. The goddess of the depths, of the night, holds these mysteries in her hands. She gathers those wounded and betrayed in her rites into her healing heart. If we are called before her altar of dark transformation, we can only bow and take our stand for the sanctity of relatedness and enduring love she has revealed to us.

CHAPTER 9

Coping with Cultural Blindness

Don't let us forget that the causes of human actions are usually immeasurably more complex and varied than our subsequent explanations of them.
—Fyodor Dostoyevsky

FOR THE BETRAYED WOMAN to realize that her hurt and indignation have roots deeper than her personal experience helps give her the strength and courage to own her truth, tell her story, and take a stand. Otherwise, it can be tough to go against the tide of conventional attitudes. We live in a culture that dismisses and downplays both emotional pain and the abuse of power. Raised in this atmosphere of denial, we hardly know what betrayal is, much less what it takes to recover.

Contemporary culture does not prepare us for the seriousness of the shock or the posttraumatic stress that follows. Current TV and movie-saturated stereotypes veer between images of business-as-usual, no-big-deal, *Sex in the City* bravado—get drunk one night, then move on to the next guy—and *Fatal Attraction's* rabbit-boiling, knife-wielding images of the woman scorned.

A divorce or precipitous breakup is romanticized as if it were the stuff of a high school drama, or excused simplistically as falling out of love. "Oh, well, they grew apart." "It just did not work out." "He had a midlife crisis." Infidelity has almost become a joke, in the news on a daily basis, the stuff of gossip and scandal. It is so commonplace we never even think about the destruction and pain involved, as we sweep the anguish of each story aside with a shrug. In this climate, until we are betrayed ourselves we are blind to the desolation of such life-transforming events.

In the first tremors of the aftershock of Rob leaving, when no one had a clue what I was going through, I got a lot of suggestions from friends and family. I was advised to count my blessings that he was gone, to let go, to get over it, and to move on as quickly as possible. I was plied with well-meaning platitudes: "Men are like buses: One leaves and another pulls in,"…"Just be in the moment and be grateful for what you have,"..."Whatever happens is the highest good." Sometimes support from friends took the form of attacks on Rob that were only too easy on my ears: "You dodged a bullet,"..."He was a cad/a liar/sleazy/a loser—good riddance!" Forgiveness was advised by my spiritually minded friends as the quick ticket to recovery and the best way to demonstrate my love, as in "If you love someone, set them free." Just "let go and forgive," and the pain will disappear—so I was told and believed myself.

All too often I was encouraged to cheer up, take a class, make new friends, volunteer, hike, or practice more hot yoga, all of which I tried. No one particularly wanted to hear that I was as full of holes as a Swiss cheese, ready to check myself into the nearest psychiatric hospital, commit some unspeakable act of vengeance, or wander in front of a passing car. I wanted to say to those who offered advice, "Hey, I would 'let go' if I could—meanwhile, I want to strangle you for suggesting it." I was doing everything in my power to pull myself together, but nothing was working. When no one seemed to get the seriousness of what had happened, I felt more and more alone and misunderstood.

Beyond the first few weeks, as a culture, we do not easily tolerate the grief and despair that follow the sundering of deep bonds. We acknowledge physical pain but talk little about the debilitation of emotional injuries, and even stigmatize emotional and mental illness. In our happiness-obsessed, "Prozac nation," we consider intense suffering an aberration or an indication of weakness. I am convinced huge numbers of people silently endure protracted experiences of physical and psychological pain such as I experienced.

The hypervigilance, heartache, obsessing, and grief that I went through for years are examples of the kinds of suffering we shunt to the catchall categories of depression or self-indulgence, and treat with drugs, if we treat them at all. Sadness is linked with depression and perceived as dangerous. We dislike and shun people we judge to be "wallowing" in such personal pain. Symptoms are rarely seen or understood as natural responses to the trauma a person has suffered.

Why? Because emotional pain makes people uncomfortable. Those who have not faced the depths of their own pain—and so few of us have, where are the models?—are doubly afraid or ill at ease when they see another suffering. Even those who know we must be hurting and want to help probably feel awkward or clumsy and do not know what to do. This cultural atmosphere of denial of suffering makes the blindsiding of betrayal even more severe.

In New Age, politically correct crowds, where attitude is considered the sole determinant of the impact an event has on a person, it gets even worse. No matter what happens to you, you get to choose the version of "reality" you want to live with—as if there were no interpersonal facts, only interpretations.

The upshot of this perspective is that a person's suffering would vanish if only they adopted a more evolved perspective, recognized the hand of God at work, and stopped seeing themselves as a victim.

Some recommended, if I was serious about healing, that I take "one hundred percent responsibility for everything." Others suggested more benignly, "With a couple, everything is fifty/fifty." This was also one of Rob's favorite lines. I searched diligently in myself to find the "fifty/fifty responsibility" key that I, too, believed must be at work in any relationship of depth. To no avail— after this experience, I could no longer accept the neat, tidy, appealing formula meant to erase all blame and resentment and instill instant forgiveness.

Suggesting that I take responsibility for my victimization seemed to me an iteration of "blaming the victim" that only further burdened my fractured heart and mind. While there may be truth at the deepest spiritual levels that the victim of abuse or accident or crime shares responsibility, on the human level, generalized prescriptions like this skip over the hard facts of what has happened. For most of us, prematurely adopting these rosy perspectives before we accept the facts and move through the pain amounts to a classic spiritual bypass.

Before the traumatized psyche can make such a lofty philosophical leap, we have work to do. I needed to see and feel into my situation for what it was interpersonally, psychologically, and socially before I was anywhere near ready to graduate to the big picture and appreciate whatever divine purposes the betrayal may have held. I needed to pass through layers of distress and loss of faith in myself, in others, and in life itself.

The Stigma of Victimhood

We need to de-stigmatize *legitimate suffering* if we ever hope to move beyond our fixation on instant happiness and claim the deeper truth of our soul. We live in a world that not only rejects emotional pain, but reveres power and control and disdains victims and losers. Most commonly, in addition to nursing a broken heart, the betrayed must carry the burden of the powerless loser, who, clearly, brought this situation on herself. You hear: "You must have provoked him," or "Surely you saw it coming," or "You chose him, after all." These common judgments, also known as *blaming the victim,* add to the humiliation and social stigma of the betrayed and absolve the betrayer.[1] Attitudes that blame you for your pain and brush off the abuse barely hide a disdain for the powerlessness of victimization. They reveal a collective wish "to exorcise the specter of the rejected individual."[2]

The term *victim* has even become a dirty word in some circles. If someone claims they have been injured in a relationship—especially if their wounds are not physical—they are charged with not taking responsibility for their part; for wallowing; for vengefulness and rage; for emotional instability; for taking pleasure in suffering; and finally for taking satisfaction from forming a new and exciting identity as a victim!

The simple fact is that when someone you have trusted turns on you and tears apart your world with complete disregard for your pain, you have been profoundly violated. Your psyche has been shattered and permanently altered. Your recovery is far from guaranteed. You have been emotionally and spiritually raped. Tellingly, you are just as suspect in your complicity as you would be if it were a physical violation. Regardless of his or her conscious intentions, childhood wounds, needs, or sensitivities, the betrayer has psychically eviscerated you and left you with injuries that will impact the quality of your life going forward. It is natural to respond with shock, outrage, and panic.

Letting the truth of what has happened penetrate takes time, but recognizing the depth of the violation, naming betrayal as betrayal, begins the healing. It is an essential first step. When we genuinely pass through the pain and face the truth, there are no steps we are allowed to skip to come out looking better. That is why, when people, even with the best intentions to help us, turn aside and reject our blame and rage, our sadness, our denial and longing, it only sets us back.

Once we let ourselves off the hook and acknowledge we have been victimized, we can stop pretending we are fine and stop trying to be spiritually correct. Grounded in the facts, we can proceed with more clarity to deal with the consequences. Most important, now we can take the necessary steps to take care of ourselves, calm our distressed nervous system, and find the help we need to face our battered condition and get on with the regeneration of our heart and soul that can restore our faith and trust in life.

We can begin to surrender to the burning grounds without the crazy-making beliefs that nothing much has happened or that some inherent defect or wrong attitude of ours is to blame for our distress. In time we may indeed come to see the entire drama as orchestrated by larger forces than we can comprehend, but for me, anyway, that shift came much, much later.

THE LEGACY OF DOMESTIC VIOLENCE

People do not like to talk about it, but we still live in a patriarchal world. Abuses of power have been a routine aspect of patriarchal culture, so it is natural we take them for granted. We have made some strides in the past half-century toward greater equality, but the legacy of masculine privilege and values runs deep.[3] It is this cultural milieu that has encouraged us to turn a blind eye to interpersonal trauma, particularly emotional violence and abuse, between men and women, just as it has blinded us in the past to racism and homophobia and to more blatant sexism.

As a species, we appear to be wired for violence. Just look at the daily news, the popularity of violent entertainment (movies, TV, video games, contact sports), or at the history of war on this planet.[4] Men commit the vast majority of societal violence; they support violent entertainment; and it is men who almost exclusively wage war. Debate continues as to whether the male tendency to violence is genetically determined or a reflection of cultural values.[5] When they are betrayed, it goes without saying that men hurt, too; and often that hurt will be expressed in some form of aggressive reaction. Although men are more likely to act out their rage in physical violence, it also takes psychological forms. Either way, the threat of male rage gives an underlying tension to the relations between the sexes, even in the best of times.

In 2005, one-third of all women murdered in the United States were killed by their spouse or partner.[6] Until 1976, marital rape was not considered a crime, and only became illegal in all fifty states in 1993.[7] The fact that obvious domestic violence is still the number one cause of physical injury to women points to that legacy.[8]

In this atmosphere, fully acknowledging the destructive impact of your partner's faithlessness demands education, support and a ferocious love for yourself. This is the sorry milieu in which a betrayed woman must recover herself after the severe violation of her most intimate ties. Although we are waking to acknowledge that physical battering of a partner is wrong, as a culture we are a long way from recognizing and applying that standard to emotional abuse. The facts are: *emotional abuse can be much more harmful and insidious than physical abuse.* As I pointed out earlier, at least if someone hits you or cheats on you, it is easier to see it is their problem. If the abuse is emotional you are more likely to be disoriented and to blame yourself for your distress.

The disempowering dynamics of betrayal place the betrayed at a great disadvantage with their community. The betrayer has claimed the high ground for himself. The betrayed, however, is stunned into bewilderment and helplessness by the shock. It takes all she has to even know what hit her. The betrayer has the added advantage of time to spread his version of the story while she is still reeling in shock. He may cast himself as the victim, implying he has been bearing up under her unbearable offenses all along. His claims about her faults as the cause of his brutal behavior may have an eerie echo with the mantra of perpetrators of physical battering and of rape, often expressed as, "She provoked me," "She attacked me first," or "She asked for it."

In such circumstances, others are likely to turn away from what looks like a private, interpersonal dispute, "none of my business," just another classic "he said, she said" situation you can never sort out. But the indifference to your pain can be as unexpected and traumatizing as the original shock.[9] When one friend finally said, "I am so sorry he was so cruel. It must really hurt," my heart melted with appreciation. When we are reeling with pain, we need validation and compassion.

Because the type of egregious betrayal I am describing is outside the range of so many people's experience, it is not surprising that most people do not understand the depths of the psychological destruction it often causes. In the trauma literature, the victim's response to bystander disinterest in what really happened is known as secondary traumatization. The refusal of others to see the truth of abusive behavior serves to drive the injured one into further isolation and to condone the abuser's behavior.

Judith Herman underlines this point with an observation about the human tendency to do nothing in the face of psychological trauma and thereby to side with the perpetrator:

> ...those who bear witness are caught in the conflict between victim and perpetrator. It is morally impossible to remain neutral in this conflict. The bystander is forced to take sides....It is very tempting to take the side of the perpetrator. All the perpetrator asks is that the bystander do nothing. He appeals to the universal desire to see, hear, and speak no evil. The victim, on the contrary, asks the bystander to share the burden of pain. The victim demands action, engagement, and remembering.[10]

When we have a friend, family member, or client who is reeling after a stunning betrayal, we can help by trying to give them the benefit of the doubt and hearing them out. When we are hurting, we can do our best to realize what we are going through may be incomprehensible to others. It is time to seek out those who have been there. These are the people who can validate and hold us with their warmth and understanding.

"FORGIVING THE PATRIARCHY"

Regaining a sense of our own power becomes the core work of the betrayed. This is work we also do, whether we realize it or not, to help heal the communal soul. Professor of Jungian Psychotherapy, Veronica Goodchild explains, "Each person's suffering leads to an archetypal core...if we are able to penetrate deeply enough into these altered states and *make them conscious, we will help to raise the level of collective consciousness.*"[11]

The impetus for the expansion of consciousness may be one of the hidden reasons for the epidemic of divorce, adultery, and abandonment. The invisible wounds of intimate betrayal affront a woman's soul like little else. The pain, rage and grief that arise have the power to destroy a person, or they can impel you to dig deeper than you ever have before to find redemption and healing. Embracing the pain and powerlessness with kindness calls for strong medicine. It calls for the powers of the repressed feminine in men and women.

It takes the power of fierce love to hold the pain of all these broken hearts. The epidemic of wrecked relationships is forcing the growth of love and compassion; the pain itself pushes us to say, "No!" The unbelievable suffering is a strong motivator. It gives the courage to name the problem and to take a stand against these abuses and for relatedness. It may finally be time for the eclipsed forces of the feminine soul to awaken to heal these traumatic wounds. Those of us wounded in love are potent carriers of the seeds for that reawakening.

Women are not the only ones in touch with this spirit of fierce love. Men, too, are recognizing the importance of enduring ties and how painful the old values of power and control can be. One hero of mine is a friend who went through a crisis years ago in his marriage. He fell in love with another woman and was determined to leave his wife of twenty years. After great struggle, he and his wife stayed together, and they seem to be one of the more inspiring, happier married couples I have ever met. When I asked him what happened to change his mind, he said, one day it just hit him. He realized *what it would do to his wife* if he left—and he loved her enough not to put her through that. It touches me still to have seen the power of love prevail.

In another example, years after Rob left, one of the most surprising and heartening experiences I had was when a man connected with his men's group apologized to me for failing to say or do anything at the time Rob left. He even confronted Rob about it. He was a man committed to standing up against male entitlement and violence toward women.

It is hard to exaggerate how important this was to me. Men who serially abandon women often care little about a woman's opinion but are concerned about losing status with other men. Men in leadership positions especially have the power to prioritize challenging abusive behaviors, rather than colluding by looking the other way, or worse, actually giving higher status to men who hurt or are contemptuous of women, or who try to prove themselves through their sexual conquests.

A spiritual teacher I admire, Leslie Temple-Thurston, called the evolutionary work for women and men in our time "forgiving the crimes of the patriarchy." My situation reflected only the tiniest microcosm of the problem of abuse and powerlessness we face from our collective history. To dissolve the shards left in the collective feminine heart after thousands of years of dominance of masculine values, of trauma, heartbreak, and violence against women—expressed only in part by pornography, rape, sex slavery and trafficking, genital mutilation, battering, disenfranchisement—is an order of gargantuan proportions. My immediate reaction when I hear or read about many these crimes is that they are unforgiveable.

To make a shift from so much trauma and powerlessness to forgiveness and love would be a huge evolutionary leap. Many thought leaders and spiritual teachers believe the world is ready for such a leap. Making this shift will require us to *recover the source of true power: the power of love in our own hearts*. To recover our hearts, we must be willing to dig deep to heal the hurt, rage, and resentment that protect our vulnerability and block our true power.

For women, this means we need to recognize and forgive our collusion with our victimization and oppression. Many women have learned to roll over and play dead, keeping silent in the face of abuse, accepting powerlessness as the natural order of things. Without questioning, we enable the entitlement that permits disrespect and devaluing. We are willing to carry projections of weakness, pain, and brokenness to support the prevailing image of the "strong" man and dependent woman.

Instead now, to call back our projection of power onto men, we need to learn to bear our own rage and admit our desire to do harm, without acting it out. That rage is potent fuel for dissolving separateness and connecting us to a Higher Power that knows how best to heal the pain.

What we are all up against in coping with the existential dilemmas of a human life becomes close and personal in the fires of the betrayed soul. Being deceived and dismissed makes you want to do something to stop the madness that embeds betrayal at the heart of our humanity. Bearing with the helpless frustration at having one's trust destroyed and one's partnership life derailed grows the compassionate heart. Going through our own hell reveals how much everyone suffers when we choose power over love, no matter which side of this split we prefer. What we can forgive in ourselves, we more readily forgive in those who have hurt us.

Women, because we are made to carry new life, also have a closer relationship with the body, relationship, and natural rhythms. We are equipped to know in our bones that God includes the earth as well as the sky, the feeling world of the body as well as the rational mind, the subtle world of connection as well as individuality. This knowledge is a key to learning to channel the destructive urges of ego power back into nature where they belong: into the pulsing earth waiting to receive us, into the spaciousness of the sky, and into the warmth of the encompassing sun.

Turning to face our own rage and terror teaches that these archetypal eruptions do not belong to us. They belong to transcendent realms. These painful emotions transform when we learn to root ourselves and direct their potent energies into the Dark Mother spirits of the earth. She relishes their taste; while, when we take this power as our own, it turns bitter and poisonous.

As we make our way through betrayal's trials, the dark feminine mysteries—the sacredness of relationship, body, ground, connection, sexuality, birth, and death—call out and infuse us with their wisdom. We remember what we have lost, and we know better what to value. Faithfulness to our cracked-open heart becomes the compass for following the feminine mysteries that can heal us individually and collectively. Grounded in the heart, we are empowered to take a stand for the sacredness of relationship in a world of ideals that has denied and desecrated its significance.

Betrayal can show us how to stop the cycle of violence it represents. It can wake us to our many self-betrayals and teach us to reach beyond our errant beloved to a greater love that can hold our suffering. Betrayal is a stern taskmaster, like the Zen master who whacks his students at just the right moment to awaken them. The blow smashes our small world to open us to a greater one. It is breathtaking to know in our bones, with that shock, that relationship itself is what matters most in this life. But I get ahead of myself.

CHAPTER 10

The Weight of Projection

A projection is a very tangible thing, a sort of semi-substantial
thing which forms a load as if it had real weight.
—C. G. Jung

MANY UNSOLVED PUZZLES REMAIN about the uncharted subtleties of relationship. The last chapter took our focus to the environment of the larger world and how it can make us blind to relational values and violations of those values, such as betrayal. As we return to the struggles of the inner life in relationship, I want to explore one question that kept coming back to me pleading for an explanation. Since a subtle-body bond involves both individuals, how is it that one person experiences so much distress and pain, while the other goes off with a little guilt, possibly, but primarily lighthearted, liberated, and carefree? What is it that permits one partner to deny and dismiss this immense relational reality, while the other resounds so viscerally with its depth and significance?

When we are betrayed, we are traumatized and disempowered, and the betrayer is not; that much was clear, but there seemed to be something more to explore. Engaging this question took me further into the subject of the subtle-body and its relational dynamics. Inevitably, it led me to considering how the psychological defense mechanisms of splitting and projection operate in partnership.

It is a dangerous business to try to assess someone else's motives or state of mind. Analyzing another's behavior probably reveals our own frame of mind as much as theirs. It was Mark Twain who said, "When we remember we are all mad here, the mysteries disappear and life stands explained."[1] We do not have to go far into an exchange laced with projection and splitting to appreciate his wisdom. In close relationship, we enter a hall of mirrors where each person's madness reflects back at them in the perceived actions of their partner.

Be that as it may, I found it impossible not to try to understand what to me was Rob's mind-bending behavior. Human beings are designed to make meaning. The mind can never find the ultimate truth but is nevertheless driven to make sense of our lives—never more so than when we are fragmented into meaninglessness. The consequences of projecting and the splitting that goes with it are part of all close relationships, but may never be more severe than when we betray and are betrayed. These dynamics offered at least one explanation for the vast contrast in the experiences of the two people involved in abandonment and betrayal. They gave my mind a port in the storm of hurt and confusion. Maybe considering your situation from this perspective will do the same for you.

The Return of the Repressed

I believe that most often when we are driven to break our agreements and to betray, or whenever we move to hurt the ones we love, we do so to escape from our own unlived pain. Whatever interpersonal drama of childhood we carry in our bones, we are at risk in our closest relationships of falling prey to a classic reenactment, or return of the repressed, as Freud would call it.

As intimacy grows, our partner's behavior inevitably stirs our unhealed hurts, fears, and longings. Franciscan Thomas Keating makes the point how increasing closeness brings on our shadow: "Difficulties arise whenever a committed relationship is succeeding. Love makes you vulnerable. Your defenses relax and the dark side of your personality arises."[2] Under pressure, we tend to project these intolerable feelings and assume our mate is the problem.

We act out unconscious feelings every day, but not every projection justifies a betrayal. In our interactions with each other, it is a matter of degree and depth. Bonded partnership engages our vulnerabilities like little else in life. Access to each other's defenselessness and the temptation to misuse that trust when we feel threatened gives betrayal in love its deadly sting. Once we make the mistake of making someone else accountable for our demons, we need only take a small step to justify hurting them to protect ourselves. In this way, we become the unwitting perpetrator of hurts we suffered but have not yet faced. We do to our partner what was done to us.

When Rob left with coldness and contempt and accused me of a litany of terrible sins against him, it was as if he was addressing someone else in the room, so far off were his accusations from the reality of my deepening devotion to him. It seemed he was looking at me through glasses colored with hurtful images of his past, now cast upon me. I shook my head in disbelief and could not make a match between my truth and his claims about me.

Yes, I have my blind spots, my "shadow issues," and Rob was likely more aware of them than I was. But because I knew him so well, I could not help seeing the hurts from his prior relationships flash through my mind as he spoke his words of contempt and rejection. His past included abandonment, divorce, betrayal, infidelity, violence, and more. Now he was betraying and abandoning me in a barely disguised rage; surely, he would connect the dots.

My cracked-open heart went out to him. For a while, I could feel the impossible pain he was feeling that enabled him to treat me so harshly. I believed that in a close partnership, what touches one, touches both. I implored him, "Please don't do this to yourself." But he could not hear me; he flatly rejected my perspective, as I did his.

PROJECTION AND SPLITTING

Projection develops as a primitive defense mechanism early in life. It arises from unconscious feelings and unwanted parts of ourselves. Some of our personality characteristics do not fit our self-images and disturb us so much we try to banish them. One common way we conveniently disown them is by transferring them onto another person. This transfer unfolds outside awareness, and is a way the ego-mind manages its self-images and averts attention from early pain.

Without conscious effort to do otherwise, we are likely to split off and project what we cannot bear, routinely attributing to others our own feelings, motives, and attitudes. Our judgments, prejudices, and biases against certain people or groups of people often reflect what we do not want to admit about ourselves. Splitting and projection are applicable not only to intimate partnerships, they are also what create enemies at any level of human connection.[3]

The psyche is capable of slamming a door on any aspect of experience when we feel overwhelmed or threatened. When we project what we do not care to feel or see about ourselves, we virtually split ourselves in two. A successful split demolishes emotional memory in a strange amnesia. We become indifferent and calloused to the part of the psyche that we cut off in ourselves, but highly sensitive to it in others. We do not want to feel our anger, for instance, so we block and prevent anger from coming to awareness by being righteously indignant or put out whenever we perceive anger in someone else.

In a partnership, projections of idealized and despised qualities can come to dominate our interactions. The process has an automatic, uncanny quality that is easy to miss. The projector causes the person targeted for the projection to embody his same split-off feelings. Almost like a form of hypnotic induction, the projector's behavior toward his partner evokes precisely the feelings, thoughts, sensations, and behaviors that the projector does not want to acknowledge as his own. It is truly amazing how it all works so subliminally.

Rarely, do we recognize how we pressure or provoke our intimate partner into enacting certain behaviors. The projecting person, for instance, may not be able to tolerate feelings of needing his partner's attention and affection to feel okay about himself. At the same time that he projects his intense need and fear of rejection onto his partner, he ignores her more often, puts other people and activities ahead of her, dismisses her concerns, arrives late, puts her on hold, and so forth. When she is treated this way, she will tend to believe in her feelings of rejection, missing the energetic transfer from her partner. If she reacts with hurt or anger, protesting his withdrawal and disrespect, he may tend to counter with even more dismissiveness or with accusations, problem solving, or analysis about her "symbiosis," neediness, or dependency problems.

The more the projecting partner induces the other to act out his or her inadequacies, the more evidence he or she gathers to support a belief in the other's problem, making it easy to avoid acknowledging that the distasteful behavior in the partner is an intolerable aspect of his or her own makeup. The longer the projecting goes on, the greater the polarization becomes. The projected partner is likely to end up treating his partner the same way he treats that aspect of himself: by devaluing and rejecting her.

The more the two partners' subtle bodies blend, the more substantial their projections are likely to be. Carl Jung studied projection primarily in the context of the psychotherapeutic transference relationship and believed it was through the subtle body that projections are carried and transferred between people. He described projections *as actual energetic phenomena that had substance and weight.*[4]

You can begin to notice your projections when some behavior particularly bothers you in another person. A red flag can go up to remind you to check for the same tendency in yourself. On the other hand, if you are the recipient of a projection, you may notice you feel manipulated to behave in a way that is alien to you, as if possessed by an outside force to act in uncharacteristic ways.

When we betray or are betrayed, we become particularly susceptible to projection and splitting. The shock of abrupt abandonment removes resistance and turns us into a virtual magnet for projected energies of hurt, powerlessness, and rage. In the months and years after Rob left, I often felt flooded by what I believed to be his unacknowledged feelings, as well as my own. One day, I sat down and made a list of more than twenty states of mind that had been alien to me before he left. I believed most of them to be Rob's "emotional stuff" that I was now carrying. Often I felt suffocated by the heavy weight of these foreign feelings, as if a big pile of debris had been dumped on me—who knew being "dumped" (on) had a literal meaning!⁵

Many of the overwhelming feelings bore no relation to anything I knew about myself. Yes, my own unconscious patterns were coming to light. I had a lot to learn about myself with the help of this crisis. Nevertheless, from my years with Rob, I recognized many components of *his* behavior. For instance, I had grown accustomed to his anxiety and moodiness as part of his temperament, including his fears around his physical sensitivities; his extreme safety precautions in the house and wherever we went; his concerns about what others thought; his fears of rejection, abandonment, and engulfment; his insecurities about himself; and his despair concerning his health were just a few of the fear patterns I knew well in him.

Here now, uncharacteristically, I felt these exact feelings inside me: humiliation, guilt, and shame; the ongoing anxiety, paranoia, and fear of attack; and feelings of despair and abandonment were the most obvious. During the relationship, I had noticed how I tended to pick up his feelings. If he was angry when we went to bed, sometimes I knew it best not to sleep with him, or I would wake up in the same frame of mind.

We spoke about this phenomenon, and I blithely even tried to clear and transform some of these feelings in myself "for him." I admit in some ways I believed that Rob could use my help in the emotional department of life. This was one way my own tendency to superiority and power came into play, trying to be a helpful, healing "savior" to the weakness I had projected onto him.

CARRYING YOUR PARTNER'S FEELINGS

Women often do carry their man's feelings, since men tend to be more cut off from their emotional bodies. As women, we learn that this is one way to manage and survive with a wounded man (and we are all wounded, men and women alike). As part of the covert agreement for keeping the peace, the receiving partner cooperates by taking the disowned feelings right in—"Let me take care of that for you, dear"—like a sponge. I was only too willing to accept Rob's idealized projections, but when he began to turn against me with deception and devaluing, I smarted and began to protest, seeing finally that this was a crummy deal.

Within a relationship committed to seeing and breaking these codependent, mutually reinforcing patterns, both partners can break the cycle of projecting and carrying each other's feelings. It pays to set a pattern early in a relationship to reality-test about projections. I had confidence that Rob and I were regularly checking in with each other this way, but even that intention, obviously, turned out to be no guarantee. Our blind spots are legion. It takes committed effort from both people to do the hard work of recognizing and taking back disowned feelings. When one person starts stonewalling, for whatever reason, how are you to know?

Both need to be willing to identify and name their feelings, refuse to carry those that do not belong to them, and face painful truths about themselves. Nevertheless, should you come more into your strength and refuse to continue to carry a projection, be warned: No longer taking on some quality or feeling you have absorbed all along is likely to upset the equilibrium of the relationship. Your refusal can cause your partner to fly into a panic or rage at the shame of needing to feel and re-own the intolerable feelings he has become accustomed to you carrying. He may well accuse you of betraying him! One example of this is when I finally refused to go along with Rob's insistence that I was insensitive and responsible for his allergic reactions. He immediately claimed victim status due to my intolerable lack of empathy.

So take care when you begin to name projections you have carried for your partner, or your partner begins naming yours. You probably are entering extremely sensitive places that have been carefully walled off and are painful to see or acknowledge. Treading in this delicate psychic territory can easily trigger terror, rage, and abandonment—killing the messenger can be the gut reaction, especially if you clumsily touch an early wound in someone you have been, until then, colluding with to protect. For some people, blowing their cover, not upholding their self-images, is unforgiveable, the worst imaginable crime for which you will have to pay.

Once your partner has physically left you, of course, you have no further opportunities to reality-test, to share the burden of working out projections. You are left to deal with it all yourself. Rob slamming the door on me, his unwillingness to hear anything I had to say, or, really, to acknowledge my feelings at all, was part of the traumatic shock that turned my world upside down. Not only had he casually annihilated me, now he seemed to be taking pleasure in watching the anguish his rejection caused. The things Rob did and said were not neutral; his remarks and behavior were startlingly precise in targeting my most raw insecurities.

He was a tuned-in, intuitive man—it is not as if he was not aware of what would devastate me. Sharp remarks of cruel, cold indifference were his primary weapon as he coolly erased me from his life. I continued to be dumbfounded by his sudden animosity. In my research, I learned how common this disempowering, lover-turned-stranger pattern of splitting and cutting off is, especially when men leave. You become the scapegoat for their pent-up rage at womankind. It is annihilating to be casually dropped as if you never existed by someone with whom you have shared such close bonds. It is the psychological equivalent of them killing you.

When the psyche splits, it makes a radical break into the opposites of good and bad. Splitting has an either/or quality that makes one unable to integrate the bad with the good. We simply *cannot tolerate* the opposite quality that we are projecting. Seeing the other person as "all bad" allows us to classify ourselves, by contrast, as morally, psychologically, or spiritually superior. The psyche abruptly cuts off any positive memories, feelings, sensations, and thoughts associated with the person, relationship, or situation. The partner becomes the embodiment of evil in the mind of the betrayer. Under the sway of splitting, we can justify the most brutal treatment in the name of self-defense.

In one instance I perceived as splitting, the night he told me he was leaving I suggested to Rob that we each take the other's part in this stay-or-leave polarity. Taking on the role of the one who wanted to leave, I would recount what I found trying in the relationship; and he, playing the part of the one committed to stay, would recall what worked well between us. Still imagining we both wanted to bring consciousness and honesty into the relationship, I thought this might be a good way to center and put things into perspective.

He agreed, but when it came time for him to focus on the positive parts of our relationship, he said he could not think of a single thing. After a long pause, he finally said, in a deadpan voice, that the only enjoyable experience he could recall in six years was when we once went on a bike ride. Otherwise it had been a "conflict-ridden and joyless" relationship. Weeks later, he amended his list to say "maybe 20 percent" of the time had been enjoyable. In relationship crisis, what looks like a dishonest denial of the facts by a partner distorting events to cast us, or the relationship, in the worst possible light often simply reflects the painful result of unconscious splitting and projection.

I have remarked that when Rob left, any ambivalence he had disappeared suddenly. From loyal fiancé he morphed to attorney-for-the-prosecution against me. He was uncharacteristically self-confident in his certainty about my faults and his lack of love for me. Weeks later, he wrote that from the moment he left, he had not had a single second thought about leaving—"not one thought, feeling, sensation, or urge" passed through his mind, as he put it, to reconnect with me now or ever again. *Ouch.*

When Rob went on to claim he had stopped loving me long ago and had already grieved the loss before he left, I was dumbfounded. I inquired, when and how had he grieved? I asked why, if he was finished with me so long ago, he continued to plan the wedding with enthusiasm, to tell me repeatedly that he loved me, virtually until the day he left, and even to deny he was thinking of leaving when I asked him point blank the day before? Most important, I wanted to know how he could possibly make love, such hot and crazy, soulful, eye-gazing love—Oscar-quality performances—with me several times in the weeks leading up to his departure, including a few days before he walked out? Needless to say, I was stupefied when he replied that he had no memory at all of any lovemaking. *Really?*

Being on the receiving end of this apparently disowned part of his psyche, I, far from having no memory, was left with our sexual connection etched into my body and soul. With my love and trust only deepening as the wedding ceremony approached, never had I been so open to him as I was in those times together. These intimacies embedded themselves in the marrow of my bones. Moreover, in light of his deception the memories were drawn into the vortex of the trauma. I was plagued by repetitive visceral intrusions of our sexual connection that took years of trauma therapy, grieving, and somatic healing sessions to clear. During this process, I could not help but feel I was carrying not only my own deep body memories but those disowned by him as well.

When you receive the negative projection of sudden psychic splitting from a committed lover, it not only undermines your perceptions and trust in yourself and in the other person, it is also confusing and crazy-making. When such profound splitting goes on with no return to center, the two persons involved quickly inhabit different realities. The chasm can create a total communication breakdown, as the reality of each person denies or opposes that of the other. That surely was my experience.

Even in my shock and with my own tendencies to projection, I could not stop believing Rob had panicked and acted out his painful feelings toward his mother and other women he felt had hurt him. I reasoned I must be the scapegoat for that unprocessed pain. But he assured me that he did not feel threatened at all when he left. He claimed his decision was cool-headed, arrived at in a moment of clarity, after months of soul searching. Of course, that meant he had been deceiving me all that time, which I did not want to believe. I will never know how much truth he was expressing and how much easy rationalization. But his complete denial of the splitting, panic, and seizure of power looked clearly to me like textbook delusion. Meanwhile, he apparently believed that I was a demon incarnate, out to guilt-trip him into ruining his health and his life by sticking around.

Regardless of what he said, I still needed to find a way to deal with the weight of Rob's projections. This was easier said than done. Unlike my own feelings that were trying enough, I could not process or befriend or transform *his* feelings.

Without going into a description of the entire process, I'll summarize by saying that I finally went through a series of *depossession* and *soul retrieval* ceremonies with a shaman. The shaman identified, called forth, and cast out several malevolent "beings," and confirmed the projection hypothesis in unexpected ways. Her explanations reinforced my experience of autonomous, foreign substances that moved and felt like Rob's anger and fear, bent on my destruction, prowling about my emotional body launching random attacks.

She believed that Rob had unconsciously cast into me these aspects of his emotional body. In turn she claimed that he had taken my heart, confidence, and strength with him. That fit. The shaman extracted the malevolent presences, journeyed to retrieve my lost soul parts, and cut the energetic cords along which the projections presumably traveled. She confirmed that the connection was draining me of courage and personal power and transferring it to him. How strange! But how true to my inner experience.

Around this time I had what to me was a momentous dream:

With Rob nearby, I walk into his bedroom at his new place. It has an empty, Spartan feeling. I spot a black velvet watch box on his dresser that I open. In it I find a heart-shaped, deep violet jewel. It is radiating, pulsing with life and energy, almost like a living heart. I recognize it is my heart! Although I feel a little guilty, I have to take it back, especially as I sense Rob is planning to give it to someone else. I put the box under my coat and quickly slip out the door. I know he will not give it to me; he needs it and will be very angry when he discovers it missing.

This dream gave me hope that I might reclaim my heart after all—that beauty, joy, and light might be returning to my days.

WITHDRAWING PROJECTIONS

Someone I loved once gave me a box full of darkness.
It took me years to understand that this too, was a gift.
—Mary Oliver

It is an accepted psychological notion that everything that irritates us about others can lead us to a better understanding of ourselves. Betrayal provides a pressing opportunity, a rare chance, to go through the hard work of dissolving our own inner splits. Healing these splits through bearing both sides of our own opposite qualities is essential medicine for resolving whatever hurt caused us to split off part of ourselves in the first place.

As the betrayed, I, too, claimed the high ground in the rounds of blaming and anger. For a long time, I projected my power and rage onto Rob. I felt I was the innocent, helpless victim, wronged by his rejection and brutality—was it not obvious? While there was truth to this claim, as long as I could not own my own malice and rage, I was doing exactly what he had done to me: splitting and projecting my blindness and resentment onto him.

Sometimes I was able to perceive the other side of his behavior—the fear and pain that had triggered his actions. I struggled to bring together the persecutor and the victim in myself (when I wasn't convinced he was a conniving sociopath). It also worked to experience as directly as possible the part of me that felt compassion and cherished him and not just the part that detested and feared him. This inner work with someone who has seriously harmed us takes patience and can be the work of a lifetime.

As the dismantling of our delusions unfolds, the insight dawns that getting lost in an extreme emotional reaction to something or someone signals we are likely projecting some quality or feeling we cannot bear. The initial insight only begins the work of taking back, integrating into our self-picture, bearing the feelings of the projection. Regardless of the methods we choose to re-own our projections, the challenge to our self-image—an image that has been built on repressing at least one side of these very qualities—can be daunting.

Embracing both sides implies willingness to recognize unpalatable truths about ourselves and to burn through the pain the discrepancies cause. Re-owning what we most revile in ourselves becomes one of our major tasks as we move along betrayal's winding path into the darkest corners of our being. The hard work of recognizing, reconciling, and either disclaiming what is not ours or re-owning what is (such as power, wisdom, or love), becomes the inner work of the maturing of consciousness in the dark night we will take up in part III.

It made sense to me that the shattering had brought my own unresolved fear and rage lurching out of the unconscious. Projections need a hook in the psyche in order to latch on and keep their hold. I knew I had plenty of wounds to hook on. I had been wrestling with my own inner violence for decades, as an ongoing project. The unresolved feelings from birth trauma and other early-life experiences of perceived abandonment or family conflict had been exacerbated by the trauma and brought to light to be held in conscious awareness.

Taking back projections means immersion in a cauldron of churning opposites; it means suffering our illusions. In other words, it is powerful. We do whatever we can to help the dissolving of the splits. I prayed for myself and for Rob; I practiced Buddhist *tonglen* meditation, taking in the resentment and blame and sending out forgiveness. After cycling around into one side, then the other, of vengeful tormenter and terrified, helpless victim, I caught a whiff of hopelessness that my own efforts would ever amount to anything but continual flip-flopping from persecutor to victim. Until, one day feeling a thorough failure, I finally gave up and resigned myself to this madhouse of opposite tendencies. I was in dire need of *the help of the miraculous.*

In contrast to the evil we so readily see in a betraying partner, it takes a grace we cannot commandeer to burn through the biased belief in our own innocence, as well as to endure the sting of seeing our own characteristics reflected in behavior we most detest in him or her. When I felt most discouraged in the morass of analysis, blame, and heartache, I finally had no choice but to bring both sides to the altar of the heart and surrender there. In moments of surrender, I handed over all my healing strategies to a Higher Power I did not understand but knew more and more was my deepest truth. I turned over my concerns, my questions, and my entanglement with both the unholy projections and the sacred ties with Rob. This prayer of offering became my final refuge for dealing with my traumatized psyche and the subtle-body connection that lived on in me.

I read in a new light the many stories of Christ casting out devils and was encouraged that I was not forever doomed to these torments. My compassion grew for my own helplessness. I began to welcome both the tormenting persecutor and the broken child inside. Each time I acknowledged in myself a hint of what I intuited Rob had projected onto me, I sensed our common humanity and a small healing took place.

Poet Greg Kimura captures the essence of what I have been trying to convey here in this excerpt from his poem "Sacred Wine":

> *The ancestors say: the world is full of pain,*
> *and each is allotted a portion.*
> *If you do not carry your share,*
> *then others are forced to carry it for you.*
> *Sit with the pain in your heart.*
> *Hold it like a sacred wine in a golden cup.*

Sitting with the pain in your heart as if it were a sacred wine in a golden cup—that is also a nearly perfect description of what we must learn to do as we journey deeper into this dark transforming night of the soul.

PART III

Seasons of the Hollow Soul

CHAPTER 11

Facing the Trauma

Trauma is hell on earth. Trauma resolved is a gift from the gods.
—Peter A. Levine

E VEN AS I WRITE, I am still amazed that it took so long for me to recognize how traumatized I was by this abandonment. Although I had undergone trauma-reduction sessions in my training, and read a number of trauma-related books, including *Waking the Tiger* by Peter Levine and *Trauma and Recovery* by Judith Herman, both classics in the field, even counseled people in shock, it never occurred to me that being abandoned as an adult could be so traumatic. When I myself was overwhelmed, I needed help to recognize my condition.

Toward the end of the first year, struggling to cope with what felt more and more like mental illness, I came upon Susan Anderson's work. Anderson made the descent into the underworld herself after her husband of twenty years suddenly left her. A therapist who specialized in treating abandonment survivors, she wrote about her groundbreaking research with a large sample of women in *The Journey from Abandonment to Healing*. Her work helped to bring the emotional crisis of the trauma out of the shadow of trivialization and into the light of greater understanding that it deserves.[1]

The more I learned about trauma, the more I realized how well it explained not only my physical symptoms, but also the emotional extremes and mental turmoil I was living with every day. Most of the women Anderson interviewed used intuitively the word *trauma* to describe the shock when their source of comfort, protection, and warmth is cut off. The sense of shattering at the initial moment of being deserted—when the wound to the core self was inflicted—is the first, nearly universal, sign of the shock.

To review what happens physiologically at that moment—the emotional brain signals immediately the release of masses of adrenaline and other stress hormones and puts the psyche into fight-or-flight mode. Simultaneously, the mammalian part of the brain goes haywire in an effort to reconnect us with our lost source of sustenance and support. In this state, we startle easily and have trouble sleeping, eating, resting, and even functioning.

The traumatized psyche kindly puts the effects of the trauma on hold by going into denial for a honeymoon period (not the honeymoon I had envisioned), which, many agree, often lasts about three months (although delayed PTSD symptoms can appear many months or even years later). The numbing translates into simply not feeling anything, and not believing our partner has gone. It takes time for the psyche to reorient to such a drastic shift in its reality before it begins to unfreeze around the moment of shattering.

The experiences of many women confirm how common the symptoms of denial and disbelief are. One woman told me it was five years before she could feel *anything* about her husband of twenty years leaving her suddenly. She thought she had just brushed it aside and gone on with her life as usual. When she was not working at her job as an elementary school teacher, she busied herself playing golf and bridge, attending a reading group, and otherwise preoccupying her body and mind. Ultimately, she developed severe headaches, but even then she learned to live with them and did not relate them to the betrayal. Finally, one of her daughters convinced her to enter therapy, and only then did she begin to confront what had happened.

When we are finally ready to face it, the shock of the moment of desertion has likely already been deeply etched in traumatic memory, and PTSD has likely set in. Brain studies consistently show that when PTSD develops, it involves actual structural changes in the brain, specifically the hippocampus, the amygdala, and the medial frontal cortex.[2] Practically, the damage means you lose the ability to concentrate, to recall recent events clearly, and to switch off distressing thoughts, feelings, and memories. Awash in ongoing survival alerts, you become anxious, obsessive, and hypervigilant.

As I discussed in chapter three, we keep finding ourselves dragged down by the undertow of distressing flashbacks, reliving the shock over and over again. The memories reappear in insistent, unpredictable, invasive replays, like those I have described. We are shocked to realize the betrayer is lodged at the center of the tiny torture chamber that has become our world. The mind has riveted on him as both the source and the solution to the pain.

The Pain Is Real: The Biochemical Storm

The torments of the betrayed heart and mind are difficult to believe. Yet we are apt to question and doubt the pain because it is "only emotional." When asked, we might say that it feels "as if" the hurt is "real"; we temporize in this way to avoid the charge of exaggeration. As I mentioned earlier, science is finally proving that the feeling of being hit by a bus, stabbed with a knife, or kicked in the gut and left to die is not simply a metaphorical dramatization. With current technological advances in neurobiology, MRI studies have validated what many have long suspected: Heartache can cause the worst kind of pain. Research shows that the psychological/emotional pain of rejection travels along the same pain-processing pathways as physical pain and registers as an equal threat to survival.[3]

The intensity of the shock and subsequent stress of any loss of a loved one can alone lead to such severe heart pain that the symptoms are often mistaken for a heart attack. This condition, known commonly as *broken heart syndrome* (also called *stress cardiomyopathy*), sends many to the emergency room. Several times, I myself was a heartbeat, so to speak, away from calling 911 for my heart pain seizures. The doctor who introduced broken heart syndrome to the public compared the traumatic stress of getting a Dear-John letter to that of having a .44 magnum shoved in your face.[4]

As far as our brain is concerned, the pain we feel in rejection is no different from a hot-oil burn or a knife wound. In fact, because of the other parts of the brain that get involved in intimate rejection, the torments go beyond those of physical pain to moral, existential, and spiritual suffering.

In an ironic twist, rejection also reactivates the same center of the brain that fires when we first fall in love, inflaming desire for the abandoning partner to mythic proportions. This is also the same center, the caudate nucleus, that fires up when we experience addictive compulsions, such as to nicotine or cocaine. Researchers have learned that the caudate nucleus releases the pleasure chemical dopamine, which drives goal-oriented motivational states—in other words, craving, longing, addiction, obsession, and compulsion.[5] Recovering from romantic rejection not only hurts, it emulates—not metaphorically, but viscerally—withdrawal from a cocaine addiction.

In a bonded relationship, the brain produces relaxing opioid chemicals that give us a sense of safety and comfort, which we take for granted until they are withdrawn. A long-standing relationship helps regulate many psychological and biological functions, and meets countless physical and emotional needs. In a nurturing relationship, body systems have been accustomed to high-circulating levels of oxytocin, the soothing, bonding hormone. When we are abandoned, it abruptly cuts off oxytocin, and our system goes into wild disarray, similar to what happens to an addict going cold turkey off a highly addictive drug. Since we are hardwired to avoid rejection, the nervous system keeps sending out life-or-death *signals to reconnect,* which amount to nothing less than the most intense cravings of your life.

I thought I was being amusing when I told my friends in Chicago, with whom I stayed for three months during the worst time, that their place was a rehab center, but apparently I was speaking more truth than I realized. With the pain and pleasure centers of the brain lighting up simultaneously, a rejected lover lives in a crossfire. You are desperate to reconnect with your executioner, but you are also angry, confused, and terrified by how much he has hurt you. Your hormones are pumping the accelerator and the brakes at the same time, throwing you into a neurochemical torture chamber. All you want to do is find a way to stop the pain, when you are not contemplating ways to maim or torment him—revenge, too, as we shall see, falsely promises to make the pain stop.

THE VICTIM/PERPETRATOR LOOP

Ongoing trauma changes your brain in other ways. The dialog between primitive and more evolved parts of the brain that normally allows for reason and common sense to prevail gets derailed. When we dissociate, our survival instincts take over. The psyche regresses and reverts to primitive defenses, including splitting the pain and aggression into two separate compartments. Rage and terror take over as protests and protection against the pain. Analyst Donald Kalsched in *Trauma and the Soul* calls these traumatic defenses the trauma vortex, or *self-care system*. According to Kalsched, this internalized split functions to keep the central treasure of our existence—the wounded, innocent soul child—safe, but hidden and buried away.[6]

The self-care system pushes aside the former sense of self and begins to take control of the interior landscape. This is another way of understanding what it means to have our identity shattered and no longer know who we are. In this dissociated state, the mind splits into protector/persecutor and a wounded child/victim and loops back and forth between the two. In the throes of the trauma vortex, we tend to vacillate between fear and rage, between feeling under attack and wanting to kill someone. The protector takes the form of a malevolent or, at times, benevolent presence whose purpose is to hide and hold together the innocent core that is under assault. In time, however, the intense aggression of the protector/persecutor can function more like an autoimmune disease than a guardian. That is, each time we feel hurt or vulnerable, it turns against these most vulnerable inner parts and we attack and blame ourselves for our weakness, rage, and pain.

The zeal of this primitive safeguard helps to explain the sense of ongoing threat that has replaced our usual state of mind. It is the protector who interprets every situation as a threat of retraumatization and adopts an antilife

stance of attack to meet any new experience. In the throes of PTSD, even per-
fectly neutral situations are considered potentially dangerous, a reason to fight,
freeze, submit, or flee. Connecting or relating do not even enter the equation.
For years, every time I encountered Rob, I panicked and froze. Even the idea
that I might see him, even hearing about him, started my heart pumping and
my stomach churning with anxiety.

This high-octane split in consciousness explains many of the debilitating
symptoms of PTSD. If not treated, this defensive looping radically changes
your quality of life. Trauma victims exist in a state of low-grade, chronic suffering, oscillating between the two extremes of victim and perpetrator, cut off
from their authenticity and soul life. This is why it is important to get help
as soon as possible to begin to reset your traumatized brain and reclaim your
dissociated soul.

THE ORDEAL OF WITHDRAWAL

When the denial finally lifts, we enter a stage of "withdrawal," described by
Anderson as "one prolonged state of emotional emergency, a tumultuous and
intense time of great stress."[7] The withdrawal symptoms are confusing because
we do not commonly appreciate what happens when we become attached to
someone. The unmet, natural instinct to bond produces terrible longings of
expectation, craving, seeking, and a sense of distraught loneliness, which, if
we cannot find some way to distract ourselves, eventually fill every waking
moment. The longer the impulse to bond is thwarted, the greater the stress
becomes, taking us right back to infantile fears and despair.

In my experience, the withdrawal symptoms are the worst ordeal of
betrayal—the most stressful and humiliating trial. You lose control of your
thoughts, feelings, and sometimes even your behavior. In a recent MRI study,
people in the early stages of rejection reported thinking of their lost love 85
percent of their waking hours, and all of them said they yearned to reunite
with their partner.[8] In this time of utmost vulnerability, you are like an orphan
abandoned in a foreign land, and you naturally want to reach out to your
former source of protection and support to comfort you. This longing is part
of the archetypal core of betrayal; it happens biochemically, naturally, to most
everyone in this situation.

Biochemical withdrawal is part of any attachment loss, but when attachment is torn by unrepentant betrayal, it adds additional trials. During the
withdrawal phase, which comes and goes and can last months, if not years,
despite your rational intentions otherwise, the early brain views your rejecting partner as the remedy to take away unbearable distress. The urgency to

reconnect with this person who has inflicted so much pain comes on power-fully, unexpectedly—as a natural instinct, like hunger or thirst. Any dignity you have managed to salvage is likely to be trashed by the gnawing urgency arising from the mental, physical, and emotional pain that overwhelms your normal ways of coping.

The kindest, but most difficult, thing you can do for yourself is to cut off all contact with this person until you can resolve the trauma. Otherwise, the sense of powerlessness in the face of the imperative of the primitive psyche to reconnect with someone who abandoned and no longer wants to have any-thing to do with you can be humiliating. It can overtake you and drive feel-ings, thoughts, and actions that destroy any remaining pretensions you have to willpower, intention, and rational thought.

This is the phase when you will likely have the strongest impulses to con-tact your betrayer, for what seem like the best of reasons. You may also be highly motivated to enter another relationship to try to soothe your longings for connection. To avoid the pangs of withdrawal is also why the chances are high the betrayer has someone else in his sights or has already replaced you.

Besides the withdrawal symptoms from the shorn attachment that can make you crave your lost love like an addict craves a drug, betrayal brings yet another crazy-making factor into play: The shock of being left actually increases the intensity of the bonding with the person who has hurt you. I had never heard the term *betrayal bonding* before, but I found out fast what it meant—and not just in theory, either.

Betrayal Bonding

You cannot believe it when it happens to you, but anyone who has been through betrayal knows too well the disturbing truth: *The more someone hurts you, the more difficult it is to break the connection.*[9] As we have seen, being betrayed signals life-threatening distress to your brain and floods your sys-tem with the survival hormones for fight or flight. These hormones create neurological conditions that perversely strengthen the bond beyond the ties that existed previously in the relationship. In an atmosphere of confusion and fear, mammalian bonding actually intensifies. This phenomenon is known as *trauma* or *betrayal bonding.*

Betrayal bonds contribute to the unholy cords that tie us to an abandon-ing or betraying partner. These ties can grow quickly or over time. They are most often created by a form of emotional abuse, characterized by a pattern of alternating cruelty and kindness. After your partner hurts you emotionally or physically, he shifts to attention and warmth to draw you back in and set up the conditioned association that relief will come from the same source that caused the pain.[10]

Under these conditions, the early brain centers that connect your partner with comfort and love begin to see him as someone who can relieve the disorientation, fear, and pain and return you to safety As long as the traumatic pain remains unresolved, the early brain interprets the hurt as a signal that you need the abuser—no matter what your neocortex says—to relieve what it interprets as a life-threatening situation. Remember, in a traumatized state your rational mind has gone pretty much offline, overrun by survival instincts.

For the early brain, the equation in betrayal is blatantly straightforward: Your betraying partner must return to relieve the very pain he is inflicting, or you will not survive. To your dismay, you have become intensely focused on, and loyal to, a person you distrust, fear, and now may not even like. The sense of compelling attraction that rejection stimulates adds fuel to the opioid withdrawal of partnership loss. These two involuntary, biochemical reactions that you are powerless to control can craze your addled, betrayed mind with longing, and contribute greatly to your sense of helplessness.

Family service caseworkers who work with abused children describe this phenomenon when, for instance, the battered child clings to the abusive parent. One social worker friend of mine recalled an incident when she needed to take a four-year-old girl away from her mother who had been abusing her. The child had cigarette burns up and down her arms, some fresh and bleeding, that her mother had inflicted on her as punishment for misbehaving. Yet the child screamed piteously, struggling in my friend's arms, reaching out, and pleading to be returned to her mother. Tales of battered women reuniting with their abusive husbands point to the same phenomenon.

Whether the violence is physical or emotional, no one is immune to developing trauma bonds. They come with our mammalian inheritance, although a childhood history of extensive trauma may have set the neurophysiological stage for their reenactment later in life. When a pattern of trauma bonding develops in a relationship, it generally grows stronger the more time passes, and only reveals its intensity in outright abandonment, betrayal, physical violence, or other major abuse. The chances are high that, by the time someone abandons his or her partner, it is the final slap in the face in an ongoing pattern of psychological abuse and progressive disempowerment the victim may hardly have recognized.[11]

If you are experiencing the symptoms of trauma bonding, it is another sign your system is in shock, and you likely will need help to calm and reprogram your nervous system. You need a trusted friend or professional to help derail and redirect the destructive bonding. You need reassuring touch, the language of the early brain, to help soothe the distress and come back into relationship with the world. With help, you can more readily find the strength and support to face the genesis of the traumatic overwhelm—the fracturing of your core self—and, ultimately, to face and heal the hidden existential suffering that is part of our human nature. But that comes later.

AND THEN THE OBSESSING

Meanwhile, the pull of the trauma, along with the need to reorganize the shattered psyche, leaves you prey to the furious force of the obsessed mind. In response to the shock, the alarming, invasive preoccupation with what happened takes you completely by surprise. No one I spoke to or read about was prepared for the debilitating burden of obsessive thinking. Obsessing is a harrowing plague, and I would be remiss if I did not talk about it in more detail. Preoccupation with someone you consciously want to put out of your mind adds to the ongoing sense of shame and helplessness that characterizes PTSD.

My disoriented psyche revolved around Rob as the heavens do the North Star or some galaxies do a black hole. Just like subjects in the love and rejection MRI research,[12] I spent almost every waking minute captured by memories and images of what happened, along with endless protesting imaginary conversations. Worse, Rob invaded my dreams at night. Every day I would wake up thinking about the situation, and every night I would fall asleep doing the same. For more than three years, my mind would not stop trying to make sense of the senseless, so I despaired of ever getting my life back.

I began to wonder if anything else in the world existed besides the sights and sounds of the betrayal scenes and the time-warp after-tremors of how Rob's deceptions played out. I felt like I was in a scene from the movie *A Clockwork Orange,* tied to a chair, alternating images of a Jekyll and Hyde Rob, earmarked to unhinge me, being blasted into my head 24/7. In my day-to-day dealings, I smiled and tried to act normal, while I held close the deep, dark secret that my mind was constantly preoccupied, rerunning tormenting background clips of what had happened. I could not let anyone know about the situation; it was too insane. I felt so helpless and assumed being so out of control proved some inherent defectiveness of mine that had finally been revealed by Rob's leaving.

Obsession is said to be a defense that occurs when we isolate feelings from thinking. So often it was written off in a sentence as the by-product of repressed rage, but I could not make the connection. I felt "in touch" with my rage, but that did nothing to stop my obsessing mind. After betrayal, the anxiety and pain are so intense that, paradoxically, thinking about the person who has hurt you brings a measure of equilibrium. The preoccupation both agitates and soothes the nervous system. Whether you need to calm down or wake up, the mind reverts to its now-favorite subject—your betrayer. He resides at the center of the trauma vortex, both as a shield against and an invitation to the disintegrating threat at the core.

I did not realize what a powerful protective shield my thoughts were creating to keep me from falling apart; I only despaired at finding how much I had lost control of my mind. I tell you this so you know you are not alone in trying to rein in your bedeviled, runaway mind. I can only tell you that if you are obsessing, you are still in shock. You are in the throes of a traumatized psyche trying to protect you from a threat long passed, and a frustrated primal instinct to bond run wild.

I wondered had this anchoring of my psyche in relation to Rob been going on throughout the relationship? Could I have been this intensely dependent on his actions and attentions, only hiding it from myself? The answer was no. At the time, I had no idea that fixation on the trauma is a classic PTSD symptom. I thought I was hopelessly weak, while all along my mind was heroically involved in an effort to hold me together and to protect me from feeling the massive, annihilating hole in my chest until I was stronger. When we incorrectly diagnose our symptoms, it is difficult to know how to treat the disease.

Now I know and want for you to understand also, this is what betrayal trauma does to a person—you shatter and regress. No, you were not pathetically dependent on your partner. But after this emotional assault, you are now. The pain rules you, but will eventually lead you to new depths of heart and soul. Most everyone regresses to survival fears and obsessions when they are abandoned—and hardly any of us dare to admit it because of the stigma and shame.

How naïve I was in those early months, imagining my rational mind could still exercise control over the obsessive play of thoughts and feelings driven by such powerful instinctual, archetypal forces. To get through my days, I tried many, many things in addition to meditation and prayer to recover my equilibrium. I was determined to make the pain, longing, and crazed preoccupation stop, to reconstruct some version of a normal life. I tried therapies, body work, psychics, classes, retreats, groups, volunteering, exercise, entertaining, travel, the list went on and on.[13] My habit of self-reliance and my belief that I could handle the situation on my own had gotten me this far in life, and I was not about to give up now.

Several rounds of trauma therapy the second and third year finally began to calm my nervous system. Three months on the Mendocino coast helped, too; the ocean gave me perspective. Otherwise, I am sorry to report, nothing held my interest for long or could staunch the poisoned wound maddening my mind. I had stamina, but this was like trying to participate in life with the emotional equivalent of a bad flu; or to try to listen to music with loud static constantly delivered to your brain.

Activity generally made me feel worse, not better. I participated halfheartedly in these activities and often left early, anxious to get home. Regardless of what I tried to do, I could not concentrate, and my mind dragged me back to its preoccupation. The open wound was like a magnet that attracted thoughts about the situation every spare minute to try to staunch the bleeding. Time and again, I learned that the kindest thing I could do for myself was attend with care to the screaming feelings—and not keep trying to screen them out by changing the channel with company, events, and activities. The best environment for me was solitude. I needed to crawl into my proverbial cave and lick my wounds until the dark night that was descending on me finished its work.

One thing that helped me in my time alone you may want to try. Find a personally meaningful image to pair with the painful thoughts and memories. If you have an image of God, of beauty, nature, or love that speaks to your heart, make a practice of bringing it to mind when the trauma memories or obsessive thoughts arise. In this way, image speaks to image, and a larger truth may soften the grip of the past. A strong image can remind you more directly than words that there is more to the situation than the pain.

Spiritual Healing for a Spiritual Crisis

To sum up the topic of trauma: It is important to realize that *time alone does not heal trauma*. If you have even an inkling that you may be living with the symptoms of the complex trauma that can result from betrayal, I again recommend that you get professional help.[14] Find someone who will not invade or abandon you to hold your hand as you slowly unravel the shocking events that brought on the distress. Treating trauma directly not only helps you deal with the physical symptoms of shock, but it also points you in the right direction along the trajectory of transforming the pain into a more soulful life. It will not necessarily eliminate your pain or save you from the other trials of this testing, but it will provide a firmer foundation for the work your soul is calling you to do.

Recovering from such intense interpersonal trauma involves more than waiting it out, calming down, and pulling yourself back together. In time, you realize trauma therapy is just the start. The depth of crisis that betrayal precipitates *requires spiritual healing.*

Ultimately, only timeless presence contains the magic ingredients that can ease the frozen hurt of the traumatized soul. The medicine that heals comes from *returning consciously to the moment when the pain imprinted* on the psyche—not in a dissociated state of mind, dragged back through intrusions and obsessions, but with grounded presence. But trauma constricts consciousness and puts us in a Catch-22 situation. That is why we need help, both human and divine. Any time, but especially when we are traumatized, being in the moment is easier said than done.

The shock and pain of trauma drive us into the present as the only real refuge; but at the same time, forces within cause us to want with all our might to resist, to defend, to escape—not only from the suffering, but also from the light and love waiting in the here and now. I tried everything in my power to "be in the moment." Sometimes I even succeeded: for a few moments, an afternoon, I would feel victorious, hopeful, only to be plunged into despair when, inevitably, I found myself again lost in the distressing feelings and thoughts. In this way, I discovered that whenever I gave up the search for solutions to lessen the pain and admitted I did not know what to do, I was living on an important edge.

Realizing *I did not know* the answers to the questions my mind relentlessly wanted answered, and admitting my powerlessness over my life, brought both relief and terror. "I know" had always been one of the ways I defined and protected myself from insecurity. Not knowing what to do or how to be was a huge blow to my familiar identity. Without that crutch, I felt all the more lost and alone.

Finally, it dawned on me that the natural desire for pain to go away prevents us from accepting our circumstances. Following advice from a wise friend, I asked myself, What if these replays never stop? What if they never go away? What if I have to live the rest of my life with this empty ache, with this run-away, obsessed mind? I began to stop fighting and, in a leap of faith, to surrender the preoccupation and pain to a Higher Power I did not even believe in. The broken heart knows better than the sophisticated mind. During the worst times, I prayed a lot. I dropped my thoughts and feelings into knowing hands; I turned them over to a God I did not understand but was coming to hold dear, and just rocked my brokenness with all my heart.

CHAPTER 12

An Archeological Dig into the Past

*There were many ways of breaking a heart. Stories were full of hearts
being broken by love, but what really broke the heart
was taking away its dream—whatever that dream might be.*
—Pearl Buck

WHEN BETRAYAL BREAKS YOUR heart, you grieve, not only the loss
of your love, and the loss of faith and trust, but most fundamentally,
the loss of your broken dreams. Lasting love in partnership had been my most
important value and dream; I did not realize how much until it was taken
away. Throughout my adult life, I imagined that relationship held a key, not
only to happiness, but also to the enigmas of my soul. I believed in love! The
purpose that gave my life meaning revolved around finding God, love, and
my higher self in *relationship*. I wanted to co-create this higher plane of living
with another person more than anything else. I thought of it as my mission,
my presumed path to truth and love.

Sinking now into the swamps and cauldrons behind the closed doors of
my psyche, I found mixed motives had been at work in what I believed was
a purely spiritual yearning. Relationship *was* my heart's ruling desire, central
value, and life path, but I had confused the path with the destination. In ways
I did not realize, I believed that the finger pointing to the moon was the moon
itself. I had been mixing up primal yearnings for connection from my earliest
life with the longings of my soul. My hunger for the infinite was attached to
something finite: to an idea of love, to another person, to relationship itself.

Soon enough, the abandonment revealed my clay feet. The traumatized
infant that emerged to rule my psyche overwhelmed any spiritual identity and
purpose I had constructed around my relationship with Rob. In the face of
this child's despair, every otherworldly goal seemed ethereal, faraway, unreal;
and they *were unreal* to her. The Holy Spirit could not walk with her and hold
her hand or drive her around town. Spirit could not share concerns about her

day, or cuddle with her in bed on a cold night, or keep her company on a rainy day or a long weekend.

At every turn, I would hear this small voice inside asking, "Where is Rob?" Despite every reassurance from my adult, rational mind, I found myself continually sidetracked by this inconsolable child. Whenever I dropped inside, I would find her curled up in a little ball, terrified that she could not survive without him, but, primarily, simply not wanting to. My adult self understood that Rob was no longer good for me and that the question I "should" be asking was "Where is God?" but nothing I did could persuade my child's heart to stop wanting what she wanted. To her, it was as if the sun had permanently set, and she was condemned to living forever without warmth or light.

Learning this truth about the power of the intense longings of the little one inside me was humiliating and mortifying. Her uncontrollable desires destabilized my pride—my identity as a mature woman and seeker of truth and spiritual awakening. When I was honest with myself, I had to admit any experiences of the Divine I had known (and I imagined there were so many!) were eclipsed by the desolation and the drives of my child's heart. What I thought I wanted and what this ordeal actually revealed about my priorities added more self-blame and shame to the stormy brew inside. But, ultimately, it brought the balm of truth to my troubled soul.

OUR EARLIEST WOUNDS

The heart broken in love opens like an archeological dig into the past. The velocity of fracturing draws you down, down, down through layers of feelings, strategies, and beliefs that have been protecting the heart from a primeval pain. The depth of the desolation stunned me. The grief and longing came not from this particular loss alone but from events much further back—from infancy and childhood, from my lineage, from the collective experiences of humanity, and perhaps beyond, from lifetimes or dimensions we can hardly comprehend.

Because trauma disconnects the rational mind from the primitive brain, it reveals our primal imprints in high relief. We find out what has been laid down as the foundation of our identity. Sitting with my distress exposed a terrifying ancient injury; a wound hidden deep inside was torn open and exposed by the abandonment. I began to viscerally live out what I believed I had understood for decades: Our earliest relational traumas form the bedrock of our identity.

We come into existence in relationship; our sense of self is rooted in relationship.[1] As we emerge out of the dark cave of the womb and our symbiosis with mother, we recognize ourselves existing *with* another being. The sense of dual unity, of two-in-one, becomes an essential part of who we think we are and how we relate to others. The satisfying warmth of merging with Mom in the cocoon of the mother/infant twosome imprints on the psyche as a prototype of ideal relationship, of life as it should be.[2] But that is not all. Abandonment, frustration, and fear also impress on the brain as an expected pattern in relationships.[3]

The most dependent creatures on earth are humans beings. We are profoundly social animals, hardwired to fear abandonment as a threat to survival because, as newborns, we will, in fact, die without care. That is why loss of attunement and attachment early or later in life signals to the brain a life-or-death threat. Birth itself can be understood as our first betrayal, and infantile experiences of abandonment, although repressed out of awareness, our earliest wounds. What a shock it must be to be suddenly separated from our mother, cast out of the warmth and connection of the womb.

Even the most caring parents cannot protect their child from the shock of birth or from the perceived abandonments of infancy and childhood. Psychologist Judith Viorst describes the trauma of a mother's inevitable abandonment of her child: "The presence of mother—our mother—stands for safety. Fear of her loss is the earliest terror we know…. Yet all of us are abandoned by our mother. She leaves us before we can know she will return. She abandons us to work, to market, to go on vacation, to have another baby—or simply by not being there when we have a need of her."[4]

Although we survive her absences, they leave us with fear, and if we are deprived for too long, "…we may sustain an injury emotionally equivalent to being doused with oil and set on fire. Indeed, such deprivation in the first few years of life has been compared to a massive burn or wound. The pain is unimaginable. The healing is hard and slow. The damage, although not fatal, may be permanent."[5] Here was another way to describe the "primitive agonies," as Winnicott so names them, that underlie our personality defenses.

Regardless of the quality of the mothering we receive, abandonment happens to us all. This is why abandonment is archetypal. Being deserted takes us back to our origins and causes most everyone to panic and regress. Italian analyst Aldo Carotenuto summed up the situation, "We were all violently expelled from a paradisiacal original condition, and our lives are spent in the attempt to heal the wound."[6] To use another familiar image, the orphan lives in us all.[7] The "orphan" is a metaphor for our primal experiences of dependency and abandonment, of expectation and deprivation, of shame, loss, and loneliness. These long-buried, early survival fears come to awareness to add their painful potency to the hunger for our lost mate.

Many traditions recognize this outpost of human life. In Buddhist terminology, we have been catapulted into the realm of the hungry ghosts who yearn but can never be satisfied.[8] In Christian terminology, abandonment and betrayal recapitulate the torments of the cross. Another image that describes the anguish of the betrayed state of mind comes from Greek mythology: that of Tantalus who must endure the eternal deprivation of nourishment he sees but cannot grasp. He stands in a pool of water with food and drink visible, yet just out of reach. However we imagine them, these extremely unpleasant sensations of not getting what we most need to survive take us back to our earliest days. These primal agonies coalesce to form a solid state of deprivation and shame at the foundation of the core self.

Until something forces us to face our early pain, we barely comprehend the degree of sheer terror we experience as a dependent infant with no capacity to grasp that a frustrated need does not necessarily threaten our existence. Before we are shattered or deeply loved, our defenses protect us by banning these unendurable feelings. Any time we come close to this underground angst, it reverberates, like a raw nerve hit by a dentist's drill without Novocain, and we reflexively contract against the hurt.

A Speck Adrift in a Cold Night Sky

For decades I understood the theory that our ego grows out of our early experience and exists in relationship, but now I got to live out the implications of that theory. After Rob left and I first experienced this anguish, I was still new to this freshly excavated inner territory. I had no idea that psychic torment could hurt more than physical pain. Perhaps that is why I remember so vividly the first time I landed in this isolation chamber, a place I was to inhabit often in the months and years of my undoing that followed.

I had left town for a few days and came home the day after Rob moved all his, and some of our, shared belongings out of our house a month after he announced his departure. I was roaming around our roomy three-bedroom place by myself, absorbing the sense of his absence. When I went into the now-empty corner bedroom we had shared, the dull ache in my heart seized up into a stabbing pain so sharp that I doubled over. My knees weakened, the room started to spin, and I had to lie down on the floor to keep from fainting.

That is when I began to whimper like a baby, terrified of the pain. I rolled into a little ball against a gnawing nothingness that poured over me like a black sea. I have never felt more isolated, alone, and exposed in my entire life. I was afloat in a cold night sky, a speck adrift, at an unfathomable distance from anyone or anything. Finally, after what seemed like hours, but was likely minutes, the freezing grip of the emptiness relented. Still spinning, I opened my eyes, caught my breath, slowly pulled myself up, and made my way to the phone to call someone I knew would care about me. Uncharacteristically for my self-sufficient self, I stammered, "Will you help me?… I really need a friend."

Friends can hold your hand, but no one else can pass through the antique pain that betrayal uncovers. Similar states of the infantile experience of abandonment occurred frequently as I deepened into my unknown self during this siege. I learned more about the infant psyche than I ever wanted to know. From raising my daughter, I recognized a few familiar reactions. When infants or children first sense the absence of their caretaker when they need them, they protest, scream, and cry out for the caretaker to come. Protesting, longing, and tears alternate with fits of rage. The longer the separation between caretaker and child, the longer no one comes in response to the protest, the more the rage gives way to despair.[9]

As time went on and Rob did not return, my despair mounted. When I was home alone, primal sounds poured out of me in intermittent waves. I was like a puppy on the first night away from her littermates and mother, who initially barks nonstop, then pauses when there is no reply, and, finally, starts to whimper piteously. Sometimes I would wake wailing and crying, making sounds distant and unfamiliar—scary, animal, infant noises, plaintive "Mommy, Mommy" cries. These distressing sounds were carried on unstoppable waves of sorrow, like a force of nature refusing to be held back. The grief seemed to come from ages past to be poured out into the night. I gave myself permission for this powerful release, against a mind aghast at my behavior.

Betrayal falls on you as a catastrophic, irreversible loss. I imagined, and others have reported, too, it registers in the brain like the amputation of a limb. As time goes on, you experience phantom pains for what is lost that pass into intensified grieving and a pervasive sorrow that seems it will never end. Gradually, you slip into that dark shade of sorrow we call despair. During the long outpouring of grief, you cycle from longing to protest, to rage, to despair, and back again. In my regressed state, I recognized not only how I missed the comfort of Rob's presence, but also the panic I must have felt as an infant when Mother was not there when I needed her.

I even quizzed my mother about my birth. The circumstances she described supported the sense that I had excavated a buried trauma from my earliest days. After nearly forty hours of labor, my teenage mother had an emergency Caesarian, and I had to be resuscitated for twenty minutes before starting to breathe. My mother nearly died from complications and needed special care. Although my father visited, I was kept in the hospital nursery until my mother recovered enough to see me—eight days later. These early experiences apparently lived on in me.

As I moved from protest into despair, I felt a complete stranger to myself, yet oddly connected to others in similar pain. Primarily, I felt I was carrying Rob's abandonment pains as well as my own. In these deep waters, I found it was not "me" crying, rather, I was part of a community of sufferers, crying the cry of all children abandoned and alone, the archetypal orphan. I sensed something extraordinary and deep moving through me. The unmooring of the early implicit terrors of no-mother-when-needed was revealing both what held me back from a more soulful life and what pointed me forward. Consciously suffering the early torments was clearing the way beyond my wounded humanity to a deeper source of support and love than an imperfect mother or caring partner could ever provide.

SHAME AND THE BASIC FLAW

Rob's 180-degree turnabout, his sudden withdrawal of warmth and love, threatened to destroy me, but also handed me a key to my deeper self. I had the chance to change my relation to this terrifying sense of betrayal and isolation that lay at the roots of my being. Most of us have erected many compensating layers of personality to cover the torments of the primal agonies we suffered as babies and toddlers. Although this amalgam of dreadful sensations does not fit neatly into any emotional category, for convenience, I will be using the word *shame* to label these early pains. Shame lies at the core of the basic flaw I mentioned as an underlying feeling of defectiveness, fear, or badness; an inconsolable, gnawing emptiness; a sense that something vital is missing at the core.

As infants and children, we experience shame when instinctual needs for food, shelter, soothing, and, primarily, attachment to our caretaker go unmet. Unmet needs are terrifying threats to survival for babies; the painful sensations arising from lack of attunement, helplessness, and fear are traumatic. Our early shame is ubiquitous; we generally do not notice it, like the air one grows accustomed to breathing in a smog-filled city.

Normally, we do our best to keep our shame under wraps; we avoid situations and people that stir these feelings. Betrayal changes all that. Like putting a match to dry kindling, it threatens to turn the embers of early shame into a blaze of self-hate. When I began to recognize it, I was amazed how much shame I felt after Rob left me. Being tossed aside and replaced is deeply shaming in itself, regardless of earlier trauma. As I learned to bear with these punishing sensations, an image of the shame formed in my mind and in my dreams of a wild, tormented child, sitting in the corner of a damp, dark dungeon, in rags, with matted hair, who screamed and raged if anyone came near her.

When we are discarded, we must endure being treated like an object. In speaking about rejection, Czech novelist Milan Kundera linked shame to being objectified: "The transformation of a man from subject to object is experienced as shame."[10] The shame of objectification includes sensations of helplessness and isolation at being treated as someone who does not matter, someone despised and rejected, or worse, as someone who does not exist. When a new lover is involved, as in a classic betrayal, it is as if you are a throwaway, replaceable, like an old toothbrush. In addition, we carry not only our own shame, but also that of the betrayer, who is often shameless about what he has done.

Touching into this shame, or basic badness, feels so awful because, given the truth of our spiritual goodness, this is one of the biggest lies that we tell ourselves. Each time we unconsciously identify with feeling basically bad, we *betray the goodness of our deeper selves*. When we believe ourselves to be a defective thing, we cannot help compulsively looking outside for something to compensate and fill us up against the pain. In ordinary consciousness, under all our sophisticated defenses, most of us live in the muted pain of this continual self-betrayal, completely missing our own preciousness.

I had stumbled on a critical archaeological find. During the years when, day after day, I fell into these infantile states of mind, I became more convinced that shame was the pivot point around which my entire personality had developed.

I had hit upon *the Achilles heel of my false self.* Under my personality, I believed I was this crippled, terrorized, and shameful person. In this state of mind, reflecting the natural self-centeredness of the infant, I believed my own unbearable defectiveness was the cause of anything that happened to me or anyone close to me. The shattering revealed the source of my isolation and attachment hunger: alienation from my own goodness, from my own heart. Seeing my loss so clearly, I was powerfully motivated to offer love and nurturing to this outcast, terrified part and bring her home to my heart.

UNREQUITED LOVE

Nothing else wounds so deeply and irreparably. Nothing else
robs us of hope so much as being unloved by one we love.
—Clive Barker, *Absolute Midnight*

Being abandoned by the one you love offers a crash course in early shame and abandonment, but that only begins the excavation. You discover not only the roots of your heart's desires, but also their close cousins: loneliness, craving, and longing. When the one you love leaves you, you are thrown into the throes of unrequited love—defined as being unwanted by the one you most long for and feel you most need. This state of mind is no fun, to put it mildly.

Unrequited love epitomizes the mutually incompatible drives that dominate your rejected psyche. You might also call this state *forlorn resentment* or *frustrated desire*. In this afflictive state of mind that has become your new abode, you are under the sway of a biochemically activated, involuntary longing for someone you also fear and resent. Knowing that rejection sets off a neurochemical storm may help to take the frustrated longing less personally, but, still, we have to get through it.

Despite my intentions to "turn toward the pain," it seemed insane to open and welcome *these* particular feelings. The unrequited longing pulses with an erotic intensity that is best described as *craving*. That word seemed extreme to me until I went through this and experienced a ravenousness that could only be described as craving. When I encountered this hunger for Rob, I was pretty sure I knew what primal agonies meant. Each cell in my body cried out for him, as if I was literally starving for his company. The sensations were like stinging nettles inside me. At moments, I sensed myself as nothing but a walking mass of thousands of ravenous mouths. In a clamor, they cried, "Feed me, feed me!" The tiny mouths opened and closed like famished baby birds whose mother has flown away, reaching for their lost source of nourishment and protection.

Willing and good intentions alone are not sufficient to bear with such torturous sensations. We need support and kindness, some balance of goodness, to not fall prey to identifying completely with this early suffering. One skill from my practices that helped was learning to intersperse letting myself feel these unbearable feelings with taking breaks—excursions into relief. I would touch the longing lightly; then turn to focus on anything that offered a hint of pleasure, safety, goodness, or solace. I would hum a lullaby to myself, go out and gaze at the sky, sit in the warmth of the Northern California sun, or absorb the many pinks at bloom in the garden.

Under the spell of yearning, I learned a lot about unrequited love. For instance, the punishing sensations have a paradoxical, sensuous quality. Disturbingly, I noted that the craving actually turned me on, as if the pain mixed with rage oozed a tantalizing life force. Psychodynamic theory teaches that unrequited longing may, indeed, stem from an eroticized wound where, in the past, our passion, need, or longing was mixed with fear or pain, as might happen with a rejecting, abusive, or indifferent parent. If you are the dethroned oldest child at two-and-a-half, as I was (and Rob also, at 18 months), you are likely to have plenty of early feelings of envy, loss, and abandonment.

In Freudian terms, our early wounds are naturally eroticized, supposedly so that we will be attracted to situations that give us the opportunity to try again to repair the harm done. When the early trauma of feeling unloved by those we have depended upon for survival stirs, Eros pours forth to attract similar conditions. If we are reinjured in these circumstances, however, the cut of the old wound widens. That is why it is so important to get help when we are falling apart and not just tough it out and imagine time heals all wounds.

You might say my nervous system was calling out in a compulsion to repeat the trauma/abandonment from my birth or the birth of my premature sister. Somehow, however, I had managed to get through six decades of life before this blow brought me to this desolate core. Why now? I will never know. Depth psychology can be helpful for navigating this suffering, but does not explain everything. I only know that I was drawn into a depth of openness by my love, Rob's promises, his nurturing, and our mutual commitment to healing. I trusted him with my earliest vulnerabilities, as I had no one before.

Ah, me, the perils of trust and love. No wonder we armor ourselves against it. Rather than reject love as protection, I prefer to believe when we are brought to our knees like this, we are finally ready to take the plunge into the mysteries of brokenness and suffering.

The Demise of the False Self

Never are the differences between the languages of the heart and the mind more obvious than in times of great heartache. When I was on the surface, in adult mode, I would reason, "Rob is not my mother or my god, I do not need him to survive and thrive." I could temporarily organize myself to get some distance and relief. The well-thought-out talks I gave myself had, however, virtually no impact on my underlying feelings. Despite the protests of my rational mind, on this preverbal level, I continued to feel only Rob could ease the pain. Every memory, thought, or feeling about him hurt and stirred the longing. He was like a shard of glass implanted in my heart. Hearing about him was excruciating, and yet I wanted to know how he was doing, as a mother would a lost or troubled child. In this way, I experienced both sides of this parent/child dynamic with him.

These early feelings of shame and craving seemed to hold "me" together in a compelling way. I both clutched at and resisted the suffering with all my might. My psyche clung instinctively to the distress, like Harry Harlow's isolated baby monkeys clung to their wire surrogate mothers. On a visceral level, the angst felt like a familiar, albeit painful, home. I reasoned that being in relationship with a rejecting, non-caring person whom I believed I needed in order to survive offered the strange security of the familiar.

Understanding can give a false sense of control, but it cannot replace the somatic release of this ancient pattern. This deep body work is essential to the transformation of abandonment trauma and the building of a new identity. Our sense of self is rooted in the body. I could not think myself out of this. I needed to feel through these torments if I was to have a chance of getting to the other side.

My mind was busy trying to protect me from and hurry me through a difficult truth about my nature I did not want to face. With the desolation touching the ground of being I had worked my entire life to hide, I had to admit that suffering was not an extraordinary occurrence caused solely by Rob's unconscionable behavior. No, suffering was a *substratum of my existence,* and I needed to come to terms with it, and that takes time.

Moving one's center of gravity from the sense of deficiency and fear to communion and love requires a monumental shift on many levels: physical, emotional, mental and spiritual. The false ego self can barely endure the loss of the foundation on which it stands. Only the awakening heart is powerful enough to penetrate these wounds with the love they need to dissolve into a larger sense of who we are. Only the warmth of the deep heart provides a truly safe haven. As my images of the false self—"defective me in relation to a powerful, shaming other"—began to dissolve, it challenged my limits,

When the ego self is under siege by love, it fights back. My deficit sense of self based in shame and longing struggled to resuscitate itself over and over again. It held me in the grip of my former nature that had, after all, gotten me quite far along in life. I could not believe the isolation, the pervasive sense of badness I felt during this meltdown time. Being bad, flawed, toxic felt like a birth defect, as if I was born emotionally crippled. This ontological shame alternated with episodes of hollowness and barely tolerable nonexistence in an all-out war to resist the love that was dawning in my soul.

When what we believe we want most in the world—in this case, my mate, "my true love"—is denied, it feels to our early self as if life is no longer worth living, and the world is coming to an end. In a way, the world as we knew it is coming to an end. Moving from shame to love leads through a wilderness of emptiness and existential loneliness when we no longer know who we are or why we are here. In time, I learned to remind myself that the closer I was to my essential goodness, to my true heart, the more my dying self felt its demise as a terrible, unendurable tragedy I could not survive.

THE MISPLACED LONGING FOR THE DIVINE

What is hell? I maintain it is the suffering of being "unable to love."
—Fyodor Dostoyevsky

The longing for the Divine is said to be the fiercest passion of the soul, a passion that can only truly be satisfied by communion with our source, the ground of being, with love, with God. Experiences of the Divine come to us however, through the world of form, and we naturally confuse the source of the spiritual nourishment we crave with the everyday experiences. When we succumb to this level of confusion, which we all do, people and things become our gods. Gradually, we idolize and bind ourselves with chains of steel to whatever we have mistaken for the Divine. We all do this. When we make this basic mistake, we close our hearts to love and court addiction. In this way, you could say we are all addicted to something.

We may point fingers at the obvious substance addictions of drugs, alcohol, even nicotine or caffeine, and imagine ourselves at least above such weak behavior. Behavioral addictions, such as sex, gambling, shopping, TV or Internet compulsions, even reading or exercising, most anything we do, may look more acceptable, but are often fueled by the same inner emptiness and longing.

No matter the addiction, our compulsions point to our deepest pains and show where we are blocking the deepest love. Psychologist Marion Woodman said addiction is a kind of wound. She also said the god can be found in the wound. Betrayal helps to show just how much our addictive tendencies have set into our partnership or marriage. The more transcendent experiences we have had with our partner, the more likely we are to have confused them with the Holy Spirit, and the more we will suffer the wound when they are taken from us.

I believed that my desire to love, to know truth, and to experience freedom comprised the most important things in my life. My spiritual ideals influenced where and how I lived—the partners I chose, my friends, my work, the choice of a school for my daughter. When I saw these ideals so quickly eclipsed by my broken heart's yearnings, I was beyond discouraged. My grandiose image as someone dedicated to enlightenment pretty well collapsed. I saw that I did not know myself at all. I had been totally delusional about myself—my values, wishes, and priorities. I had imagined my life on the pages of *Shambhala Sun* when it belonged in *True Romance* or *Cosmopolitan*. I began to think my entire life had been wasted on imaginary pursuits and was a sham.

The esoteric truth is that many of us in modern culture, men as well as women, have misinterpreted our yearning for union with the Divine as a futile search for "the one." We spend our lives seeking the soul mate that will complete us and take away the hollowness inside. In this mistaken longing for an idealized other, we do not realize how we forsake our own souls.

When we create deep bonds with another person, the love and loyalty are real, but they get all mixed up with dependency and attachment, which limits our capacity to love genuinely. James Hillman described the tendency to attach to and idolize other people: "Others carry our souls and become our soul figures, to the final consequence that without these idols we fall into the despair of loneliness and turn to suicide. When we use them to keep ourselves alive, other persons begin to assume the place of fetishes and totems, becoming keepers of our lives."[11]

Until we know in our bones that another person cannot satisfy our true heart's longing, we will keep looking in all the wrong places to quench what is actually a deep-seated desire for our spiritual home. Analyst Jacqueline Wright writes about how we need betrayals to move beyond the primal urge to search for fulfillment in partnership. "We relive this primary emotion [the betrayal of birth] in every relationship and encounter, every loss, as if it were the first. If we can work through the sense of abandonment and isolation, it can make us aware of the impossibility of being fulfilled by another.... But for the psyche to bring to birth what it carries, it must suffer the loss of these betrayals. Relationships cannot in themselves heal the basic betrayal and ache of being a separate individual."[12]

Many of us use relationship as a defense against the hardest, but most essential, fact of our human condition—*how much we suffer from our separation from God*. I sigh as I write this, knowing it is true, yet thinking how betrayal must be a lesson in tough love. Most of the time, I would much prefer the coziness of a faithful partner to facing my "existential separation from the ground of being"! To the ego self, incapable of comprehending the love of the deep heart, God feels almost like a booby prize when you lose in love in such a harsh way.

The difficult truth remains that our relation with another person, while it can point the way and be a wonderful solace and support, and may even be our path in life, can never fulfill the emptiness and loneliness at the core of our being. No matter how compatible we are as partners, how passionate or ethereal the attraction, or how reassuring or resonant the connection, we have to walk the lonesome valley on our own to get to the home that lies on the other side of our existential desolation.

SURRENDER AND GRACE

All along, I understood that the intense longings I felt for Rob must have a spiritual component. Every spiritual seeker has learned that our desires are misplaced yearnings for God's love, right? Nevertheless, my consciousness was too wrapped up in wanting the pain to stop and wanting Rob's love to get near such wisdom in practice. I was not going to lie to myself about this if I could help it. I had to admit, despite my intentions to be kind to myself, I often hated these terrible sensations of frustrated longing and could not shake the belief that they indicated something terribly wrong with me—not some call for love from the depths of my soul. In this condition, we are badly in need of help. In time, I realized, that is the point.

Often, I felt like I was standing on a board and trying to lift it. I kept blaming myself for the despair and could not find a way to either accept or stop it. If only I could shift from knee-jerk recoil to one of welcoming this wretchedness! This had been my intent all along, but putting such radical acceptance into practice when everything in me was screaming "No!" was going to take more than good intentions. Acceptance takes two essential components the mystery set in motion by betrayal germinates. It takes surrender, and it takes grace. I was incapable of commandeering either one.

One afternoon, in the quiet of my living room, I was struggling with the starving sensations in my chest, gazing absentmindedly, as I often did, at an image hanging on the wall of Kwan Yin. The picture of the Buddhist goddess of compassion was given to me by Dennis as his final gift and often brought me solace. In this instance, I was bordering on despair, certain I could no longer endure my helplessness before these torments, when a small miracle happened.

A warm aliveness began to seep through the sensations of hollowness and desolation. A palpable presence moved inside my body, like thousands of tiny kisses. Starting precisely at the painful center of the now familiar ache behind my heart, a sweet substance began to fill me. Tenderly, "someone" whispered my name and enfolded me in warm, caring arms. And I was relieved, for the moment, of the great burden of my bereft self. As I let myself fall into this sudden, light fullness, I began to feel the delicate fabric of my connection with the life all around me, and it breathed hope into my soul.

I still do not know from where the love came that penetrated through my despair. I could only call it grace. I knew from my many failures that I could not generate such love on my own. I could invite, I could ask, I could even beg; but I could not compel. In the long mortification of the dark night, I reached many points of desperation like this. Looking back, I believe these moments of giving up brought on a surrender that finally allowed help to enter. I did not know the meaning of these longings. But I felt in those moments how they reached far beyond Rob. My deepest unrequited loving was for this mysterious aliveness and warmth I was powerless to create; it was for a love I could not explain; it was for God.

I wondered if the warm presence might have appeared in response to the perseverance it took to welcome and remain open, however grudgingly, to the terrible early feelings. Could I take some credit? The patience itself was a form of asking, was it not, a surrender to the mystery of suffering, a stubborn faith? Staying with our feelings implies a willingness to be helped, when everything wants to shut down.

It reminded me of what it takes when you are first learning to listen to a Wagnerian opera. If you can stay in the opera house through two or three hours of the shrieking onslaught of monotonous voices, some time into the third or fourth hour of a five-hour performance, the music starts to sink into you, to sing through your cells with an unparalleled beauty and meaning that makes the wait more than worthwhile.

For whatever reason, that day in my little living room, tenderness penetrated the pangs of craving and the stinging nettles to reveal a soft underside—a field of caring presence greater than the desperation. As this warmth saturated the suffering, it brought tears of surprise and relief, and dissolved a layer of my ancient enmeshment with the abandoned infant, and the primal shame that went with her. It also unpeeled a layer of my visceral conviction that Rob was the source of this love for which I longed.

In this and subsequent graced moments, when that exquisite gentleness seeped through me, it quenched my longing and my loneliness, and I was held and at home. Sometimes that presence came simply as warm aliveness; other times as a mild, golden light; or as tiny blooming flowers; or, my favorite, as thousands of caressing kisses. In the years of suffering and struggle, these moments of dawning love were rare but vital consolations in learning to embrace the holiness in the pain. They brought hope and helped fuel my nascent faith it might be a benevolent universe, after all, and that we are not isolated and alone, floating in cosmic space.

CHAPTER 13

The Problem of Pain

God whispers to us in our pleasures, speaks in our conscience,
but shouts in our pains. It is his megaphone to rouse a deaf world.
—C. S. Lewis

IF YOU ARE A seeker like me, in the turbulence of betrayal you seriously
reconsidered your commitment to loving, to living a life of depth, and to
"waking up." Once Rob left and I suddenly no longer cared about kindness, or
truth, or God, or enlightenment, making the pain stop became my new god.
Give me back my illusions, I pleaded. *Please, I do not care if I am superficial and*
deluded; please, just make the pain stop! As much as I protested and pleaded,
however, I could not retrace my steps. It was sobering to realize that once we
have started down the slide into the mysteries of the soul, we cannot go back,
even though we may kick and scream and struggle with all our might on the
way down when we realize what we have gotten ourselves into.

The descent is not for everyone, and at times I wonder if it is wise for
anyone! Either way, we have very little choice. When wisdom traditions and
teachers advise us to turn toward our suffering, they are proposing a radical,
fundamental shift in the way we relate to life. To stay safe and alive, we have
learned to avoid as much pain as possible. Instinctively, for survival, we move
away from pain and toward pleasure. In this species-wide condition, we are all
wired to avoid pain; and thereby to resist a central ingredient needed in clearing and opening the heart.

All of us, by the time we are adults, have enclosed ourselves in protective, self-satisfied psychological cocoons, in self-images, and in the roles we
play. Wrapped in our self-contained worlds, if we do not move beyond our
ego's comfort zone as we age, we become locked more into our routines, and
become more estranged from one another and from our lives. As Pema
Chodron explains the situation, "It is hard to know whether to laugh or to cry
at the human predicament. Here we are with so much wisdom and tenderness,

and—without even knowing it—we cover it over to protect ourselves from insecurity. Although we have the potential to experience the freedom of a butterfly, we mysteriously prefer the small and fearful cocoon of ego."¹ We get by, learn to survive, and can live our entire life in this self-protected way. If, however, we are called to growth of consciousness, something more is asked of us, something that goes against our nature.

Either through spiritual practices, creative endeavors, or life circumstances, our defenses are cracked open. We find ourselves backed into a corner where, if we want to go forward in depth, meaning, and love, we must turn toward suffering. Like a salmon swimming upstream, we need to turn against the powerful, instinctual current to do otherwise. Or perhaps we just need to stop long enough to hear a buried, ancient longing for something more, also part of our nature—Jung called it *the religious function*—that impels us to make the turn toward pain and suffering. Until we make this turn (and even often afterward), our suffering just feels pointless and wrong.

PAIN OR SUFFERING?

A number of my spiritual-minded friends and more than a few acquaintances, trying to be helpful, and maybe just the tiniest bit impatient with me in my prolonged distress, gave me pep talks to remind me of the difference between pain and suffering. Human beings cannot avoid pain—*pain*, they explained, describes the actual physical sensations we feel. If we stay with sensations of hurt, without elaborating with the mind, pain is quite manageable. *Suffering*, on the other hand, we create ourselves by coloring the events in our lives with inner commentary, judgments, and interpretations, all of which add geometrically to the physical pain. This idea is gospel in New Age spirituality: Suffering is optional. We suffer only because we identify with the pain and with the delusional story we tell ourselves about it.

From this point of view, if you are suffering, the remedy is obvious: You simply need to detach and let go of your interpretation. At the very least, take an appropriate distance, and quietly observe whatever is disturbing you until it changes, which will be soon if you stop identifying with it and apply the right attitude. In a fatherly attempt to help me be strong, one friend who avidly practices Zen advised, "Wake up. Be firm with yourself—just say *stop* to it all!"

I was very familiar with the theory behind this advice, and I had already tried to apply it in every way I knew how. In my traumatized condition, the effort to "just say stop" was discouraging, humiliating, and, frankly, impossible. The fact is most of us who have been traumatized and broken open will suffer relentless pain that begs for distractions and numbing, no matter what we do. Advising someone going through this much suffering to "just say stop" was like telling a person with third-degree burns all over her body to just stop hurting.

In actuality, the transformation of intense psychic pain into fruitful or "conscious" suffering requires a radical receptivity of heart and soul, an expansion and rewiring of the nervous system that most of us have yet to develop. If we are lucky and graced, we may use being broken open to take baby steps to go against our aversion to suffering, to feel into the mysterious roots of pain. But expecting the pain to stop, if we just get it right, oppresses and discourages the soul.

I was reassured when I came upon Tibetan master teacher Chogyam Trungpa speaking to this idea that we can somehow skip over suffering if we are only awake enough:

> The idea of egolessness has often been used to obscure the reality of birth, suffering and death. The problem is…we can easily entertain or justify ourselves by saying that pain does not exist…. This is just cheap escapism…. "There is no one to suffer, so who cares? If you suffer, it must be your illusion." This is pure opinion, speculation. We can read about it, we can think about it, but when we actually suffer, can we remain indifferent? Of course not; suffering is stronger than our petty opinions.[2]

Because I had spent hours every day trying to apply these beliefs, trying not to identify with "the pain body," the obsessive thinking, and the despair, I knew in my bones the truth that suffering was stronger than my opinions. Attachment may indeed create suffering, but in our human condition, *we are, by definition, attached.* It comes with the equipment.

SUFFERING IS NOT OPTIONAL

When we reach our pain limit either physically or psychologically, *suffering is not optional.* We can accept this truth more easily with what we consider to be purely physical pain. But when we are shocked into feeling places of deep-seated emotional patterning, the reason for our suffering is less clear. It just feels wrong; and we find out we cannot leapfrog from our foundational attachments to detachment. We cannot simply will away the sense of self that gives rise to so many of our painful feelings, thoughts, sensations, and beliefs.

When life destroys what has given us structure and meaning, we suffer, and suffering shrinks consciousness to the pain at hand. When higher faculties go offline, forget about enlightenment, forgiveness, or unconditional love. If we are fortunate, the distress may initiate a dark night of the soul in which we maintain a vague intuition that something extraordinary is going on. That intuition may help us not to succumb to depression, addiction, or acting out to cope with the relentless pain.

Loss of what has given you purpose, security, and identity registers as a grievous threat, and a threat it is. Willingly suffering the unraveling of our attachments brings death to an entire way of being. And, however delusional our life and self-images turn out to have been, dying still hurts.

Through suffering the demolition of our safe ground at the hands of our trusted partner, we learn how much we humans exist in an impossible situation over which we have little control. Bearing the healing crisis after learning we have been living a lie begs for kindness and compassion. Our orientation to reality is being realigned. In this time of disorientation, the ground we have stood on for decades has crumbled under us, and it is frightening and grievous. Now we see how much help we need, how little we know, and how dependent we are on forces we do not understand. Imagining that we somehow can control our reaction and simply erase our suffering with the right attitude or practices denies our humanness. We need to lighten up our expectations, cut ourselves some slack, and tread gently while we are being schooled in the mysteries of suffering. One suggestion for the more serious among us: Allow plenty of time for margaritas and movies!

DEPTH DEPRIVATION

When we endure a serious betrayal, the first noble truth of Buddhism that "all is suffering" seeps as a reality into our bones. And we see why we need to learn to befriend suffering. Many spiritual traditions teach that any deepening of inner life must bring an awareness of underlying suffering. Trungpa, for example, pointedly reminds us, "Pain is very real. We cannot pretend that we are all happy and secure. Pain is our constant companion."[3]

Even in times of complacency and well-being, when we stop to be open and alert enough, we find low-grade anxiety, compulsions, restlessness, and dissatisfaction underlying our usual busyness and distraction. Before crisis and loss strike, most of the time, we live on the surface of life where we feel less pain. But the result is we suffer from chronic "depth deprivation."

Awareness practices encourage deepening; but depth both attracts and frightens us. Sustained awareness tends to reveal the wonder of whatever we focus upon, whether it is our breath, the sky, a lover, a new baby, the garden, or our pain. We "see" the beauty of what we attend to. Some say attention is the beginning of love. Sustained presence opens us up beyond the three-dimensional world we take for granted. It unfolds a vertical dimension, a qualitatively more interior aspect of whatever we attend to.

Awareness unveils previously unrecognized beauty and meaning; it hints at the miracle of existence. Awareness, however, *also brings our underlying suffering to the surface.* Love, inspiration, and beauty flush whatever stands in their way into consciousness. Much of our surface personality reinforces our habitual depth avoidance. Our ego defenses help us avoid pain we have carried for a long time, and leave us unprepared when pain enters our life in overt and obvious ways we cannot avoid.

Demonstrating how close the usual cover-up of our schemes and strategies is to the unconscious pain we habitually carry, author Annie Dillard described the extreme pain of burn victims: "Once I read that people who survive bad burns tend to go crazy; they have a very high suicide rate. Medicine cannot ease their pain; drugs just leak away, soaking the sheets, because there is not skin to hold them in. The people just lie there and weep. Later they kill themselves. They had not known, before they were burned, that the world included such suffering, that life could permit them personally such pain."⁴

Severe physical or emotional pain forces serious existential questions: "Why is this happening to me?" and "What is the point of so much pain?" Suddenly, we want to know the answers to these questions with great urgency.

Wisdom traditions are built around offering answers to these questions. They suggest that pain, when met with awareness, is a necessary ingredient for soul growth. Suffering taken rightly can be medicine for our soul sickness. Pain can lead us out of our usual ego-tight cocoon and become a catalyst for healing our sense of isolation and separation, and depth deprivation.

James Hillman describes betrayal as medicine for our soul sickness. He makes a case that betrayal comes as an imperative from our inner being, as a dark means for forging a connection with unconditional love and forgiveness. The shock of betrayal forces an encounter with the Higher Self, which is always experienced as a defeat for the ego. Clinging to the ego self causes suffering; but, at the same time, ego-shattering can be a potent remedy to destroy the ego's control over our lives. He goes so far as to suggest that the *growth of soul through the crushing of the ego* may be the primary reason betrayal is designed into the scheme of human life, and possibly its only positive outcome.⁵

The shattering, humiliation, and helplessness at least temporarily relieve depth deprivation; betrayal takes us down and wakens us to an unpalatable, but profound truth: The way to the love we most want is through the deepest pain we most do not want. The last thing we consider possible in the midst of what seems like our wholesale destruction is that the torments of betrayed love could be delivering medicine for the healing of our lives. In fact, just the opposite seems true. The infusion of grace that enters through our broken dreams appears at first to sicken, weaken, and destroy what had been working well for us. It just seems wrong.

MAKING PAIN AN ALLY: CONSCIOUS SUFFERING

Suffering can also be too much. It can overwhelm, as if the doctor over-estimated the dose. With intense pain, throw all bromides out the window. Now whenever someone says "Whatever doesn't kill you makes you stronger," I just shake my head. Suffering causes too many people to die inside, if not physically, to escape the pain. Human beings need to learn how to befriend suffering if we ever hope to save ourselves and our planet. There is too much suffering to keep acting out unconsciously, smoothing over pain with denial and platitudes..

We have two options when betrayal shatters our comfortable existence: 1) We can pass through the hell unconsciously, by acting out, repressing, denying, or losing ourselves in the distress; or 2) we can turn mindfully toward the pain. We choose the second alternative with the hope that it will lead us out of the crisis to an expanded, more meaningful life. Most likely, when life takes us down, we will spend time in both these states of mind.

To learn to befriend and not simply indulge our suffering, we need to differentiate between "good" and "bad" pain. We need to recognize when we suffer consciously and when we are suffering unconsciously. Bad or unconscious pain indicates fruitless suffering that hardens and reinforces our sense of being an isolated, separate being. Even if we do not repress, act out, or drug the pain, but feel it, the ego can use pain to craft or reinforce an identity. The ego is happy to take any experience, however painful, to enhance itself, thus the advice to quiet our interpretations is not all wrong.

That is why, after betrayal or any trauma, we are at risk for adopting a victim identity. Unconsciously identifying with suffering can silently reinforce our small self in numerous ways. Pain can intensify feelings of worthlessness, specialness, outrage, or brokenness. We might imagine, for instance, that we are the most hopeless case ever, that no one else would fall apart the way we have; or we may channel our pain into resentment at the perpetrator, reinforcing our powerlessness. Conversely, we may inflate with the idea that we are a cut above most people, especially deep and spiritual because we are enduring more pain than anyone ever has before. Or, we may adopt a Captain Ahab identity, driven by vengeance to destroy whoever harmed us, our version of Moby Dick. I tried on all these victim hats in my struggles with pain.

"Good" or conscious suffering, on the other hand, asks that we bring curiosity and kindness to the hurting places inside. Good suffering can eventually transform our relationship to the pain itself. To me, transforming suffering became the Holy Grail of this expedition. As we change our relation to pain, it changes the quality of our connection to everything else in our lives.

"Accepting what is" is one way to describe conscious suffering. Acceptance is not a tough assignment when our lives roll pleasantly along in our comfort zone, and we like the way events are unfolding. Oh, what a different story when things fall apart, and we are thrown into trauma and torment. Even when we intend to suffer our pain with mindfulness, to pick up "our cross" willingly, our instincts and past programming immediately confront us. Our hidden beliefs and opinions that suffering is wrong interfere with the conscious intent to listen directly to the messages in the pain.

The Longing in Pain

Gradually, as I began to see how much I did not understand, I realized I also did not understand the meaning of pain. Suspending my judgments, stories, and beliefs, I began to listen more directly to the sensations in the most unbearable feelings. That is when I was surprised to discover a wise longing in the pain. I sensed that pain is a mystery, a messenger knocking on a door I needed to open, a prayer from my deep heart. It was a gift that was mine to offer. Offering was a gesture of surrender to a higher intelligence that understood more than I why this betrayal was in my path.

Habitually, we suffer unconsciously, resisting, fearing our grief and pain. The worst part is that right at the point of our greatest vulnerability, when we feel the most pain, we automatically abandon or shame ourselves. Most of the time, we do not even recognize what we are doing. Aggressive states of fear, shame, anger, and yuckiness come over us in conjunction with pain with such familiarity, we just keep sitting there until they reach breakdown proportions. This self-attacking tendency may be the source of all violence in the world and the reason "peace on earth" begins with taming our own inner aggression.[6]

Knowing that suffering is an integral part of the human condition can help come to terms with pain, but radical acceptance of suffering, making pain an ally in our yearnings for love, is a subtle art—I almost want to call it a martial art. Conscious suffering scares us, and mobilizes our defenses as if we are going to battle. When our ego nature fights back, it takes a warrior disposition to endure the struggle that ensues. Our innermost being, when it breaks through, threatens our old nature. So we panic. We reach out for anything to hang on to—thoughts, feelings, self-images, other people, addictions, manic busyness, or spaced-out distractions. This resistance too is okay and to be held with gentleness as where we need to be.

Painful situations are like Olympic events. There are degrees of difficulty that count as factors in one's "performance." Making it through a betrayal is an extremely challenging event to pull off with grace and ease—like executing a back 4½-somersault dive! We deserve to give ourselves points for getting through it at all. Destruction of what has been most important to us seems the worst that could happen and precipitates our oldest fears. It takes a warrior's courage to face them down.

It can be amazing to realize that the Divine comes near to us right in the heart of pain and problems, that pain itself is a prayer of longing for an enduring love. The suffering betrayal brings signals the nearness of an ineffable mystery that draws us on. We are being schooled to say yes, to welcome, the suffering. This *radical acceptance*[7]—our eventual yes to what is, regardless of our gut recoil—remains an inscrutable component of recovering from the cataclysm of betrayal and from any big losses in our lives.

I do not like to admit that I, or anyone else, may require pain and suffering to grow in depth and heart. Nevertheless, I must reluctantly admit that I have come to believe that many of us do need to be broken down to touch into our soul's potential.

In the intensive care ward of the psyche, where we have landed, we are asked to trust that we are in good hands. We are being treated for the intractable disease of separation from a source we long for and need beyond anything in this world. It takes radical surgery and strong medicine to turn away from eons of programming, karmic tendencies, or "original sin"—those deeply grooved habits of security and identity—toward the compassionate wisdom in the heart of pain.

Dark Nights of the Soul

The operation we need to bring us out of our depth deprivation and delusions takes place in darkness. That is, we do not and cannot know what is happening to us during the surgery. While intellectually I understood that healing could come through accepting suffering, for long periods of time I felt cut off and confused. My mind and my body were as if living on different planets, speaking different languages, in orbit around a different sun. My intuition, my psychological savvy, my spiritual senses, my faith all had disappeared into the distress.

Primarily, I could not shake the main question that pained and unnerved me: If I had been wrong about something as important as this relationship, this central facet of my life, how could I ever trust myself again? I lost confidence in my perceptions, beliefs, memories, and judgments. With no inner compass to guide me, often I felt hopeless about going forward. For long periods of time I felt adrift, lost, uninterested in living, covered in a fog of inertia and psychic pain, until I found myself asking, *Why go on?* I wanted to believe this suffering had a purpose, but waiting in nowhere land for some sign of life returning for so long, I was unconvinced. Yet, I intuited vaguely that something more was moving in my depths beyond the distress.

After a serious betrayal, once we are ready to face the shock head on, we are likely to be launched into what is known in psychological circles as a "night sea journey" and in the mystical tradition as a "dark night of the soul." John of the Cross, the sixteenth-century Spanish mystic and Carmelite monk, first used the term *dark night of the soul* to describe this distinct phase in spiritual life. He saw it as a purifying passage that reveals painful truths, but is ultimately full of hope and promise.[8]

The dark night is a transitional time of profound inner struggle, expressed archetypally in the stories of Christ's temptations in the wilderness and of Buddha's confrontation with the forces of Mara. It is represented by the passage to the East on the medicine wheel, by the symbols of crucifixion, abduction, devouring, or dismemberment. It has also been depicted as entering the lion's den, being thrown into the pit, marching into hell, abducted into Hades, or being lost in the wilderness or the desert.

In the life of the spirit, the dark night is a rite of passage, an initiation into a new state of consciousness that can reconnect us to the higher reaches of our nature. Jung knew the dark night as part of the individuation process. He described it as the night sea journey—an archetypal voyage through regression, depression, and neurosis, during which we withdraw all interest from the outer world and are submerged by inner reality. He called it a "descent into Hades and a journey to the land of ghosts somewhere beyond this world, beyond consciousness, hence an immersion in the unconscious."[9]

When the darkness falls, suddenly you are no longer normal. Usually precipitated by loss, the shock takes you into liminal time to become a dweller in the land of in-between, not yet having relinquished what promised fulfillment in the past, nor yet been transported to a new way of being.

When Jung unearthed images from medieval alchemy that offered profound insights into the individuation process, they included the dark night, referred to as the *nigredo* or blackness.[10] Graphic descriptions of the blackness from alchemical texts include death-making, rotting, decomposition, dismemberment, stabbing, decapitation, mud, slashing, carrion birds, the dying of the old king: all metaphors that give a flavor of the ordeals one must pass through during this winter time of transformation. In describing what it takes to individuate, to grow in depth and authenticity, Jung said "...the individuation process is, psychically, a borderline phenomenon which needs special conditions to become conscious."[11]

During a dark night passage, you are taken into "borderline" inner terrains where you begin to feel you could be losing your mind. The brokenness of betrayal provides the "special conditions" where the borderlands of consciousness come to awareness. These scary, but promising places are those populated by *both the madman and the mystic*. The trip to the hinterlands in the dark is not for the faint of heart—not that we have much choice. During this descent, the initiate vacillates between the glorious and the wretched, between agonies and ecstasies, between madness and mysticism.

When my spiritual director suggested I consider that I might be involved in a dark night of the soul, I doubted her. But eventually, understanding the trauma as an initiation into a new phase of spiritual growth enabled me to frame the misery as a test of faith. This context helped me endure with more patience what seemed to be interminable disorientation with highly uncertain results. From this perspective, passing through a dark night is an honor, a time when we are ready to be redefined and to transform our relationship to ourselves, to God, and to the meaning of life. Realizing you are partaking in the mysteries of a *spiritual testing* that goes beyond psychological insight and healing, helps restore the trust and dignity betrayal tramples.

Would it not be great if we could keep this viewpoint in mind and feel honored that we are finally ready to be divested of our delusions! Unfortunately, until we get beyond the worst times, it does not occur to most of us that we are involved in anything remotely spiritual. Likely, we have rarely felt less "enlightened." Under these unsettling circumstances, we are less inclined to embrace the suffering and more apt to be pleading to have our sleep restored and our comfortable lives back as soon as possible—*please!* As F. Scott Fitzgerald put it, "In a real dark night of the soul it is always three o'clock in the morning."[12] Ideally, we should crawl off to a cave and have someone bring us our food so we do not have to function in outer life. All our energies are needed to attend to the disintegration and dismemberment going on inside.

The mystics say when a dark night arrives, it comes as a response to a hidden yearning inside. I liked the sound of that with its promise of meaning to be found in what too often felt like meaningless madness. We have been asking for something—maybe love, maybe beauty, maybe truth, or God— the request could take many different forms, depending on our temperament, heritage, and conditioning. Likely, we may not even know what we were asking for; but, with the coming of the dark, our secret request is being granted. We are being answered, though it is not what we consciously expected or wanted.[13]

I vaguely knew I had hungered my whole adult life to learn to love. But, who could tolerate the irony of being brought to the threshold of love by losing what I had cherished most? If this betrayal was an invitation to a greater love, it went against every idea I had of what love was, and often I turned tail and begged that my life's longing be extinguished. Who needed love if it looked like this, if this loneliness, torment, and emptiness were the cost?

Though we are advised to rejoice when the darkness comes, to take it as a sign that our prayers are being answered, if you are like me, you do not feel at all like celebrating. To your ongoing chagrin, during this time, the primal woundings—shame, fear, guilt, rage—all rise to awareness to be sheared away. Often you feel sickened, poisoned, or rotten; and it can seem as if you are literally dying. We are in the throes of the symbolic death of parts of our former self. This sounds poetic and vaguely attractive—to die and be reborn—except that we cannot help resisting dying; it hurts, and we must grieve the loss.

EXISTENTIAL ABANDONMENT

Your separation from God is the hardest work you will ever do.—Hafiz

Locked in these struggles, I kept a thin thread of awareness that my distress went beyond Rob's absence. I felt cut off, not only from him and from the imagined warmth and safety of our partnership, but more important, I felt cut off from God, from the spiritual nourishment to which I was accustomed. I did my best to bring my heart into the infantile despair of "no mother" and the adult disheartenment of "no partner." But beneath this dread, I found the spiritual ache of "no God." This aching showed me ways my relationship had been helping me avoid feeling a profound, existential emptiness.

Many of our most horrible feelings, such as powerlessness, loneliness, and meaninglessness, stem from the sense that we are alone in the universe. Some traditions teach, as I mentioned, that *all our suffering* stems from this sense of isolation from God. The existential loss of faith in life itself is one of the worst torments of human nature that the betrayal of trust reveals.

Wisdom teachings suggest that the human condition includes some variation on "original sin"—the soul sickness that arises from our separation from God, from the ground of being. Stories of the fall from grace common to many world mythologies and religious traditions describe spirit incarnating into a physical body as a primordial shock. These myths convey that we experience incarnation as having been cast off, hurled out of paradise, into the constricted, fallen state of human life. The traumatic splitting from the wholeness of existence imprints on the soul as an irreparable abandonment, a state of being outcast by the source of all good.

These earliest experiences of separation from the matrix of life leave a sense of deficiency, of shameful lack that goes beyond the personal The lack registers in the psyche as a *component of basic reality* wherein shame and existence itself are inseparable. Burrowed deep in the subconscious and etched into the grooves of our nervous system, this ontological deficiency fuels the basic flaw, the underlying sense of "me" alone in an indifferent world. The sense of existential betrayal may be the deepest hurt we carry, a pain more ancient, more hardwired even than that of birth and infancy. This betrayal goes beyond the quality of our mothering. Even the most exceptionally good-enough mother cannot make up for this loss.

Analyst Heide Kolb explains our dilemma:

> A deep seated trauma most of us share is abandonment. Being betrayed right from the start. Being born into a world that is not welcoming. Being born with a soul that remembers wholeness, but cannot find it in lived life. A soul that is subjected to terrible suffering if she does not remember her way back to the source of her belonging.[14]

There is no escaping this most universal of themes: It comes with the equipment of our humanity. For life to have meaning, we must find the meaning of this betrayal, this earliest pain.

God Is a Trauma

According to some traditions, it takes a traumatic shock equal to the original existential loss to stir forces strong enough to reveal our buried grief and shame, and to restore the wounded soul. Becoming deeper and more authentic, individuating, in the depth psychological tradition, is said always to begin with a crisis, a trauma, devastation or loss. Kolb quotes Jung:

> That "God is a trauma" is an often quoted notion in Jungian thought. Jung said, "To this day 'God' is the name by which I designate all things which cross my path violently and recklessly, all things which upset my subjective views, plans and intentions, and change the course of my life for better or worse." He writes further in *The Red Book*, "The force of God is frightful," and this force is within us and we have to come to terms with it.[15]

When betrayal trauma brings on a dark night, we are being invited to shed our old nature. In that process, our attachments to the things of this world are violently under siege.[16] The time has come when we are ready (or not) to be stripped of the misplaced dreams and desires of the conditioned heart that have driven us away from our deepest wisdom to lesser things.

Whenever we attach or identify with anything, we tend to make it into a *false god or idol* that engages our attention, affection, and energy. The dissolving of our lesser gods by the luminous darkness causes much of our suffering. You might say "God's jealousy" has decided enough is enough. Whether we believe in God or not, some sense of connection, love, meaning, beauty, or purpose ties us to life and keeps us going. This indefinable faith that life is worth living is our god. We naturally tend to attach our sense that life is worthwhile, along with our deepest yearnings, to people and things in the world of form.

Losing whatever has given life meaning—what has become our god— brings the deepest despair. For me, and likely for most of us who have been crushed by betrayal, my faith in life was upheld by my belief in my partner, in our relationship, and in lasting love. Betrayal violently shattered that faith.

In the darkest times, I felt forsaken by all, but especially by a God who would allow such cruelty and abandon me in my misery. I was confronting a world without meaning, a life without value or purpose. When meaningless- ness pervades the soul, it feels as if you are living in a vast Antarctica, an end- less cold, gray wasteland. The mind whispers, "There is no God, no beauty, no love, no joy…no reason to live."

The time has arrived to come to terms with God, with the source of our life, however we conceive it, in the face of cruelty and suffering. For a long time, the question that Einstein suggested as the most important one a person can ask—"Is this a benevolent universe?"—dominated my mind. Deep down I believed the biggest betrayal was the betrayal by a God that let evil run rampant in the world. One minute, I renounced my faith and wanted nothing to do with such a heartless God, and the next I would be calling out, "Please! Help!" As the conviction in the goodness of life slips away, we are at risk of slowly dying inside. This is a time when having a spiritual friend who knows this territory can be invaluable. We need warmth and kindness to tolerate the loss of our dreams, and, more deeply, to come to terms with the evil and suf- fering in the world.

THE DISTRUST OF LIFE

Warmth and caring were, however, the last natural impulses I had toward this desolation. I recoiled at my neediness and pain. In hellish states of ancient attachment, we feel so isolated, ashamed, and alone. We need to continually lasso attention back to the goodness and simplicity of the moment. I took to praying for help and to turning to the most tangible positive sensations I could detect. Focusing on breathing, looking at colors, feeling the ground, or listening to my heartbeat granted a momentary counterbalance to the pangs of isolation. In the midst of so much inner upheaval, the urge to escape the present moment is intense, yet now we most need its sustenance.

I knew there was abundant, warm caring all around me, but I was like a person dying of thirst in the middle of a clear-water lake—surrounded by what I needed, but too angry and afraid to drink. In these states, I realized I was hitting a critical raw nerve. The meaninglessness was barely concealing a profound barrier to love: my distrust of life.

The excruciating *distrust of life itself* was the core loss I needed to learn to welcome. Feeling lost and adrift, I felt as if I were on a rolling river of emptiness that connected me to millions of others traveling along the same stream, who felt lost at that very same moment. The realization of the incongruous, shared emptiness with the community of the alienated once again gave me the strength I needed to bring kindness to the despair.

A decisive turn from feeling so lost came one day when I went out to the yard to try to take a sunshine break from desolation. As I watched the little yellow-tinged finches at the birdfeeder, my heart lifted, and I discerned that this empty meaninglessness that was eating away at me was yet another "mind thing" made up of interlacing strands of itchy, quaky terror and the sense of "me." I realized I did not really understand what these painful sensations meant or were trying to convey to me. Somehow the sweetness of the birds had gotten through to my constricted heart and released a wave of compassion—erupting from the sensations of emptiness themselves—for this terrified being I was taking myself to be.

Seeds planted in the darkest times were beginning to sprout. Looking back I see that in those moments I was learning what to trust. I trusted the holding ground of my heart to be stronger than the angst wanting to take me over. Thereafter, the terrible sensations dissolved more often with my breath into what began to feel at times like a velvet sea, a sea of love.

In a subtle movement, I began to linger with more curiosity when even the hollowness clutched at my heart, listening for what the sensations really meant. The suffering was awakening me from my usual trance, that much was certain, inviting me to something beyond the desolation, beyond this world. I began to hear a distant call through the hollowness, and to sense how the pangs were like birth pains. Something alive and vibrant, light and playful, delicious and warm was trying to break through. The suffering was murmuring a prayer for freedom, a prayer for love—no matter what life was bringing my way.

CHAPTER 14

Resentment Is the Altar Where We Go to Pray

*Knowing your own darkness is the best method for dealing
with the darknesses of other people.*
—C. G. Jung

I USED TO CONSIDER ANGER, resentment, and blame to be personal failings, compensations for something missing in my childhood, weaknesses in the formation of my character. After brewing in this betrayal, I have come to believe, however, that humans are hardwired with a drive for vengeance that must have served us at some point in time.

When someone hurts us, or someone we love, the impulse to strike back is a knee-jerk reaction. The urge for vengeance may even be encoded into our genetics as an evolutionary strategy. Was not an-eye-for-an-eye considered high justice at one time? Whatever the roots, the instinct to return pain for pain runs deep, deeper than I could have imagined.

Because I liked thinking of myself as a kind person who would not purposely harm other people, I was more willing to accept my heartache, fears, and sadness than to own up to my rage and resentment. Yet, because I was determined to stay with the truth of my experience, I had to admit that the impulse to strike back sizzled hot in my blood and bones.

As much as we may want to remain gracious and dignified and move on, many confirm that betrayal stimulates the most vengeful reactions they have ever had. Shock fuels the anger with the abnormal intensity of archetypal realms, and biochemistry is also a factor. According to Ginette Paris, "Your brain interprets the trauma of abandonment just like a physical attack and denying that such an attack causes anger contradicts the instincts."¹ Although I had spent years in therapy and trainings unlocking repressed anger, the rage unleashed by the betrayal introduced me to new levels of outrage and fury, feelings that went beyond the personal to the collective.

More disturbing than the spikes of anger was the low-key resentment that set in as a pervasive background mood I could not shake. The intensity and persistence of my ill will toward Rob made me realize that we do not know what we are capable of until we are traumatized and pushed to our limits. That people commit atrocities under extreme stress no longer surprised me. When our survival instincts come into play to test us, they readily reveal the fragility of our civilized veneer and the tenacity of the instinct to return pain for pain.

A Trip into the Heart of Blame

Stranger than a lover's love is lover's hate.
Incurable, in each, the wounds they make.
—Euripides, *Medea*

After Rob left, I did all I could to manage the 24/7 anxiety, but when the rage hit, it obliterated any wise, benevolent self-images that remained standing. Although I had read that feelings of rage and murderous revenge fantasies are common reactions to traumatic abuse, I had no idea I was capable of such malevolence.[2] Fantasies of tormenting and humiliating Rob came on at times like a flash flood. Maybe he would be in a disfiguring accident; or be covered with warts or boils; or catch some lingering, debilitating sexually transmitted disease; or become impotent, completely unable to perform sexually—that thought had great appeal. I wished for him to end up on the street, penniless. I even considered getting a voodoo doll, if sticking pins in it could actually make him suffer half as much as I had. And, if I ever heard reports of his good fortunes, I would seethe at the unfairness. It was as if my civilized superego had gone entirely offline, and I was left to contend with my unabashed animal instincts.

If your conscious attitude has been one of tolerance, self-control, and forgiveness, like mine had been, and you suddenly find yourself filled with murderous impulses triggered by the smallest thing, you can start to feel like a monster. Most of us do not like feeling like a monster, so the tendency is strong to talk oneself out of these thoughts and feelings, or to subvert them into distractions, addictions, illness, or more acceptable feelings. I could not help being ashamed of myself for entertaining such horrible imaginings and ill will.

In calmer times, compulsive, more acceptable resentments preoccupied me—cataloging his defective character traits, blaming and condemning him in imaginary conversations, making my case against him before an invisible jury. The ongoing desire to hurt and devalue him as he had hurt and devalued me alarmed me; yet my broodings felt so gratifying compared with the bottomless pit of shame, pain, and loneliness that it was virtually impossible to stop them, despite my fervent intentions to do so.

I learned that when we have been violated, revenge fantasies that mirror what was done to us, with the roles of trauma victim and perpetrator reversed, are a common reaction to the helplessness. Herman explains, "The victim imagines that she can get rid of the terror, shame, and pain of the trauma by retaliating against the perpetrator. The desire for revenge also arises out of the experience of complete helplessness. In her humiliated fury, the victim imagines that revenge is the only way to restore her own sense of power."[3] Instead of bringing relief, however, these fantasies only add to the inner torment, keeping us bound to the betrayer. They cannot be willed away, however, and represent a stage we need to pass through before righteous indignation and the difficult realization that it will be impossible to ever get even sets in.

Rage and vengeance fantasies defend against the powerlessness of being manipulated and deserted. We need to cut ourselves some slack at this survival-based reaction to trauma. Like a magic potion, rage and resentment serve as a kind of netting to protect us from the full impact of the shock. They have an amphetamine-like effect that can be addictive and give a surge of energy, confidence, and power. These reactions provide immediate relief for the battered psyche and hormonal surges to steady a tattered nervous system.

THE INCIDENT OF THE EGGS

One way I experienced the force of this impulse was through acting out my rage in the incident of the eggs. On the one-year "anniversary" of Rob's departure, I went away on retreat, and my daughter had a rare meeting with him. After long, grudging resistance, she had finally begun to bond with him as a father figure and part of our family a year or so before he left. I was so angry with myself for not protecting her, and bringing him into her life. She too was shocked by his departure, but felt they had a special relationship, and if she talked with him, it would make a difference. It took a while for her to realize how he had cut her off, too, and how much his abandonment of our little family had stirred the wound of her father's death.

At this time, she needed some fatherly advice, and reached out to Rob to ask for his help. When I arrived home the evening after they met, my usually cheerful daughter melted into tears. When I pressed her to know what was wrong, she told me. "He doesn't care about me at all—he didn't even ask about me!" she sobbed. "He doesn't even know I just graduated; he only kept telling me about bonding with his girlfriends' teenage son" I consoled and held her, but underneath, I was trembling with outrage, my fury now justified by seeing her so let down and hurt.

Later that evening, I happened upon a ready, unanticipated outlet for my outrage. On my way home from the store, I spotted Rob's easily recognizable car in a condo parking lot. I slammed on the brakes, swerved into the driveway, and pulled my car up behind his. Seemingly without thinking, I got out, went around to the grocery bag in the back seat, and grabbed the carton of a dozen eggs among my purchases. One-by-one, I took aim and pelted that hated car with those eggs. That car had triggered countless trauma reactions in me, as he nonchalantly drove past me around town. I must admit, smashing those eggs all over his car windows was wildly satisfying. All the same, I knew I had gone over the line in acting out this anger and felt sheepish, as well as enlivened, about it. I am not recommending you follow my lead.

I am telling you this story to share at least some of how I was living on the edge, trying to contain my anger, and how it boiled over in this incident. Behaving in this way helped my compassion grow for people who strike back when they and those they care about are hurt. But the potential humiliation of getting caught at these antics, I realized, made it not worth the fleeting gratification.

I cannot exactly say I was practicing the Golden Rule either: I was acting against my values, passing on the fear I felt from his indifference toward me. While I confess to reveling in the egg throwing, I was now doubly appalled at myself. I knew acting out anger was harmful, the beginning of the slippery slope that can end with outright war. But what could I do? How could I trust myself if at any moment I could lose control like that? I also knew that, considering what other vengeful options sometimes floated around my enraged, hurting mind, the egg throwing was an act of immense restraint.

Seeing and accepting this uncontrollable, malicious part of myself was one of the most disheartening ordeals of this passage. I would wake in the morning already enraged. In my futile efforts to manage the feelings, I would repeat to myself, over and over, "I am angry; I accept my anger. I am angry; I accept my anger." While I managed to restrain acting on most other vengeance fantasies, despite all my efforts, I could not prevent the continuing thoughts of resentment and revenge. They were the dark part of the obsessive flow that had captured my life.

STOP THE PAIN HERE!

Spiritual progress is like a detoxification.—Marianne Williamson

Often, it seemed that in my rage and pain, as with grief and longing, I had tapped into the experience of millions of other people who, at that very moment, were also resentful or enraged. As I intuited the universality of the angst beneath our civilized veneers, I also began to know in my bones that I did not want to inflict pain on anyone ever again; there was already too much pain in the world. It was too terrible to live with suffering every day the way I was, and I did not want to add to it. Thus I formulated a goal for myself: I would stop this pain with myself! I vowed to do whatever I could not to contribute to the recycling of violence by passing my pain on.

My resolution to not pass on my suffering gave me focus and motivation. Trying to apply it to a traumatized psyche that oscillated between terror and rage as a way of life, however, increased my dejection. Despite my passioned intention, some troubling devil in me was determined to shake Rob awake to what he had done by inflicting the fear and pain on him that he had inflicted on me. I viewed this payback as a righteous necessity to force him to acknowledge the harm he had done and to stop him from continuing to hurt people this way.

Admitting my helplessness to keep my vow before the power of this vengeful force in me led to a burning question: What is this impulse to do harm? Admittedly, this desire was mixed with an instinct for justice and the kind of care parents exercise when children need tough love to reign in their destructive behavior. But for now, my focus was on why, when we are hurting, are we compelled nearly irresistibly to hurt back?

I began to make a more studied inquiry into my drive to return pain for pain. I decided to start small and to focus as mindfully as possible on resentment and blame. I knew "How could you?!" was the question that repeats over and over in most all betrayed, bewildered minds, years, even decades, later. It certainly led the hit parade in mine. That question plagued me, probably hundreds of times a day the first couple of years, and even kept popping up years later. This seemed a good place to start.

With a little attention, I soon realized the subtext of "How could you?" was "What is *wrong* with you?" When this devaluing question dominated my mind, the first thing I noticed was how "together" I felt in contrast to how I was viewing Rob: I was clear—he was confused; I knew the truth—he was deluded; I was taking the high road—he was a low life; I was significant, above the fray, in charge of my life again—he was a dishonorable loser. I felt justified in these thoughts. *I felt like a powerful somebody.* I was fighting for the right against an obvious wrong. As I deemed him weak, dishonorable, and craven, I was, by contrast, authentic, formidable, morally superior, and self-assured.

When I was focused on Rob's weakness like this, I no longer felt like a helpless, throwaway nobody; rather, I felt like a powerful *somebody*. This blaming attitude helped me perceive myself as more solid than broken, more expansive than small, more dignified than humiliated. I could see why so many ex-spouses or former lovers settle into fixed attitudes of resentment toward those who have hurt them—how better to regain dignity, to feel better about yourself, but primarily, to protect yourself from the horrible feelings of rejection, shame, and longing? Blame helped to puff up and glue together my shattered ego. The pleasurable sensations and thoughts of superiority—I felt smug and satisfied—gave this subtle form of mental aggression its addictive appeal.[4]

Despite feeling ashamed at myself for indulging at his expense, I caught the logic of the psyche at work. Perhaps by *the simple act of blaming, the mind staves off something much worse* that can follow traumatic injury: major depression, suicidal impulses, homicide, substance or behavioral addictions, dissociative or borderline disorders, or even a psychotic break. Blame seems like nothing compared with the other possibilities of a cracked-up psyche. From this perspective, blame was a knight in shining armor, protecting poor little me from disintegrating. Well done, psyche!

As I learned to discern the calming, tingly sensations of "strong me" that accompanied blame, I dropped deeper. I noticed this sense of strength corresponded with a subtle contraction throughout my body. This hard-edged contraction formed the outline of my usual bodily sense of self. Tensing all these muscles to feel strong required an enormous amount of energy. *My "strength" consisted of sharp, stabbing sensations* that were actually faintly irritating. That is when I realized that the aggressive blaming energy was ricocheting back on my body. It was as if, with each flush of righteous indignation, I had been pricking myself with, and contracting against, thousands of barely perceptible sharp pins.

Beneath the surface satisfaction, the shell of confidence and certainty of blame, an undercurrent of violence was brewing in my body. I recognized these persecutory pangs contained both anger and fear—the barely perceptible perpetrator/victim energies of the trauma vortex. Mindfulness had given me a front row seat for watching how I whipped up thoughts of blame *to divert attention away from the far more disturbing underlying rage and terror.* Under the surface of confident self-righteousness, I found I was caught in a loop with perpetrator and victim trading time on center stage. I could not decide which side I preferred, the stabs of anger or the tightness of fear.

At times, these opposites of fear and anger came together in my awareness, and I understood these moments as shifts toward wholeness—mini-unions of opposites. Then I would experience a wave of expansion and softening into spaciousness and communion with my world.

Yet my mind always pulled me back. As the sensations of communion became more arduous to bear, I slipped back again into blame. Minutes, or even hours later, I would awaken, realizing I had gotten lost in some seemingly brilliant new analysis of Rob's character defects or the humiliating indignities I was enduring. The mind was so inventive, coming up with anything to entertain and entice me to avoid staying with the raw emotions. I concluded I was addicted to the mind activity to avoid the distress, and to the distress to avoid the dissolving into mystery.

WE NEED HEART TO FIND HEART

While blame kept my ego from falling apart, it bolted shut the door to the more subtle veils of the heart that I needed to pass through to touch into the wounds that had been stirred. When I focused on my heart in these inquiries, I realized warmth was missing. My heart was protected, yes, but felt numb, encased tightly, like bound feet in old Chinese style. Without caring warmth of the heart, I was imprisoned either in the mental state of blame or in the volatile feelings of the persecutor/victim. At this impasse, I could see why. Moving attention into my heart engaged my curiosity, but *it hurt*.

Focusing on my heart brought me right to the edge of my brokenness, where I needed help. Where we most need heart, we lock down and reject ourselves. In a misguided effort to keep us safe from further harm, the traumatized psyche directs our most vicious denunciations at our deepest wounds, making our pain the enemy.

As we get closer to the core wounds of the traumatized psyche, the inner predator/protector clicks in and turns on us, like an autoimmune reaction, attacking our most vulnerable self with arsenals of fear, shame, and self-hatred. In this threatening atmosphere, our most vulnerable selves, like scared, injured animals, are not about to come into the open.

So, what to do when we have no access to our own heart, and yet we need that heart to heal our wounds? We could use a little tenderness, as Otis Redding suggests. Even a drop of kindness applied to the pain of what we most reject in ourselves gives the needed courage to face the hurt and sorrow beneath our anger. The most direct solution is to reach out, to call on a friend, guide, or therapist for caring and connection.

If we are alone, however, and find the heart on lockdown, we can still learn to prime the pump of kindness. Visualizations, singing, chanting, dancing, affirmations, metta (loving-kindness) practice, and devotional prayer all help to soften us to the natural goodness of the heart when most needed. When I was alone and the going got rough, I sang a little chant, "Spirit, I adore thee," written by Linda Webb-Khakaba. The words and tune helped me feel held, as if in the arms of a divine mother. In this environment of tenderness, we more readily touch into prayer of the heart. The holding presence gave me the courage to sink with more willingness and trust into the hurt, as if slipping into a warm, comforting bath.

TOUCHING THE BEREFT CORE

As I eased into my broken heart, an image formed. At first I heard faint cries, and then a thrashing, howling infant came into view. As I stayed with the heartache, I found myself whimpering, sobbing, and, finally, wailing. The sounds came from somewhere, as if from another person, even another world. After perhaps twenty minutes of this outpouring, a quiet came over me, and I melted into that moment, merging fully with the arms of love that held me close. With this healing power touching the early anguish, I sensed I had come into the deepest truth beneath the rage. At the core of what I initially experienced as a powerful "me" intent on righteous blaming, I had discovered this very young bereft child. Although I had spent years doing depth work, I had never been ready to touch into the depths of this wound.

When we come face to face with our deepest pain, by definition, we are in the territory where *no love can penetrate*. The bereft infant that forms our ego core is unloved, unwanted, alone, terrified, grief-stricken, a contracted speck in the universe in great need. Our ancient identification with isolation and pain forms an impenetrable barrier to our true identity that resides in the depths of the warm heart.

This frozen infant self had come out of long hiding to be melted, soothed, and released by attention and care. Now she was dying, dissolving into a sea of love I both feared and longed for with all my heart.

The big question we face in coming back from the hurt of intimate trauma is "How will I ever trust again? How will I ever allow love in again?" We have been given an unparalleled opportunity: Being cracked open reveals ancient imprints we have been terrified our entire life to feel. But with the trauma defenses in high protective gear, how can we ever trust enough to let love penetrate this pain?

The answer is, *we cannot*. We cannot generate the love we need on demand, at will. But we can point ourselves in the right direction. We can be *willing* to trust the pain, willing to receive love and care even where it hurts the most. I noticed when I turned to my breath and let even an ounce of that life force into the fear and hurt, a warm sweetness trickled into my soul. It was like a miracle to me. The more I surrendered to the loving presence coming through the pain, the more the grieving infant poured forth her tears.

Was this grace? The exercise of an art form? Prayer answered? The ground of being? While I tried not to question this love when it appeared, I could not help wondering, was this flow coming from my own heart, from a guardian angel, or from the goodwill of others who had shown up to help take me through the worst pain? I did not know, but that tender presence became essential for recovering these lost parts of my soul. In these moments, I began to sense my anger also as prayer, a call for a love I was powerless to command on my own.

IT TAKES A MIRACLE

While these forays into the grief and pain underlying blame opened my heart and increased my faith in love, when it came to stopping the cycle of returning hurt for hurt, the progress was slow. As long as the heartache persisted, my mind started again and again down the road of malice in its many disguises. My psyche still seemed instinctually wired, and often it still seemed intuitively right that Rob should experience the very pain he caused me and my family and friends. It may be true that a remorseless person who hurts others indeed requires suffering in order to realize that his behavior causes great pain. It was not, however, up to me to be a one-person vigilante posse to bring about that justice. (Darn!) And what if I was wrong?

I had other work cut out for me. The difficulty in trying to turn around the Titanic of our own aggression when we have been hurt can birth more compassion, but a pattern as well-worn as addiction to blame and counterattack does not disappear with one realization and release, or even with several.

My anguish at the situation often dissolved into tears of tenderness for myself and for all people facing the suffering and sorrow that seem an integral part of our human heritage. Coming into the truth of my human nature, I began to sense it would take a miracle to move beyond the built-in desire for vengeance and power over someone who hurt me or those I love and, instead, open my heart in compassion and forgiveness.

Trying to stop the pain in myself, though doomed to failure, revealed a secret side of suffering. This remains one of the mysteries of betrayal I return to often in this writing: how betrayal brings you to a breaking point, to a humbling, where you taste your powerlessness, and right there, astonishingly, you pray—perhaps not in words, but in the tenor of your heart you realize your dependence on a Higher Power. Immediately, your prayer is answered and grace enters. At the moment of surrender, the *miraculous* enters your hurting, confused humanity to guide your way forward.

The time did eventually come—it took years—when, in response to Rob's continued denial and dismissiveness toward me, instead of reeling in pain and rage, my heart kindled with a flow of compassion that went out to him and answered my deepest prayers. In those moments, I felt my humanity most clearly. I realized we all carry the propensity to return hurt for hurt; we all long for love we are powerless to command, but that lives in us, hidden in our pain; and that we are all struggling for a way out of the human dilemma to find our way home in this brief, complicated existence.

CHAPTER 15

Conscience and the
Pilgrimage of the Heart

It is only with the heart that one can see rightly;
what is essential is invisible to the eye.
—Antoine de Saint Exupéry

W E TAKE FOR GRANTED our health until we are sick just as we do not notice our hearts much until they are broken. Being cracked open showed me how much I had to learn about the heart. The mystics of many traditions speak of the heart's importance, not the outer, emotional heart we think of when we hear the word, but the subtle, inner heart with intelligence and a life of its own.[1] Artist Michael Green describes poetically the inner and outer hearts:

> Within every human breast shine two mystic hearts, one hid subtly within other. The outer one loves and desires the beauties of the world, and in obtaining them is led into happiness and song; and in losing them, to grief and lamentation. But the inner heart is a secret heart, its form adamantine, and it gazes with unbroken rapture into the Great Mystery of the soul's desire. There, in the domain of neither gaining nor losing, all things are perceived truly and there is face-to-face seeing into the deepest nature of things. The light of singularity abounds in full gladness, like coming upon a light in thick darkness, like receiving a treasure in poverty; and existence is delivered from all limitations.[2]

One way to understand spiritual development betrayal calls us to undertake is as a purifying pilgrimage from the outer to the inner heart. The more familiar emotional heart can be described many ways. It is the egoic, surface, or conditioned heart, the heart of the child in us. We hear the inner heart characterized as the true, deep, subtle, essential, or genuine heart. It is also

197

known as the awakened or compassionate heart; the heart of sadness or *bodhichitta;* or the spiritual, mystic, or wisdom heart.

In our everyday life, we hardly tap into the heart's potential. What normally blocks the deep heart from guiding our lives are the passions of the surface that arise from our conditioning that trauma and pain stir into a storm. The true heart is a faculty of the soul. It is that in us that can know and be known by the Divine. On occasions when we drop into the mysteries of life—birth, death, beauty, love, suffering, and loss, to name a few—we hear the more subtle messages of the spiritual heart.

As we have explored, the cost of passing from the surface to the essential heart is often suffering. Suffering tenderizes us and rivets our attention to the calls of the deep heart. When our outer heart cracks open, it allows the influence of the mystic heart, "rapt with the soul's love," to begin to pour through us. Contemporary spiritual teacher A. H. Almaas teaches that we cannot truly know the essential heart until we have allowed the emotional heart to break. On the waves of heartbreak, remorse, and grief, we gradually travel through layers of past pain and conditioning into the dramatically different world of the mystic heart.

Buddhist teachings recognize the relationship between the compassionate heart and the broken heart. They describe the awakened heart as *bodhichitta,* the "genuine heart of sadness," whose tenderness can be felt through the soft spot, or grief point, in the center of the chest—that same familiar place we recognize in the betrayed heart that will not stop aching and becomes a touchstone for coming home to ourselves. Pema Chodron speaks of the opportunity a torn-apart heart brings to connect with this genuine sadness:

> An analogy for bodhichitta is the rawness of a broken heart. Sometimes this broken heart gives birth to anxiety and panic, sometimes to anger, resentment, and blame. But under the hardness of that armor there is the tenderness of genuine sadness. This is our link with all those who have ever loved. This genuine heart of sadness can teach us great compassion.... This continual ache of the heart is a blessing that when accepted fully can be shared with all.[3]

It may be surprising for those of us who place a high value on happiness, positivity, and pleasure to learn that the heart of wisdom is also known as the heart of sadness. We tend to think of sadness as a sign that all is not well. But when we bring attention to the heart, we learn that deep sadness can brings a grace that opens us to the life-giving truth and love of the heart.

THE MYSTIC HEART

Words are inadequate to describe the qualities of heart that emerge through consciously suffering our brokenness. Perhaps that is why it is so much easier to describe our ego fixations, issues, poisons, and problems than it is to speak about the dawning presence of an inner light, the compelling solace of stillness, the intertwining of subtle bodies, the tenderness of the breath, or the intelligence of the heart. We start to glaze over at what to the rational mind sound like mere abstractions. The world of the mystic heart can only be known by inner taste, not by the mind.

The intuitive heart attunes to another reality. Its truth is more readily conveyed by image, symbol, story, myth, music, and poetry. It vibrates with silence and the unknown. We recognize the essential heart by characteristic states of mind—such as faith, love, strength, and joy, rather than by emotions.

The inner heart is the seat of our basic goodness, "an organ for the perception of divine purpose and beauty."[4] The intelligence of the subtle heart radiates beyond the rational mind to pull together the primary aspects of our humanness. The heart connects the head with the body, and the visible world with the invisible worlds. The eyes of the heart see into the essence of people and things and look beyond appearances to invisible realities. In relationship, instead of splitting the world into you and me, the compassionate heart recognizes I and Thou.

In navigating my way through the trials of betrayal, learning to discern these two hearts was, on many days, the difference between despair and hope, and it may be helpful for you, too. On a good day, I could sense the compassionate heart coming through my painful emotions as a longing for warmth, care, protection, and a love that does not end. It was only through a growing alignment with messages of the heart that I found the strength to rebuild my faith and trust in life. Otherwise, I too easily lost myself in despair. When I felt graced with the warm presence of the loving heart, the desperation and humiliation of betrayal no longer detracted from my dignity; but softened into humility and wonder.

In our whirlwind lives, we easily mix the feelings of the past with quiet messages coming from the enduring heart center of warmth and mystery. In order to discern the heart's messages of spiritual truth, we need to listen beyond the insistent clamor of our thoughts, feelings, and sensations. Fortunately, the pain of betrayal stops us; it drives us into the slow time of the liminal world. There, the heart communicates through inner quickening, symbol, gesture, unspoken word, and flow.[5]

THE SOLACE OF SOLITUDE

It takes quiet and time alone to learn to listen to the language of the heart. Fortunately, when we are broken open, solitude beckons, and we spend a lot of time alone. Alone. I yearned never to hear that word again. Being alone comes to have new meaning after you have been betrayed. Formerly, I relished time alone and thrived on my own. But what a shock to go from imagined cozy coupledom to living on your own in a traumatized, disillusioned, single life. Loneliness comes on strongly, inevitably, with a broken heart. It is likely you have never felt this alone and weak before in your life. Going through it, you can hardly imagine its deeper purpose.

If you are like me, when you were first betrayed, you felt a desperate impulse for company to buffer the loss and separation. But betrayal also has a way of forcing solitude, as our previous social network is shorn away either literally or psychically. At the same time as we avoid social gatherings and turn down invitations to go out, we find ourselves asking, Where have all my friends gone? After the blow, we naturally pull into a shell of self-protective aloneness, like a wounded animal retreating to a cave for healing.

Eventually, we realize what we need comes most readily when we withdraw into ourselves. In this transitional time, only we can listen to our heart's call guiding us from beneath the ruins of the past. On our own, we can better listen to the messages coming from the pain and sorrow. Being alone calls as the only way to establish the faith needed to take the next step into the raw, exposed vulnerability of the heart, there to hear, sense, and feel the first pangs of conscience and the spiritual light that is dawning in the dark.

Mystical philosopher Valentin Tomberg describes how the "tension of solitude" is the element proper to souls in darkness under the sway of "attraction from above." He describes how these people feel in company "as fish [on land] seeking the sea." They find that they only breathe easily again in solitude.[6] I found I actually preferred time alone, that I could no longer relate to family and friends about what mattered most. In company, I could not find the right words; they would not understand; I would burden them with my confusion and pain. The excuses mounted as I realized that loneliness actually struck more often in the distraction of company, and I yearned to get back home and tend to the demands of my inner life.

Solitude can be a tenuous but wondrous time. There, we learn to discern the spiritual heart as a still, small voice within, like a hauntingly familiar, distant music amidst the shouts and murmurs of the betrayed mind. Being even more alone may seem like strange medicine to help cure the sick isolation of betrayed love, and yet loneliness reveals another paradox of the betrayed psyche: We must first pass through acute loneliness to learn that we are not alone. In the trials of suffering the death of our illusions, the awakening heart comes to hold and nourish us.

Living from the heart means keeping one foot in the world of form and one in the world of mystery. The mystic heart touches on another world. When it is flowing through us, it alters our state of consciousness from isolation to communion, from certainty to wonder, from doubt to faith. It dissolves our sense of *me* and *everything else*. An essential heart state permeates us with a subtle sense of relaxing warmth and wonder. In these states, we become more soft, strong, and receptive, a channel for a loving presence we have longed for and welcome with immense gratitude. Stopping to notice and mark the moments when kindness, warmth, beauty or mystery touch our day becomes an essential practice to shift our allegiance to the heart.

The Guardian at the Gate

A school I sat in cured me of hurting others.—Rabia

As I learned to listen to my heart, I found stirring a strange grief and remorse for my own past behaviors that were coming to light. The more attention I paid, the more my heart called me to an uninvited personal accounting that I twisted and turned every which way to evade and put off. I had read somewhere, and now I began to understand for myself, that conscience stands watch at the gate of the awakening heart.[6]

Part of the initiation of a dark-night pilgrimage comes from an unavoidable reconciling with the past. Many who have had near-death experiences report that, when you die, your whole life flashes before your eyes. Something similar happens in the symbolic death of personality that a dark night induces. Unbidden memories of past actions flash onto the screen of consciousness and compel your attention. Illuminated by the heightened awareness of liminal time, you see the past in a fresh, new light. Initially, it is difficult not to recoil at the expanded view that opens when conscience stirs awake this way.

In the language of the archetypes, Saturn symbolizes conscience. As the lord of karma, he stands as the "dweller" or "guardian at the threshold" to make us accountable for our actions. We must clear the holds Saturn has on us—the "debts" we have yet to pay—before we can safely gain entrance to higher realms.[7] In esoteric traditions, sometimes the dweller is represented as a hideous beast—a dragon, a serpent, a gargoyle, or even as the devil himself. Depth psychology might call the dweller a complex or the shadow; Buddhism, karma; Christianity, sin. The poetry of this phrase from Psalms, "Thou hast sore broken me in the place of dragons…"[8] described the reconciliation with conscience for me.

When we are ready to undergo a dark night, it is said that every attachment, every latent predisposition, every uncivilized instinctual tendency, all the personality characteristics from this and even past lives that have remained unconquered, every unfinished situation, and every fault, rise to awareness in the form of a potent presence.[9] Then the fight is on between the hold of the dweller and the angel of our better nature, the immanent presence of the heart. We must engage and pass through the burning grounds of this battle before we are ready to move forward into higher life and love.

The philosopher Immanuel Kant confessed that two things filled him with awe and wonder: "the starry sky above and the moral law within." I now believe we each have a moral law within, best described by the Golden Rule, which we violate at our own expense. Suffering hones our awareness of this inner law. As we begin to experience viscerally what the Golden Rule means, we learn "Do unto others as you would have them do unto you" is not just a good idea; it is moral law—the law of conscience in action. What we do to others, we do to ourselves. As our soul life deepens, whether or not we consciously intend to undertake the task of taking responsibility for our actions, the dweller brings the past to confront us. It is in the dark night passage that facing conscience becomes a required trial to clear the way for the love we need to heal us.

Terms such as *conscience* and *moral law* may seem old-fashioned and unnecessarily constraining in a New Age world of relative, subjective values. In this world, "all is well" regardless of the pain you inflict or feel; "you create your own reality" explains away all misfortune or trauma; "getting your needs met" and "following your bliss" justify disregarding others; and suffering is not real because the world we see is an illusion, and there is no one to suffer, anyway. These prescriptions work well enough when life is turning out according to our plans and desires. But when the heart breaks, and trust dies, their superficiality becomes apparent, and an altogether different truth seeps into the soul. In the midst of pain, we discover what we learned in childhood: The Golden Rule does indeed reign.

The intelligence of the broken-open heart transmits a palpable awareness of the ways in which our actions have harmed not only others, but also ourselves. As the truths of the heart dawn, we pass from the ignorance that created our everyday complacency into a purgatorial clearing; or, as I described it to myself, marching into hell for a heavenly cause.

Whatever we call it—purgatory, confession of sins, repentance, burning karma, awakening conscience, paying our debts, clearing the veils of the heart, integrating Saturn, moral inventory, or making amends—until we find the courage to admit the harm we have done, our unfelt conscience guards the door of the compassionate heart. Our debts and unfinished business keep us huddled on the other side in hidden guilt and fear. Perhaps this is why forgiveness, a complex and easily misunderstood term I will take up in a later chapter, becomes so important in the growth of the soul.

Twelve-step programs have long recognized the importance of taking a moral inventory. Their recommendation that we intentionally recall those we have harmed and make amends whenever possible reflects the imperatives of soul crafting. In a dark night immersion, we do not simply make lists of what we have done. We land directly in the territory of the wisdom heart that registers our connections and relationship to life. The knowing heart holds the unpalatable truth and the pangs that demonstrate precisely *how* we have harmed.

The pain we experience in response to our partner's actions attunes us with astonishing exactitude to similar suffering in others. In this way, we gain a growing realization of how our own actions have caused others to suffer. As our tenderness of heart grows, we actually *feel the pain we have inflicted* on our brothers and sisters. In other words, we suffer into the growth of conscience.

While I brewed in the disturbing truth that my actions had consequences far beyond what I imagined, I often turned tail and returned to the comforting illusions of my kind, harmless, well-intentioned self-images. I routinely avoided seeing my mixed motives—how anxiously I wanted Rob to suffer, for instance, and how attached I was to being right and in control.

Many turn back, or at least dawdle interminably, at the call of conscience. We are afraid to see who we really are! When we are confronted with our shadow sides, we must withdraw many projections as our illusions about ourselves die. For so long, we have cast out what we do not want to see onto others, turning the world into a replica of our unknown face. In looking into the mirror of our own evil twin, we stand before a daunting foe. It is natural to want to give up and takes courage to not shut down at this unnerving juncture of soul crafting.

GOOD TEARS: TAKING THE CURE

The most terrifying thing is to accept oneself completely.—C. G. Jung

The willingness to see ourselves unmasked, and to realize the costs of our unconscious behavior, becomes the price of shifting our center of gravity from the surface to the spiritual heart. Facing the grim facts about the harm we have done wrenches the heart awake. To the ego, the entire operation of awakening conscience seems dark, dreary, and depressing. Are we not already in enough pain? Why undertake such a loathsome task? If we take the ripening of remorse to heart, many more tears will flow in addition to those already shed in the formidable grief of betrayed love. We may wonder if we are not indulging in an orgy of self-recrimination and reinforcing our shame.

But tears of grief and remorse turn out to be good tears. They heal, like the good pain of conscious suffering; they liberate and give wings to the heart. Tomberg speaks of how tears bring grace, "Concerning the mystery of tears... The 'gift of tears' was always considered a grace from the Holy Spirit, for it is thanks to this gift that the soul surpasses itself..."[10] When we feel the impact of our behavior on others—not with the heaviness of guilt and shame of the bad girl or boy, but with kindness, the I-will-never-do-that-again kind of remorse—it is a sign we are *already in the presence of more light and love*. Love touches and melts us with appreciation for the blessing of truth, even as we are dismayed by what we see. Here is what seventeenth-century French theologian François Fénelon has to say about the dawning of conscience:

> As light increases we see ourselves to be worse than we thought. We are amazed at our former blindness as we see issuing forth from the depths of our heart a whole swarm of shameful feelings, like filthy reptiles crawling from a hidden cave. We never could have believed that we had harbored such things and we stand aghast. But we must neither be amazed nor disheartened. We are not worse than we were; on the contrary, we are better. But while our faults diminish, the light by which we see them waxes brighter, and we are filled with horror. Bear in mind, for your comfort, that we only perceive our malady when the cure begins.[11]

Facing conscience challenges us in many ways. It tests our readiness to move beyond considering ourselves special, different from, or better than others, especially those cruel others who hurt us. The heart tenderized by remorse encourages us to embrace what we detest most about others and ourselves. We begin to die to the less authentic person we were when we inflicted these harms. Compassion grows as we see we acted from ignorance, habit, or early programming. Most of the time, we did not know what we were doing; we acted out of the trance of conditioning, often even with the best intentions. Remorse wakes us to our kinship with our brothers and sisters. It breaks the heart all over again to see how we are all imprisoned and led about by helplessness and misguided motives passed on blindly from generation to generation.

I saw that the devils in me were doing most of the things I had accused Rob of doing. He hated me, but now I hated him. He deceived and used me; but how many had I deceived and used? He did not care; and how often had I been unable to care, even when I wanted to? He seduced me, and then abandoned me; I was not a stranger to seduction, I had abandoned too. He broke his promises to me; I have broken promises. He misused his power; I knew about wielding power to shore up my insecurities. And on it went. I realized I would never be able to forgive him, even if I wanted to, until I acknowledged and felt the impact of having, in however remote a form, done to others—and *especially to myself*—what was done to me.

For, above all, Rob showed me how I had betrayed myself. He came to personify an outcast piece of my own psyche that needed desperately to be seen and loved. He acted out my rejection of my own self. His actions and demeanor toward me demonstrated starkly, in Day-Glo colors, just how harshly I had treated myself, how I had habitually betrayed, devalued, and rejected myself.

It was as if, in some hidden, basement part of myself, I had spent my life punishing my own child-self for her neediness, unlovability, and worthlessness. *You want love?*—forty lashes for that. *You want recognition and acceptance?*—how pathetic. *You are afraid?*—ohmygod, don't let anyone know. And so on. Now he had taken on this tormenting task for me. Classic projection. Now my tears were softening me to accept my own loving heart, the preciousness of my own existence, regardless of what he or anyone else thought of me.

Hidden under my self-sufficient, superior, know-it-all way of being, how cruel and rejecting I had been to the scared, shamed, and traumatized little one inside. The shame and self-hatred I encountered at the threshold of my heart were fire-breathing dragons worthy of Harry Potter tales. Being willing to grieve for the pain I had inflicted on myself, to forgive myself, and let myself be loved through the torments of an abandonment I believed in my bones I must have deserved was one of the most difficult things I have ever done.

The stirrings of conscience bring both opportunity and threat. What we see threatens to bring more fuel for the fires of the basic flaw. The ego is at the ready to interpret the remorse of seeing oneself through the pangs of conscience as just another blow to pride, more humiliation, more reason for shame and guilt. If the ego self cannot be the best, it will be glad to be the worst. Remorse liberates and expands the heart. But if, in our pride, we identify with seeing our mistakes and flaws, the humiliation morphs into guilt that pulls us more tightly into our false self-images. Guilt becomes a Dementor that threatens to demoralize us into giving up on the pilgrimage to the heart's truth.

Our harshest defenses have evolved to "protect" us from these terrible early feelings of shame and guilt. When the fires of conscience turn on the light, our fear and aggression are most apt to turn on us. Right at the point where we most need to be kind to ourselves, we find out how powerless we are to rescue ourselves from our dejected state.

Rather than taking the plunge and allowing remorse to melt my heart, I inadvertently kept reinforcing "bad Sandy," subliminally berating myself for my weaknesses, my despicable behavior past and present. Fueled by the combination of remorse and desertion, without even realizing it, I fell into the trap of unconsciously assuming the situation must be all my fault. After being rejected and betrayed, we need grace, a miracle, the angel of our higher nature, to get beyond the tendency to guilt and shame. When, in desperation, I finally admitted my helplessness before my own self-rejection, I received a surge of strength to move beyond the shame. Surrender to who we are, as we are, right now, lines up our weak will with that of the compassionate power of the heart. The sad, softening action of true remorse begins, and the good tears flow.

When I could finally allow myself to feel it, tears of remorse, I must admit, were actually refreshing. Through remorse, humiliation turns sweetly to *humility*—who knew? Humility—a quaint and underrated quality of heart. When we endure our time in the dark with patience, a certain gentleness begins to blossom. The quality of humility, the softening of the hard edges of pride, is what allows grace to enter. I do not, and doubt anyone else does either, think of myself as "humble," but looking back, I see how I savored the novel taste of the flickerings of humility.

Realizing my powerlessness, my tiny size, and unimportance in the scheme of things, I felt on solid ground. I was *living in the truth* of so many dichotomies: Infinitesimal, I realized my vastness; helpless, I was empowered by grace; ignorant, I was enlightened by the wise heart, and so on. Being humiliated is no fun at all; it is horrible, in fact; but, to reach the riches of the mystic heart, apparently, some of us need to pass through this trial. Our hardened shells need to be crushed and humbled. Otherwise, how will the healing balm of conscience come through our rigid defenses, delusions, and justifications for our hurtful behavior?

I am grateful now to have had a trail blazed to deeper remorse. It remains a ready path to compassion that tenderizes many days. I do not know how else than through this suffering that this blessing can so readily enter our lives. Each time we suffer the cleansing grief of remorse, we clear a veil of the heart, and the grip of the dweller lessens. The heart expands, allowing more and more of the goodness that we are—until we are ready to let God love us, just the way we are.

PART IV

The Awakening Heart

CHAPTER 16

Grieving and the Veils of the Heart

There is a sacredness in tears. They are not the mark of weakness, but of power.
They speak more eloquently than ten thousand tongues.
—Washington Irving

NINETY PERCENT OF RECOVERING from betrayal, I came to believe, grows out of welcoming the bittersweet company of grief. Mourning is so central to healing; I wonder whether the necessity to give over to pent-up, long-postponed grieving does not compel the soul to drink the cup of betrayal in the first place. In the time out of time of grieving, transformations take place that elude ordinary consciousness. While the unlived sorrows of our past veil the heart and imprison us in a tight zone of imagined safety, mourning releases and restores the lost soul.

We do not go easily from our attachments to greater freedom—we vacillate. Do we really want this liberation that threatens to take away what we have held most dear? Partnership and who we were in relationship has given us pleasure, a sense of security, an identity. Naturally we resist the shattering and shearing away of what has been most important to us. Something in us yearns to stay on this side of the threshold before entering the downward path of dying to who we have been. For a long time, we remain uncertain.

A profound reordering of priorities is taking place that is not in our hands. Thresholds of life like this prepare us for the final crossing into death. At the moment we die, no matter how many others are with us, we know everything will be taken from us, and we will make that passage alone. Coming to terms with betrayal means going through symbolic dying: the death of who you were in the relationship, the death of the person you imagined you were in relationship with, and the death of the relationship itself, at least as it was. When *life as you knew it is gone, and you will never be the same,* you have a lot of grieving to do.

Despite grief's sacred charge, we need to school ourselves to trust sorrow. Most of us in Western society are not prepared to welcome grief, let alone to savor its shadowy nourishment. Rather, we have learned to distrust and fear the companionship of heartache and loss. Perhaps we are prudent to resist the sorrows betrayal brings. We may be forewarned by a premonition from our own hearts that, once we touch these ancient pains, we will never stop crying.

I certainly felt that way once the tears began. Rob's betrayal opened me to a seeming bottomless reservoir of grief. Over the course of the next few years, the outpouring of this ancient pain continued almost daily. Beyond my control, it came, like a force of nature, rising from depths I hardly knew existed. My psyche unleashed hundreds of hours of tears—the grief of infancy and childhood, of birth and death, as well as of the loss of my beloved, my dream, and so many other unknowns.

In the darkest times, I learned how deeply these unnamed losses were woven into the fabric of my body and soul. During the years of mourning, buried waves of unlived grief arose, as if they had been waiting, living all along in my bones, in every cell of my body, hungry for attention and care. This *unloading of the unconscious,* as Thomas Keating, the founder of the contemplative prayer movement, calls it, happened over and over again. I was alarmed by the depth and duration of my grieving and had to learn gentleness and patience toward all this inexplicable sorrow.

In *Entering the Healing Ground,* a meditation on grief and gratitude, psychotherapist and community builder Francis Weller puts a much-needed focus on the soul-healing potential of mourning. Going down into the deeper currents of life where grief abides, he explains, is crucial soul work, albeit "hard, painful and unbidden work." He shows how when we allow grief to move through us, it empties the heart of its heaviness, thins our protective veils, and, paradoxically, allows our capacity for love and for intimacy with life to expand.[1] I found this to be true. Whenever I opened wholeheartedly to the grief welling inside me, it felt like grace itself, and imbued me with subtle caring in the midst of the sorrow.

Cynthia Bourgeault also speaks of how mourning can connect us to a deeper reality, to love itself. She, too, describes grieving as a paradox, a "brutal form of emptiness." "But in this emptiness, if we can remain open, we discover that a mysterious 'something' does indeed reach back to comfort us; the tendrils of our grief trailing out into the unknown become intertwined in the great love that holds all things together."[2] We need the waves of mystic love, and the gratefulness they bring, to release what has been the longed-for prize of the emotional heart.

THE WILD ALCHEMY

Appreciation for the depth of our yearning, not its focus, holds an important key to the heart. We need to find a way to move beyond what we believe we have lost to the wordless messages from beyond in the sensations of longing itself. We need to admit that we do not know what these strange sensations are trying to tell us and simply listen and let them come. We learn this subtle art amidst many setbacks and with considerable resistance. Grief goes against our happiness-obsessed culture and our self-images that equate suffering with weakness and self-indulgence. We are unprepared for its compelling force and incessant demands.

For more than three years, when I dropped inside, I was amazed to find the swells of grief were there, waiting to break over me; then a pause, and the tension would build again to crack me open. I would notice the waves as they first appeared, rolling in, mounting slowly, as if from a distant horizon deep in my torso, crashing down in my chest, rippling through my entire body. I was in no way prepared for the depth and duration of this mourning. Like a grief-soaked sponge, I was wrung out, then resaturated, and wrung out again and again. Some days I could not stop crying and was ashamed for being in so much pain at this loss.

Grief can take many forms, besides tears—from numbness to rage, to despair, to sorrow and pain. Weller characterizes grief as a dark angel, "feral," subversive and wild, that reduces us "to our most naked selves." He poetically paints what he calls grief's muscular demands as "a wild alchemy that transmutes suffering into fertile ground...adding substance and weight to our world."[3] When we do abandon ourselves to grief's imperatives, we may not know ourselves. Who *is* this, we wonder, as we wail, flail, despair, rage, crawl on the ground, tear at our hair, or bargain desperately with God or the universe to have our beloved restored to us?

We are best served when we share our grief with others who can help hold us while we release into the unknown depths being revealed. Otherwise, with no guidance from the culture for navigating the waters of loss, it is easy to judge yourself as defective, stifle the pain, and do everything possible to pull yourself together. Though we may manage a brave, resilient front, we shut off the healing water of tears, or fire of rage, that grieving can bring. We need the support of others to get through the mysterious process of clearing the veils of the heart. I was fortunate to participate in a number of grief rituals and to have a friend or two who witnessed and held me while I raged or cried.

Often, the protracted "wild alchemy" of grieving caused me to question myself with the usual suspicions. Though I knew better, often I lacked the focus to stop my self-doubt. What was wrong with me? It did not seem right that the unstoppable tears, the whimpering, and the despair continue for so long. I believed in the process, and thought I knew how to welcome grief, but this incessant crying had gone beyond my version of healing work. Surely, all this sadness must indicate an emotional illness I should medicate. I must be depressed, clinging to a phantom, or dangerously borderline—often I felt closer to a madwoman than a mystic. Or did the tears indicate a character-flawed tendency to wallow in painful feelings, or an insidious addiction to Rob's hurtfulness? The grief of a dark night passage can fill you with self-doubts such as these.

I consulted with professionals for their advice. I was reassured by those who helped me—my grief counselor, spiritual director, and somatic therapist, intuitive healers, a psychiatrist, meditation and workshop retreat leaders, and others—that I was on track with a profound inner unfolding. Whenever I questioned them, each pointed to a certain presence that accompanied my experience. The attentiveness, maybe more like some faith in a process, over which I had little control indicated to them I was not totally gone in perversely reinforcing identification with my suffering self, as I often feared.

Depending on their orientation, they suggested that I was passing through: a dark night of the soul, an "unloading of the unconscious," a processing of collective grief, or the healing of early trauma—and that I was not simply wallowing in an emotional morass or a clinical depression, though at times I must have been. In these transitional realms, not much is clear-cut. If you are lost in a similar complicated grieving, reaching out to others for warmth, holding and reflection becomes a vital ingredient in the alchemy of healing.

Still, I admit, as self-sufficient as I have always been, I did a lot of grieving alone, crying myself to sleep, waking in despair, curled up on the couch on a sunny afternoon, incapacitated by this or that trigger. To have the courage and patience to let the tears flow in the presence of someone else, I needed to step beyond my shame that others would be repelled by how weak I was. Despite the fear that we will be rejected for the depths of our grief, support can make what feels like a hopeless hell into a propitious purgatory. Even a hint of compassionate holding can give context and direction to the suffering and subtly open us to the mystery of tears.

As our masks are shorn away, grieving tenderly detaches us from our surface heart and superficial personality. Our sorrows release soul force from frozen loss and fear, making us more substantial and authentic in our lives. Kindness toward myself, staying with the feelings, not the thoughts, the support of others made all the difference between breakdown and breakthrough.

The warmth of someone's touch kept a thread of kindness going and provided a filament of love to endure what otherwise can seem unendurable.

No one can legislate how long it will take to move all the way into the abyss of grief from a broken heart, or to climb up the mountain of dawning love into a new life. Regardless of what anyone else says or thinks about our suffering, we are still the same person inside—let us be patient and kind to ourselves while the tears reveal what our heart most needs to know.

THE COMPLICATED GRIEVING OF BETRAYAL

Betrayal brings on a complicated form of grief that sets it apart from the loss of a partner through death or mutual separation (as I discussed in chapter 6). The desolation of betrayal brings with it the circumstances to transform and complete, not your torn relationship, but yourself and your life. While strong, instinctual, emotional, and etheric attachment forces press us to try to mend the broken relationship (and for some the relationship may mend), the wisdom heart—if we can remain true to its muted but insistent call—guides us elsewhere.

We have seen how betrayal can take us into dark realms of dismemberment and the dying of our former sense of self. By grieving the loss of our old nature, we retrieve precious exiled parts of the soul hidden under the pain. We do not even know what has been lost to us through the traumas of the past. The list of possibilities is long: gentleness, strength, self-worth, purpose, creativity, vision, loving-kindness, trust, and intelligence, to name some of the most likely. By feeling the sorrow and pain of the loss of these essential parts of our nature, we bring these qualities back and weave the energies of the lost soul child back into the fabric of our life.

This reclaiming, this stitching together of pieces of the soul, takes place under the most unlikely conditions—in the dung and mud of victimhood, broken trust, obsession, yearning, terror, death of a dream, and the emptying of the basement of the mind. Betrayal delivers those borderline "special conditions" between madness and mysticism that Jung suggested are necessary for individuating, becoming who we are meant to be. It is in this liminal space that healing energies can enter from a more refined vibratory plane, and provide the catalyst we need to go this deep.

When we embrace the uncertainty and suffering at the edges of consciousness, it delivers us to another level of healing entirely. Using the language of neuroscience, Ginette Paris explains the process in this way: "The telluric intensity of heartbreak can actually cut through a layer of our complexes and addictions like a fire destroys decay, because our heart is as wide-open in grief as it was to love's bliss…. The pain will force your brain to re-organize its synaptic connections to adapt."⁴ In other words, through a lifetime of tears no longer held back, we discover a fierce yearning for greater love and wholeness comes streaming into our lives.

Grieving clears the veils of the heart to educate us about the mystery and depths of our longing. The grief has always been there. We know that now—it is true; *something fundamental is missing from our lives.* The wise heart communicates through the pain itself a subtle knowing of what we miss and need so desperately in our lives, how much we need a love that will never leave us. We need steady warmth and safety for our soul that no person, thing, or outer condition can give us. More and more we sense the desperation for this essential soul sustenance as the hidden nucleus of our suffering.

At the same time, grieving opens the heart's appreciation for life. That we exist at all is a wonder—that we breathe, that our hearts beat, that the sun rises each day, that the earth holds and nourishes us—amazing. All this everyday simplicity we come to know, through the lens of our brokenness, is a marvel in itself. In this way, mourning schools us in a new relationship with ourselves, with the world, and especially with the enigmas of suffering and loss.

For me, a life-serving presence quickened whenever I touched into the collective field of pain and realized how much suffering is impersonally woven into human nature. I came to know that, whatever freedom came from my effort to welcome this bleakness as a holy part of life, it would spread into the collective stream. I intuited time and again that it would help lighten the burden for others. I do not know how I knew this; I just did, and it lifted my heart with purpose. Stopping to sense into this greater meaning in the mystery of suffering may help you, too. From the heart of pain, we can hear the cries of the world. In your grief, you may want to try to look at others through the eyes of your pain. Just focus on your heart. It sounds counterintuitive, but looking about with a gentle focus on your personal injury, you may sense, and even hear, the cries of your sisters and brothers in the same distressing predicament. If you do, you may sense their gratitude for the attention you are bringing to the currents of hidden despair we all try to hide.

Despite blessed infusions of connectivity like this, for a long time, my beleaguered efforts to "get over" the incessant grief failed day after day, and I would feel hopeless about ever reclaiming my life. As usual, a big shift came when I stopped trying to figure out with all my healing practices how to get better and to get over it. Sensing the futility of trying to heal myself, I had to admit, the grooves of grief were too deep, too ancient, too ingrained for my tiny powers. Paradoxically, by admitting my helplessness and just allowing the powerlessness and longing in the grief and pain to flow, an important shift happened. The yearning and pain revealed themselves as *prayers for help*, desperate calls for love from the deepest caverns of the heart.

Someone had given me a card that said, "When in doubt, breath." Excellent advice! Sometimes, when I was graced with one or two conscious breaths, the gift of breath alone stunned me with its delicate sweetness, dependability, and nourishment. Breathing with a cracked-open heart relaxed and connected me to my surroundings with a melting deliciousness that reminded me of making love. I was connecting with simple moments of my life from a reservoir of resonance that I had formerly reserved for the bedroom. I found these words of psychologist Robert Romanyshyn rang true: "From grief there was blossoming a completely unexpected sensual, erotic, and even sexual hunger for the world."[5]

As I recognized my helplessness, I came to a radical conclusion, one I would often forget but kept returning to as my new, reliable ground. I posted it on the refrigerator: *All good comes from grace.* Now, when I had a moment of love or peace or appreciation, I said a quiet *thank you* to the invisible help that I intuited was with me. After so many moments of failure on my own, I knew how lost I was without it.

THE EXTRAORDINARY REALITY OF SADNESS

If you are really listening, if you're awake to the poignant beauty of the world, your heart breaks regularly…your heart is made to break.
—Andrew Harvey

In the months and years of grieving this loss, I slowly grew in my capacity to simply allow the lingering wound at the center of my heart to be there instead of wincing whenever the hurt came into awareness and feeling a failure for not healing. I started to sense the wound as a strange attractor, a portal to a mystery that urged me on. Often, as I stayed with the ache, an all-encompassing sadness filled me.

At times, sadness spread over me like a blanket and through me like air, until I was suffused with its essence. The hollowness in my heart drilled down into the center of my body and beyond, to the center of the earth, it seemed. The sadness spread to everything around me. The blue coffee cup and notepad on my kitchen table, the Audubon clock on the wall, the panes of the window overlooking the garden—all were steeped in the strange, melancholy beauty of sadness.

It was as if I had come upon an essential constituent of existence. The sorrow, like a radiant mist emanating from the cave of my heart, expanded outward—into the sky, the sun, and even farther out, beyond the atmosphere to the planets, the near stars, the galaxy, and then beyond that to the black spaces and farthest reaches of the universe. The fine, delicate mist of mourning was the essence of everything. This vision enveloped me, and I knew in my bones, *Sadness is truth*. And that truth was beautiful.

In one of the many synchronicities of the dark-night time, while reading *De Profundis* by Oscar Wilde I saw that he had concluded something remarkably similar. In his days of disgrace and imprisonment, estranged from his lover and reflecting on "lessons hidden in the heart of pain," he came to believe there is no truth comparable to sorrow. He called sadness "the supreme emotion of which man is capable." Recounting the mystery, the revelations of sorrow, Wilde described how it allows us to discern what has never before been discerned, how it nourishes the soul with refinements as nothing else can.

Wilde described how beauty and sorrow walk hand in hand to reveal the essence of true art, whose purpose he believed was the perfecting of the soul. "There is about Sorrow an intense, an extraordinary, reality...[it reveals that] the secret of life is suffering. It is what is hidden behind everything." Sadness, he explained, is always crafted by love, and has built the world. Pain, after all must be present at any birth, whether of a child or a star. He concluded that if we would know truth or love, we must give ourselves to sorrow. While we seek after pleasure, as Wilde had done most of his life, he believed that we do so in ignorance that we may actually be starving the soul of its most essential nourishment, that of sadness.[6]

As we learn to open to this difficult work, revealing the mystical roots of our personal sorrows adds more reverence for our tears.[7] As Bourgeault expresses it, "To mourn is to touch directly the substance of divine compassion. Just as ice must melt before it can begin to flow, we, too, must become liquid before we can flow into the larger mind."[8] When we embrace our hurts with care, the wounds themselves open us to a Holy Spirit at work in our soul. Grief signals a greater love knocking, asking that we let ourselves be filled with the mystery pressing upon us.

We do well to keep company with the grief of betrayal as we would a new love, close and near, appreciating this gift of grace while it lasts. Betrayal drilling into our core offers a rare chance to establish pathways into the heart that connect us to this nourishing substratum of existence, to the love that can heal our ancient isolation. In the crushed love of the emotional heart that now lies decaying, the buds of compassion sprout. As Jungian analyst Helen Luke puts it in her astonishing essay on suffering, "There is no cure for an inferior kind of love except a greater and more conscious love."[9] That greater and more conscious love emerges from the raw tenderness of the sad wounded heart, in the paradoxical joy and pain of mourning our losses.

Coming through the trials of shattered love and trust, the essential heart conveys a difficult but poignant truth. Today we have lost a love, an identity, a lifestyle, a family; but ultimately, we will lose everything. Sadness whispers, speaks, and finally shouts what we know with our minds but are now, by grace, having etched into our souls: We are only visitors here. Although we have mistaken this body and this world for our permanent home, sorrow reveals the lie we already know in our bones. Our true home is elsewhere. It is this home we miss most, and to which, through the griefs of love betrayed, we are being called to return.

CHAPTER 17

Surrendering to Grace

Learn the alchemy true human beings know
The moment you accept what troubles you've been given
the door will open.
—Jalaluddin Rumi

I AM SOMETIMES ASKED, "WHY should I pray or engage in other spiritual practices if love and freedom come only from grace?" Good question. I have asked it frequently myself. Spiritual traditions advise that, regardless of our apparent progress or failure, we do well to continue with our prayers and practices. We are co-creators in the work of awakening to the heart: When we stick with our practices, we do our part.

Practices express our intention and demonstrate our willingness to invite the Divine to guide our lives. They prepare the ground of our being for grace. Primarily, they bring us to the point of realizing our powerlessness to commandeer the one thing we most want and need: the substance and immensity of love. We can only do our part and wait for the Beloved to appear to quicken our heart and make us real. While our part may only be five percent of the equation, without it, the creation remains incomplete.

For the doers among us, this equation is daunting. We want results for our efforts, and cannot stop believing if we just "do it right," everything will fall in place according to our plan. One spiritual teacher told me that the whole purpose of meditation was to realize that we cannot meditate! Intention is in our hands, but attention is not. We simply do not have the strength to overcome either our traumas or our delusional, habitual ways of being by ourselves.

The habits of the heart formed in and reinforced by trauma have a tenacious grasp. Hearing of my exasperation at my failure to heal myself, a friend sent me Rilke's poem, "The Man Watching." The concluding lines spoke a truth I was coming to know: "Winning does not tempt that man. This is how he grows: by being defeated decisively, by constantly greater beings."[1] In the dark night, we learn how little control we have over what is most important, while we quietly come to revere the mystery that does have control. Our ego's "god complex," our penchant for taking control and doing things ourselves, cannot help but transfer to our spiritual practices. It can take many long, dark nights of futile effort before we are ready to surrender our imaginary control. This is especially true for those of us convinced we had something to do with whatever progress in self-knowledge or other spiritual gifts we may have received in the past.

After making it through the first year of continuing my practices with a vengeance inspired by pain, I felt more and more defeated with how long it was taking to feel better. Meanwhile, I was hounded by a kind of spiritual director in my head who would not give me a moment's peace, who was constantly suggesting *what I must do* to stop the pain and preoccupation, to get over it, and to move on. I could not stop thinking that if I could just get it right, the suffering would be relieved, and I would be free. But I was losing hope, feeling worse, not better. The more I tried, the worse it got. Was I ever self-willed, thinking I should have a badge of honor for not giving up! Maybe that was the point. Finally, I had to admit there was not much I could do about the wretched quality of my life. I heard all about needing to surrender to the situation, but I was clueless as to how to do that…until one night.

One night, overtaken with waves of anguish, feeling yet again that I would drown in the pain, I contemplated renting a movie, but did not want to abandon myself in this despair. As Pema Chodron suggests, when our afflictions arise, we can train ourselves to say, "Now!" Now is the time to apply our practices to what we normally avoid. So I stayed with it. My efforts to accept the pain serenely were defeated yet again. I fell into deeper despair, to such depths that I wished my life would simply end so that I would no longer have to endure this endless failure and unbearable hurting.

Previous to this trauma, mindfulness of my thoughts and feelings had always given me a "center" or ground I could trust and return to; but in this heartbreak, that ground was no longer accessible to me. I had asked for guidance on retreats, from my teacher, and from other long-time meditators, but nothing was helping. I kept losing my focus, getting caught up in the obsessing, the terrible sensations, and the grief. I was in over my head. Whatever observing I could muster was not enough to sustain me in this chamber of torments that had become my habitation.

I was sitting on the couch in my living room sobbing, yet again, at the situation, likely in self-pity, when seemingly with no conscious intent, I found myself on my knees…praying to someone or something, seeking relief. "Somebody, *please* help! Christ, Holy Spirit, intelligence-that-creates-worlds,

Mother Mary, angels of light, Tara…please, please help!" Over and over, I called out, praying for mercy from someone I needed desperately to be there, and apologizing for I knew not what—assuming I must have done something terrible to deserve this pain.

Having left behind the outer trappings of organized religion decades earlier, praying to "someone" was a highly uncharacteristic gesture that went against my supposedly sophisticated, nondual beliefs about spirituality. In that moment of drowning desperation, some other impetus moved me, and those beliefs went by the wayside. The "spiritually correct Sandra," it seemed, was being pushed aside by an unfamiliar force that took over and knew how to resuscitate my dangerously failing spirit. "Please, *please,* help," I kept repeating. The words did not seem to matter; only the imploring request and the yearning desperation rising from my suffocated, aching heart.

To my utter astonishment, within a minute or two, I felt a stream of exquisite warmth flow into me, a sweetness surround me, and a tenderness that soothed the shooting pains in my chest, steadied my breathing, and calmed my mind. Relief? Yes, relief. I softened with tears of gratitude at this wonder.

Yet, even as I felt the marvel of this miraculous comforting, my mind clicked in to regain dominance by calling the experience into question. Could my involuntary prayer really have been answered so quickly? Could this flow of warm caring I had been unable to conjure with all my efforts not be a coincidence? Or perhaps it was a regression to childhood memories of being held and soothed?

Since this nurturing current brought solace just when the pain most threatened to pull me under, I wondered if my mind—and further, if the collective human mind—invented the idea of a Higher Power, of God, as a stopgap, as some claim, so that we could bear with our inevitable suffering. But once those moments passed, I also speculated that, in times of extreme need, a natural instinct of Spirit might seize us so as to turn us in its direction. This living force of God within us is what Jung called the *religious function.* In light of this experience, this option seemed the greater truth. We come equipped with a spiritual instinct that our desperation compels more fully into awareness.

God uses despair to get through to us, to inspire us to open to the truth of our soul's purpose here on earth—to align with a greater love, with invisible realities, to remember and return home to our origins. The form our instinct for the Divine takes comes more from our background and our bloodline than from our ideas.

Pray or Go Under

"Help" is a prayer that is always answered.—Anne Lamott

When our sanity, or our life, seems on the line, surrender to something larger than ourselves—here, it came in the form of prayer—enters as a reflex of the soul. To *surrender* means: to hand oneself over, or entrust oneself, to someone or something.[2] Surrender universally comes about—in initiation rites, crises, conversion experiences, near-death or other spiritual emergencies—by being pushed to the limit, into desperation.

Jerry Sittser explains how desperation is the "first and primary condition" for true praying. We have to reach a point where it is pray or go under. In that instance of falling on my knees, when my life and soul survival seemed most threatened, some instinct moved me to open to a Higher Power; it moved me to pray. "As a reflex, prayer seems to run deep in human nature, as if we have no choice in the matter. Facing danger or difficulty, opportunity or challenge, we feel compelled to pray, even if we are not sure there is a God out there to whom we are praying."[3] I had reached the point where it was pray or go under, pray or despair; it even felt to me like pray or die.[4]

To reach this point, I exhausted everything in my power to try to handle the situation myself. Short of despair at my own helplessness, I could not manage to give up my imagined control and cry out for help. It is only at the darkest hour, at the bottom of hitting bottom that we finally give up our imaginary reins. In the instant of realizing my powerlessness, I handed myself over to a higher intelligence I somehow knew but had forgotten. In this turning-point moment, I did not know what to do, but *my heart recognized another that did*. It was in this spontaneous move from head to heart that I felt myself give over my will to "thy will:" the small self bowed to a larger Self.

Surrender signals a capitulation of the head to the mystic heart. The particular image or words—of a Sistine Chapel whitebearded God, angels, white light, Krishna, Jesus, Tara, a formless presence or creative intelligence, for instance—that come to mind in the gesture of surrender are secondary, a byproduct of the surrender itself. Background, culture and beliefs will determine the form our Higher Power takes, and that form may be a surprise, as it was to me. What matters is the surrender of control, the turning toward some agency or authority greater than our own minds. Something in us finally realizes that life has handed us a task beyond our capacities; that we need help; and, most amazingly, that help has arrived.

After this incident, during the bouts of desperation that followed, most often only a single word came from my heart through my lips: "Help!" That anxious, but sincere, single word was my prayer. Although I was keen to repeat the experience of conjuring the caring, comforting presence, I did not know how to make this grace happen again. It had taken the relentlessness of the suffering, as well as the realization of my helplessness, for this subtle movement from *my will* to *thy will* to happen.

We cannot legislate or control surrender. But we can practice our receptivity to the unknown in moments of stillness, be on the lookout for it, and welcome it when it comes. Instead of feeling like a total failure when we hit bottom, we can let out a sigh of relief as we drink in the truth of our fragile place in the scheme of things. We can celebrate rather than lament our absolute dependence on an intelligence greater than our own, and live our lives daily with a greater sense of wonder and curiosity that we exist at all.

Inevitably, we will revert to listening to the voice in our heads as the arbiter of our greatest good. Then we return to following our self-will. Normally, the agendas of our self-images—"the devices and desires of our own hearts"—determine how we live our lives and inevitably lead us into more suffering. In my case, I unwittingly sought to preserve my self-image as a perceptive psychologist, lover, and spiritual director, a person who had all the answers, who knew how to heal myself and to ameliorate the situation. Shoring up our self-images like this takes up all our psychic bandwidth with worries, strategies, plans, and agendas, and prevents us from hearing the call of Spirit.

As we rely less and less on our plans and schemes to direct us, we are able to go more often with the flow of life. Some days, all it took was stopping to take a breath into my heart for the shift from head to heart to happen—from my plans, to listening for the unknown to unfold. Each time we pause to listen to the "blind stirring of love," as the anonymous author of the mystical classic *Cloud of Unknowing* calls it, we call on the hidden companion that abides in the heart, and when she appears, soften for a moment with a flush of mystery and gratitude.

THE SUFI TREASURE OF THE HEART

As the dark night does its work of clearing and opening the heart, whenever we take two steps forward, there is, inevitably, one step back. Even before this cracking open, I often wondered why trying to be a consistently loving person always seemed doomed to failure. You, too, may have noticed that the more openhearted and loving you feel one day, the more likely you are to be sullen and irritable the next. I have lived with these frustrating swings for years, but the terrain of betrayal exaggerated the extremes. Just when I was starting to feel like the lovable, kind person I always believed myself to be, I turned into

Cruella de Vil, ready to pounce on anyone unfortunate enough to cross my path.

The Sufis, the mystical branch of the Islamic tradition, offer an explanation for these swings and the necessity of surrender that not only provided a framework for the arc of this book, but also helped me to be more kind to myself on the inevitable Cruella days. The Sufis envision the heart as a treasure fought over by both our ego and our spirit. Ego and spirit have been given equal power in human nature, and they are engaged in a never-ending battle to commandeer the prize of the heart. In their ongoing struggle, sometimes one prevails and sometimes the other.

When the heart listens to the ego, we are prevented from hearing the call of spirit and instead pursue our fear-based, security-driven interests without much regard for the world around us. That can make us like the bull in the china shop, damaging other people's feelings and disregarding our own early needs. Wrapped in the cocoon of our little world, we go obliviously along, until a glint of failure, betrayal, remorse, or tragedy—or beauty, nature, or kindness—turns our heart again toward the voice of spirit within.

When the heart listens to our spirit, defenses melt, and we fill with tenderness, gratitude, love, and compassion. But, soon enough, as we have seen, terrified of the dissolving force of love, the ego becomes threatened and mounts an all-out campaign to regain control. The ego-self activates powerful defenses—anger, addictions, procrastination, physical ailments, hurt, despair, fear, superiority, power trips—to reestablish its ground. To our continuing dismay, it seems we have no control over whether it is the ego or spirit that takes command of our hearts. And it is true, we are delusional in imagining we have control.

The Sufis explain that the ego and the spirit have been given equal power in the human soul, not to continually frustrate us, but so that *our free will can realize its profound need for God's assistance.* In the midst of our most helpless moments, we finally are forced to admit our powerlessness. It is then that we discover a tiny point of true power. By acknowledging our inability to control our lives, we have begun to let in the mystery of the Divine. With the guidance of the Divine, spirit fills our hearts and prevails in our nature.

It must be said, however, that, for most of us, surrender to a higher intelligence does not flower in a once-and-for-all moment, like Saul's conversion on the road to Damascus. Rather, it grows slowly and with much struggle, especially when we are lost in the trauma vortex of intense feelings and flashbacks. The ego does not let go easily—as it should not until we learn, step by step, to open to the sanctity of what hurts most. We need time to trust the dark messenger of suffering and to rebuild our ground on that mystery. For this next round in the spiral of our lives, we want our ground to be the authentic depths of the heart, informed by higher love, not the beguiling, familiar defenses of the past.

When the ego is pressed to admit defeat in the light of a Higher Power, the good news is that it does not go all pathetic and weak on us, as we might have feared. Nor does it disappear. After all, we need our executive function to live our lives and for that we need our ego intact. What we discover is that the ego has been a problem only in usurping control that does not rightfully belong to it. When we find the strength to surrender, our control center softens and steps back, moving into its rightful place as a servant and instrument of the grace that guides us toward the rule of the loving heart.

The Call of the Cross

Nobody who finds himself on the road to wholeness can escape
that characteristic suspension which is the meaning of crucifixion.
—C. G. Jung

I should not have been surprised that my continuing desire to listen to the compassionate heart through the ordeals of betrayal would draw me back to the images of the faith of my childhood, to the mysteries of the religion of love in which I was raised. Underneath layers of rationality and scientific curiosity, I have a devotional nature that could not be denied in this crisis.

I had left the outer trappings of Christianity long ago for the reasons so many leave. I saw dry dogmatism, empty ritual, and lifeless rigidity, along with the exclusion from grace of huge portions of the world who do not believe similarly. I was also repelled by the central image of the cross that I viewed as a sick symbol of torture that enslaved people in guilt.

Maybe that is why I struggled with an old sense of embarrassment, a nagging intellectual cynicism and doubt, and a lingering questioning of my motives before writing this section. I was concerned that I might turn many readers off with the subject of how, during my blackest moments, the inner experience of Christian symbolism came to illuminate certain truths for me.

All the same, I realized that the religious function of the awakening heart takes myriad forms. For some, myself included, its devotional nature—an innate inclination to give oneself to someone or something—emerges to help cure a despair that would engulf us. As I mentioned, that devotion can come clothed in many forms, including many that are secular, such as devotion to art, nature, creativity, animals, literature, or music, depending on our temperament, background, and culture.

During my blackest time, about the same time that prayer came bursting into my days, I had another set of arresting experiences. My attention began to be drawn to strange, luminous *crosses,* of all things. These crosses suddenly showed up seemingly everywhere: on hilltops, hotel room walls, on necklaces, tattoos, bumper stickers, even in my dreams and imaginal life. The crosses must have been there all along, but these crosses were different; they gave off a compelling glow that took me aback. Their emanation reminded me of the soft luminosity in Rembrandt's paintings of biblical scenes, particularly one called *Christ Healing the Sick* (also known as *The Hundred Gilder Print*). I later even found a print and framed it.

When I first noticed one of these crosses, I recall rubbing my eyes, thinking I must be tired or my eyes were hazing over because of something in the air. But the incandescent glow persisted. The crosses drew me in. They spoke to me. They spoke messages of promise in a silent language, symbolized by the aura of warm light that encircled them.

Finding myself called back by the intensity of suffering and the numinosity of the central symbol of a religion I had left so long ago challenged significant intellectual, emotional, and spiritual edifices I had built in the course of four decades. Stunned disbelief and, frankly, fear were my initial reactions to the experiences. My rational mind went into overdrive, rejecting the images and my response to them, labeling them as another aberration of my disturbed mind. Amidst all the mental commentary, I thought, *so what?* I do not have to listen to this. My heart was responding to the message of these crosses, bypassing my dumbfounded mind that had deserted these symbols long ago. I was learning to distrust anything that came from the voice talking in my head. After all, look where my "brilliant mind" had gotten me. Now I was determined to listen to my heart, which spoke an altogether different language.

Often my eyes welled up with tears at the sight of these crosses. Their messages reached me, as if *someone* was speaking to me, *someone* aware of the suffering I was enduring, *someone* offering warmth, understanding, and consolation. The energies of my devotional heart that had been directed at Rob were now being absorbed in spontaneous, adoring relation to an intangible, sacred something symbolized by the image of the cross. Against all logic, an ineffable presence pierced my heart and brought a paradoxical calm that infused and soothed me.

Crosses began to appear more often in my inner life, too. In daily meditations, they initiated an even stronger gravitational pull to an unknown silence within. Sometimes the quiet quickened—how else to describe it?—and the perception of a resonant living presence in my heart became more vivid. As I paid less attention to my mind's chattering disdain, this indwelling presence grew stronger. In inner gesture, I let myself go into these infusions of what I understood to be grace. I took the hand of this companion presence mediated by the symbol of the cross, reaching out for it when I felt lost, adrift, or overwhelmed by pain. Surprisingly often, this caring presence responded by twinkling alive in my chest, gently nudging me out of my morass with a tenderness that dissolved fear and pain.

In these moments, I glimpsed the deeper truth of who I am. I was not my traumatized body or mind. I was not the aching emptiness. A much more authentic me than I had ever known was being held in, and was part of, this vast, warm embrace. Later, I learned that the sweetness of this presence fit the descriptions monastics call consolations, sent to weaker souls to buoy up their faith during difficult passages. I immediately signed myself up for the weaker-souls category, seeing how badly I needed these infusions of love, of warm caring, considering how lost had I been in the isolation of trauma and despair.

I can best characterize whatever wisdom kept me from blocking or denying these experiences as a strange attraction to do-not-know mind, to silence, nothingness, stillness, to a black hole in the center of my chest where the complex message of the cross settled most strongly. In time, as I rode along the waves of the heart, a growing reassurance settled in, along with a tentative relaxation of my resistance to these images. I even bought an antique crystal rosary to use in my meditations, and felt the power of the prayer that lived in the beads.

I concluded that, for some of us, there are points in spiritual development when we absolutely need to engage the devotional heart.[5] For those "spiritual but not religious" types, this means that our ideas about the supremacy of nondual awareness in the growth of soul may need to be set aside. Specks that we are in the infinitude of the universe, we will have to admit we do not really know what orders of existence may lie beyond human consciousness, or what form they need to take to get through to us.[6] To add to Shakespeare's famous line, "There are more things in heaven and earth, Horatio, than are dreamt of in your philosophy"...or your religion, or your cosmology, or your psychology.

Perhaps I should have expected that betrayal would enliven the ancient roots of Christian imagery in my soul. I had already noticed how in the Passion narrative, betrayal is stacked upon betrayal: Judas agrees, for thirty pieces of silver, to take the soldiers in the dark of night to the place where he knows Jesus can be found and arrested; the crowds who had hailed Christ only days before as he entered Jerusalem on Palm Sunday turn against him, calling out for Barabbas rather than Jesus to be pardoned; fearing Caesar's displeasure, Pilate symbolically washes his hands of Christ's blood even though he knows the man he is condemning to death is innocent. Finally, comes the ultimate betrayal: Jesus crying out from the cross, "My God, my God, why hast thou forsaken me?"

Said in whatever form, the final words, "Into thy hands I commit my spirit," cannot come easily in the midst of torture, as the story reveals, not even to one blessed with complete faith. "Why hast thou forsaken me?" describes the soul's most desperate cry and expresses what I believe is the core betrayal wound of human nature. To receive and offer unconditional love in the midst of such existential pain must be one of the most difficult tasks for any human being. Yet from such a place of desperation, at the point of our greatest fragility and defeat, yielding to the cross allows grace to infuse us with love.

The symbol of the cross spoke directly to my torn-up heart of a love that could sanctify even the most dreaded torments of life.[7] Now I think, is it not obvious, *betrayal nails you to a cross*? Betrayal crucifies your pride and tortures the desires of your childhood heart. The mystery of the cross points to the redemptive power of suffering, and reveals the illusion that we know what is best for us and our loved ones.

Our cross—what is most unendurable in our life—keeps reminding us that we do not know the meaning of what is happening to us or to others in pain. It says we are not in control of the events of our lives. It reminds us also that there can be no new life, no resurrection, without some form of dying or crucifixion. Most important, it encourages us to "pick up our cross" and turn away from the human instinct to avoid pain.

To die to the past, to become who we are meant to be, we must eventually go against our human nature. Jung wrote about this need to go against oneself to become fully human. He wrote, "Whichever course one takes nature will be mortified and must suffer, even to the death, for the merely natural man must die in part during his own lifetime."[8] For Jung, Christ's cross was the most compelling and perfect symbol of how mortification or suffering met by loving acceptance can bring forth a life of greater authenticity.

SELF-BETRAYAL AND SEPARATENESS

It is as if we have been designed with a defect woven into our being—our sense of separateness from the mystery all around us. If we allow ourselves to feel the longing and desperation that isolation brings, the pain serves as a trapdoor to the vast heart of our spiritual potentiality. At the point of utmost despair, we discover the disconcerting truth: We cannot help but betray ourselves every day. The betrayal of the Higher Self through the ascendancy of ego consciousness is built into human nature. In our separateness, we are all broken-hearted at this betrayal.

In the life of the soul—we do not know why—it is often a human betrayal that reveals the truth we work so hard to hide from ourselves. Betrayal urges us to venture beyond our tenuous détente with our separateness from the mystery we carry in our hearts. When trust is destroyed, and along with it our masks, our security, and our identity, we can no longer wall off this primordial pain.

Instinctively, we cry out from the very depths of the existential wound at our core. We can no longer hide from the facts: We are profoundly cut off from our own authenticity, from our own hearts, from God. We live imprisoned in an aging, dying creature; insecure in, yet denying, our mortality; knowing in our depths that one day, we do not know when, everything we love and care about will be taken from us in death. We each carry a bottomless grief at our condition, but few talk about it.

When crisis strikes and reveals the truth, we saw how story and myth can help move us beyond taking the pain so personally. Myth helps to connect us with the archetypal essence of the situation. When the crosses appeared, I reread the Passion story, "the greatest story ever told," and was astonished to recognize the ordeals I faced in my most difficult moments portrayed there.

As just one example, as I read about the night at Gethsemane—Jesus does not want to be crucified and prays, "Take this cup away from me"—I realized the scene illustrates with poignant dimensionality how suffering can provide the raw material for a radical transmutation of being. But first, it puts us to the test. As long as things are going our way, the willingness to surrender the illusion of personal control goes untested. But are we really willing to follow a higher will if it means humiliation, torture, and death to what we believe to be most important in the world? Our professed love of truth, of God, like our love for one another, knows no depths if it has not gone through the "trials of Gethsemane", and we have not found a willingness to give up our will, our fervent desire for things to be other than they are.

The language of image and story speaks to and helps heal the soul. Your psyche may offer different symbols or metaphors to help synthesize your suffering. I have suggested many in this book. Are you lost in the wilderness, drowning in tears, suffocating, knifed in the heart, broken in pieces, dying of thirst; or are you alone in a foreign land; an orphan left out in the cold; or, are you, too, on the cross? Whatever metaphors best speak to you about your descent into darkness and dying, let them guide you into the wisdom of the collective heart of suffering. You may begin to welcome and encourage their presence, and let them open you more fully to the full range of your humanity.

Whatever forms the trial takes, the cross becomes the place where we learn to *surrender self-will*, those misdirected desires and cherished illusions that normally direct our lives. To recognize and honor the mystery of the cross you bear, you can look to whatever in your life is "killing you" right now. The place where we carry the unquestioned belief that we know how things should be, that this should or should not have happened, becomes our crucifixion hill.

No one wants to be betrayed. The fact shatters your life and reveals how misplaced your desires have been. Realigning misplaced desire or self-will is like setting a broken bone. It hurts. What is asked of us is a personal or collective crucifixion, *willingness* to endure in faith the suffering of realignment with a higher will than our own.

No matter what form our cross may take, the question becomes: How do I find the willingness to bear what feels unbearable? As unnerving as surrender has been for my-self sufficient, self-willed temperament, I have come to feel a welling of glad sadness when "the unbearable" rises up again. If I am attentive, at the.first sign of loneliness, sadness, or resentment, I recognize a softening coming, and I try to stop what I am doing, take a walk, or get myself some privacy—if I am with others, a short trip to the mini-retreat of the bathroom perhaps. These feelings signal that my heart is calling me to listen to prayer. I want to listen and to open to the mystery that lies in the suffering that is ripening in my soul.

I do not see how we can sidestep the passage symbolized by the cross, call it what you will. With enough time, we may even come to honor and respect this torturous time for its preciousness in the life of the soul. I am not there yet, but I believe the day will come when I may be. No matter where we are in the evolution of our soul, when we feel forsaken by all, including God, we are at a precipice. I encourage you to listen closely to what your pain is shouting at these times. "Go deeper, go deeper," my longing says to me. At these moments, we have reached the growing edge where human reaches out to Divine, where saying yes, surrendering to what is, against all inclination otherwise, leads to the silent mystery, the Christ consciousness shining in our core.

CHAPTER I 8

The Holy Grail of Forgiveness

Forgiveness, like humility, is only a term unless one has been fully
humiliated or fully wronged. Forgiveness is meaningful only
when one can neither forget nor forgive.
—James Hillman

FINALLY, WE COME TO the subject of forgiveness. I reined myself in to not
include it earlier in the book. In the quest to recover as quickly as possible,
forgiveness can become the sought-after Holy Grail, the magic remedy that
will wipe away the brokenness and give us back our lives, or so we are told.
Everything you read, from self-help to depth psychology to the wisdom traditions, and just about everyone you talk to, will tell you: When you have been
badly hurt, to get over it, you *must* forgive, let go, and move on.

In trying to apply this advice, I learned that striving too soon, or maybe
ever, it depends on the circumstances, to forgive a serious betrayal raises the
bar to an impossible height for a mere mortal. Pushing to forgive is a setup for
frustration and discouragement. Trying to forgive before we are ready almost
guarantees we will bypass our own suffering. For most of us facing betrayal,
true forgiveness is an ideal to aspire to rather than an accessible way of being
in the world. We may wish to forgive, but like so much else that involves our
depths, forgiveness grows underground in mysterious ways that are not in
our hands. And it can take many years of outright, implacable unforgiveness
before coming to fruition.

I speak from experience, because, believe me, I did try to forgive.

I religiously included forgiveness practices as part of my meditation and
prayer time. I spent two entire years every day working the exercises in *A
Course in Miracles,* the primary focus of which is learning to forgive, and
meeting weekly with a support group. I knew that no decent person would
inflict these torments on someone else, if they knew what they were doing.
I told myself over and over, Rob did not know what he was doing—as in

"Forgive them for they know not what they do." Sending him loving-kindness and acknowledging his pain and my own contribution to the situation became an integral part of my daily routine.

Nevertheless, my traumatized state of mind would have none of it, and needed a different medicine. Outside the time of sustained attention on my practices, and sometimes even with a fierce focus on them, I continued to revert to resenting and blaming Rob. Was it not obvious what he did was unforgivable, degrading, cruel, manipulative? My reptilian and limbic brains, caught in the trauma loop of rage and fear, stuck relentlessly to their truth, even as my neocortex tried to let him off the hook with sophisticated explanations about his suffering, past life karma, unconscious reenactment of his early trauma, his "mother complex," projection, patriarchal conditioning, and so on.

Frankly, trying so desperately to forgive him only showed me how far away I was from being the kind, forgiving person I imagined myself to be. Trying to change my attitude about what happened—"It was meant to be," "All is for the best," "He did the best he could"—proved equally futile. Applying these platitudes was like putting a Band-aid on a gaping wound. After many exhausting, futile efforts, in which I felt like an utter failure, I finally recoiled at trying to forgive someone who did not care and still had no remorse for his part in throwing me into this hell. I resented that I should have to be the one to do all this work to heal the connection on top of dealing with the trauma and pain.

That is how I learned that, until we have faced our shattered condition, stepped into the unknown, and gone through the difficult clearing of our own hearts, forgiveness is just another ideal that burdens the betrayed soul.

What Is Forgiveness?

Love and forgiveness are not for the faint-hearted. —Meher Baba

I have used the term *forgiveness* often in this writing, and the idea is a cornerstone of my understanding of the higher purposes of betrayal. But for a long time, I hated the word and still feel ambivalent about using it. That said, as it is not going away, I want to discriminate between everyday forgiveness we generate with our minds and forgiveness that emerges from the awakened heart.

Forgiveness comes easily enough with the little offenses of life. When *I* forgive *you*, I acknowledge that you have done something hurtful to me. This level of everyday forgiveness has its place, when, for instance, someone steps on your toe by accident and says, "I am sorry." You can easily forgive the injury. Or even when we react in anger and say something unkind, we may apologize and be forgiven. In these instances, we recognize that, in our common humanity, we all make mistakes and can act in unintentionally hurtful ways.

After a serious betrayal derails your life and ushers you into a personal hell, however, the intention to forgive is not enough. Nothing less than spiritual grace can bring the forgiveness needed to release us from those torments. When I use forgiveness in this sense, I am describing a quality that arises from the heart over which we have little control. Forgiveness, like God or love, attempts to name an indescribable state of being, a higher state of consciousness that recognizes the dream of this life and the mystery that lies behind it.

In spite of the challenge of reaching such a lofty state of mind and heart, many of us still rush, like I did, to try to forgive. At every step in our anxiousness to move on, we are tempted to bypass the destruction we need to face to clear our hearts enough for true forgiveness to blossom. Before we are established in the heart of compassion that inherently forgives, we face the danger that forcing forgiveness will launch us into a "spiritual bypass." Conveniently sweeping our despair, hurt, and rage underground, we are at risk of imagining ourselves in some exalted state of consciousness. This reasonable inflation only adds to our denial of the destruction and the work we need to do. We long to pull ourselves together, as if everything is behind us, and all is well. However, only after we have simmered in the dark, severed attachments, and crumpled self-images may true forgiveness arise.

This was my first real lesson in forgiveness: We cannot force forgiveness. In the dark night, the belief that we are in control of our lives is already on the chopping block. Trying to forgive is just another way we are brought to our knees concerning who is in charge of our lives. Just because we think it is an appealing goal, we cannot make ourselves forgive, except superficially, any more than we can release entrenched attachments or early trauma, or instantly become more loving or awake because we decide to.

Nevertheless, faced with the extremity of our reactions when we are traumatized, we cannot be blamed for trying. Forgiving looks appealing, like the magic bullet that will obliterate the pain and madness. Or to use a different metaphor, when you are trapped in persistent hurt and resentment, forgiving looks like a get-out-of-jail-free card.

According to Judith Herman, forgiveness fantasies are often a way for trauma victims to manage their outrage. "Revolted by the fantasy of revenge, some survivors attempt to bypass their outrage altogether through a fantasy of forgiveness. But it is not possible to exorcise the trauma, through either hatred or this brand of love. Like revenge, the fantasy of forgiveness often becomes a cruel torture, because it remains out of reach for most ordinary human beings.

Folk wisdom recognizes that to forgive is divine."[1] This is the sorry truth for the spiritual superegos among us yearning to show how kind and forgiving we are: We are not yet divine!

Through my failures at trying to forgive prematurely, my soul was teaching me that forgiveness lies not in attitudes, affirmations, visualizations, prayers, or meditation practices, but *at the very center of our wounds.* We cannot travel to ground zero of our suffering until we are ready, nor without the help of a grace that is not in our hands. Coming to terms with our own suffering, including seeing ourselves in ways we can hardly tolerate, must come before forgiveness has a chance. After being hit with the two-by-four of abandonment and poisoned with the venom of betrayal, we can no longer fool ourselves that we are basically nice people. The truth of our ongoing malice takes guts to admit.

When we are honest with ourselves, we find, that while we cannot truly forgive, we still cannot escape the urge to do so. When we have been deeply hurt, forgiveness takes on great importance, as Hillman suggests in the epigram that started this chapter. Hillman has a lot to say about forgiveness in his pivotal essay on betrayal I have quoted from often. Neither trust nor forgiveness, he believed, can be fully realized without betrayal. He recognized how crucial it is after a betrayal to at least grapple with forgiveness: "If one has been led step by step into an involvement where the substance was trust itself, bared one's soul, and then been deeply betrayed in the sense of handed over to one's enemies, inner or outer,…then forgiveness takes on great meaning."[2]

Without it, we find ourselves trapped in a cactus patch of unforgiveness, barely able to move without feeling the pricks of resentment and blame. We sense how much we need forgiveness to heal our own poisoned mind and broken heart. In the desire to heal our own pain, we are highly motivated to learn what forgiveness is all about. Otherwise, what impetus do we have to learn this subtle art?

LETTING GO

Until we have seen someone's darkness, we don't really
know who they are. Until we have forgiven someone's darkness,
we don't really know what love is.
—Marianne Williamson

When I saw how difficult learning forgiveness was, I figured I would just focus on "letting go" and cultivating a positive outlook. Before my world exploded, I had been a worshipper at the church of spiritual science, of you-create-your-own-reality and the Law of Attraction, so, naturally, I tried to apply those philosophies of mind to the situation. I determined to focus on the positive, to let go of negativity, to list appreciations, to be grateful for what I had, and to visualize my core value of loving into a cheery future. These efforts, along with forgiveness proper, however, were doomed to failure.

I remember one Sunday, probably into year three, when I was sitting at the Zen Center at a talk being given on the crucial importance of "letting go and letting be" for spiritual well-being. A well of tears poured from my eyes at the defeat I was feeling facing the insurmountable task of applying this simple first commandment of spiritual life. Like trying to forgive, trying to let go of broken trust and a fragmented reality before I was ready dug the groove of disappointment with myself even deeper.

Letting go and forgiveness have many properties in common and share similar misconceptions. A big part of the problem in understanding both comes from the structure of the English language. *Letting go* and *forgiving* express an action, something we can exercise our will to accomplish. In every-day matters, sometimes we do manage to disregard the hurts that come our way. When it comes to dealing with entrenched defenses and early wounds, however, we enter a terrain outside the reach of the personal will. This is where forgiving and letting go are no longer willed actions but, at best, intentions.

We may start with an intention, but soon enough learn that both forgiving and letting go are art forms that take time, practice, and grace to develop. Both express a stance of *engaged receptivity* to an inner unfolding outside our control. In situations involving great psychological harm, we cannot decide to let go, choose to let go, or will to let go; letting go and forgiveness *happen* to us. Hillman addressed the difficulty of actively trying to forgive a serious betrayal in the context of the ego's limitations:

> We must be quite clear that forgiveness is no easy matter. If the ego has been wronged, the ego cannot forgive just because it "should," notwithstanding all the wider context of love and destiny. The ego is kept vital by its *amour-propre*, it's [sic] pride and honour. Even where one wants to forgive, one finds one simply can't, because forgiveness doesn't come from the ego. I cannot directly forgive, I can only ask, or pray, that these sins be forgiven. Wanting forgiveness to come and waiting for it may be all that one can do.[3]

Trying to let go or to forgive when our brain is shouting "no, no, no!" is another futile effort, again akin to standing on a board and trying to lift it. Forgiveness and letting go can both begin to flow through us, as if by some miracle, when the nervous system has calmed down and the heart is ready. Before that time, my best advice to you is to be kind and patient with yourself, to allow your self images to marinate in the suffering of their undoing with as much gentleness as you can. In the medium of kindness, our attachments slowly release their psychic glue, and release us into the arms of a new loving heart intelligence that effortlessly "lets go."

In the dark night, where we learn that we are not the architects of our good, the more we try to do it ourselves, the more our dependence on higher powers becomes ever clearer. As the skin of our old nature sheds its unconscious attachments, we begin to feel glimmers of true forgiveness. Forgiveness is the natural condition of the heart cleared of its protective defenses. As the heart's veils dissolve, the higher heart's awareness exudes forgiveness as part of its intelligence.

We cannot know the source or the timetable of these alchemical mysteries, or how far along we are in our soul's unfolding journey. We may forgive tomorrow, next year, or never. It is no small accomplishment to trust the truth of our experience, however unpalatable. Wherever we find ourselves, there we are. What can we do in this uncomfortable waiting time while we are stewing in resentful thoughts and feelings we wish would leave us be? We can make our primary task a little simpler. We can focus on accepting the situation and ourselves just as we are. This is task enough!

SELF-FORGIVING ACCEPTANCE

In the aftermath of betrayal, to accept what happened became for me a more worthy goal than forgiveness because it was more realistic. I learned that we can aim to wholeheartedly say yes to the hand we have been dealt. Saying yes to what I instinctively resisted with all my might pretty much pushed me to my limit. I began to think of acceptance as the first chord in the forgiveness symphony. *Allowing the truth* of the terrible feelings and humiliating situation to penetrate us deeply is powerful medicine that can restore our dignity and be deeply healing in itself.

If you are willing to patiently stay close to the truth of your experience, you can test this theory yourself. If you pay close attention to what still most bothers you, to *what you cannot yet forgive*—the most troubling scenes, remarks, and behaviors from the betrayal—you may find the entry point for clearing an ancient, deep pain. Look right where you cannot forgive, where the hurt, anger, and obsessiveness grab you again and again, where the *how could he?* sounds the most shrill. There you will find the kernel of the still-hidden pain that keeps you captive. Right there is where you need to hug and hold yourself with all your might. You are getting close to the initial wound that caused your system to go into shock, where the trauma defenses are most intense.

Since the spiritual substance we call forgiveness lies in the very center of our deepest wounds, allowing those injuries into awareness is a necessary step in releasing their power to heal. Resentment is like a flashing red arrow point-ing to the wound. At this delicate juncture, we need to go slowly, to bring kindness to our bitterness and blame until we are ready to feel the unbearable sensations we call shame, pain, helplessness, and grief that lie beneath.

The waiting and acceptance of our prickly defensiveness can be the most difficult task. If you are like me, you are likely to add more shame to the pain by rejecting yourself, believing you "should be over it" by now or at least be capable of being more gracious and tolerant. I made it a practice, when I found myself disappointed at my unforgiving anger and hurt, to repeat over and over to myself: "I am angry; I wholeheartedly accept my anger"...or my obsessive-ness, or my self-pity, or my loneliness. Acceptance puts a spoke in the wheel of the blame and lets in a ray of kindness, the healing ingredient we most need. This is self-forgiveness, putting your own oxygen mask on first.

Forgiveness itself, like higher love, develops as the fruit of long days and nights of this kind of acceptance, of gentleness and faith that we are in good hands. When we understand that we cannot force the alchemy of letting go and forgiveness any more than we can coax a peach to ripen in midwinter, we begin to better appreciate our human situation. We have to wait humbly in the cold—blaming, ungrateful, and miserable though we may be—for sum-mer, when the suffering finally bears fruit. Meanwhile, acceptance of what we cannot change, patience, and as much tenderness toward our attached, unforgiving selves as we can muster are the order of the day.[4] We may not be able to forgive an unrepentant betrayer, but we can lower the bar and learn to accept him, ourselves, and the situation as it is. That in itself is quite an accomplishment!

LONGING FOR REMORSE

As anyone who has tried to forgive from their heart, and not simply their mind, can attest, our way is made all the more impossible if we hold on to any expectations of the person we are trying to forgive. If we feel that before we can forgive our offender he must express his remorse, then our peace of mind remains tied to his behavior. Yet, without that participation, any forgiveness we muster is all the more likely to be forced or premature.

It is easy to understand why we long for remorse from the offender. You sense how much his acknowledgment of your pain and his part in inflicting it could help you with the difficult task of cleanup after this demolition derby of your life. And, in a sense, that intuition is correct; in practical terms, we do require the other's participation to forgive and certainly to heal the relationship.

Despite the accepted wisdom that in order to heal you must forgive, independent of the actions or attitude of the person who has caused you harm, our human nature rebels against this advice, and for good reason. Forgiveness without remorse goes against our sense of fairness, justice, and, let's face it, simple common sense. When acknowledgment and remorse from the betrayer are absent, as is often the case, it feels as if the betrayal is continuing, getting worse and worse. Even the New Testament, which recommends forgiving your brother seven times seven times a day if necessary, adds the condition—"if he repent."⁵ The betrayer's disavowal of responsibility, or superficial apologies, increase your already heavy psychic burden. Trying to forgive someone who sees no reason and has no interest in being forgiven puts us in a double bind. Hillman saw clearly the difficulty of forgiving under these circumstances:

> But forgiveness is so difficult that it probably needs some help from the other person. I mean by this that the wrong, if not remembered by both parties— and remembered as a wrong—falls all on the betrayed…If only the betrayed senses a wrong, while the other passes it over with rationalizations, then the betrayal is still going on—even increased. This dodging of *what has really happened* is, of all the sores, the most galling to the betrayed. Forgiveness comes harder; resentments grow because the betrayer is not carrying his guilt and the act is not honestly conscious.⁶ (my italics)

While the betrayer's remorse could take some of the load off our shoulders, all the writers I have read on the subject, and most of those I spoke with, agree that remorse from the offender is highly unlikely. As long as it takes us to forgive, it may take that long or much longer for an offender to find the strength to bear this much self-knowledge. Our continuing insistence on that remorse, while it might make us feel better, grants the betrayer continuing dominion over the quality of our lives.

Moreover, if we push for the betrayer's acknowledgment, at best we may get premature apologies that are likely to be disingenuous. Premature apologies go hand in hand with premature forgiveness. Apologies offered primarily to alleviate the betrayer's guilt or assuage his self-image only add insult to the injury. Minus heartfelt remorse, true caring, and efforts to make amends, a halfhearted "I'm sorry" or a laundry list of regrets merely reinforces the sense of being dismissed and manipulated.

Think about it. Why should your betrayer take responsibility for what he has done? Even if he could see his damaging behavior through the haze of male entitlement and denial in our culture, what motivation does he have? Why should he go through the suffering of seeing the pain he has inflicted when he has plenty of reasons and a supportive milieu to keep on with denial?

Right now he is likely not suffering. His life is rolling merrily along on the wheels of his delusions and self-image (just like ours), enhanced by the power surge of having left you behind.

While we are all deluded and full of ourselves in one way or another, ask yourself, is this person ready for the deeply painful level of self-knowledge it would take to admit such harmful behavior? People who are prone to betrayal manage their pain by passing it on to others. This is the defensive style that has gotten them through life. They will likely need to be seriously broken down before they can even start to see the impact of this habitual harmful behavior that gives them security and power.

I still believe no one would do this to someone else if they knew what they were doing—that became my forgiveness mantra. Even if a person acted intentionally to hurt you, they still do not know what they have done to you or to their own soul; and for now they do not want to know. They may lack the resources, the courage, and insight to go through such a shattering; and it may simply not be the right time for them.

I told myself, look how long it has taken you, with full intention to struggle with your own demons around this pain! It takes ripening; it takes strength to feel our own pain, to admit our weaknesses; and mostly, *it takes grace* to realize how we have hurt others. It is highly disturbing and destabilizing to our self-image, as those of us who have come to face our own conscience know. Who are we to know the timetable of someone else's soul unfolding? Most of us were unprepared and blindsided by our own. It has been humbling to see how intent I could be to play god and regulate someone else's conscience.

Considering these questions may be as painfully disillusioning for you as it was for me. Like me, you may come to realize there will be no "closure," or repair, or reconciliation, or resolution to something that was so important to you. If there was significant acting, hypocrisy, and deception in the relationship, the man you knew has likely vanished anyway, and you are dealing with a virtual stranger.

Accepting this truth means melting down what has been your relational reality on the deepest levels. You are left to ask yourself: "Who was this person I believed I was with?" "Who is this person now who treats me as if we had never known each other, much less lived together, slept together, perhaps had children together, and woven our lives together for years?" Most disturbingly, you will need to ask, "Who was I in relation to this fantasy man?" Getting to the bottom of questions such as these with someone with whom you have created a deep bond allows no simple solution. This is why coming to acceptance of the situation, while a reasonable goal, can still be a long, arduous process.

I was so removed from his reality that I even had ideas about including Rob's perspective as part of this book, but that was not to be. After long periods of no contact, and sporadic attempts to have a real conversation with him to sort out what happened, I reluctantly had to admit he was not available, either not able, not interested, or not willing, to engage meaningfully with me, not to mention do the hard work to resolve what went on between us.

All I know is that after every encounter, I was slammed right back into the trauma vortex, for days or weeks at a time. I continued to be stunned at the radical shifts in his personality. His seductive charm would lure me in, only to face an abrupt shift to indifference, condescension, or other bombshells. Every time I showed up with him, I was like the mole in the whack-a-mole game; or like Charlie Brown with Lucy when she encourages him, then pulls away the football every time. He was dangerous for me to be around. Sadly, I reconciled myself to the fact there was nothing I could do.

RECIPROCAL FORGIVENESS

Beyond acceptance and short of waking up one day with an enlightened heart, I have come to believe that for practical purposes, forgiveness after betrayal must take place in relationship. It takes two. Bringing forgiveness into such a severe rupture of trust requires that the person who has hurt you acknowledge what they have done; and you need to be willing to find a way to let them back into your trust. In the ideal world, the offending person needs to be willing to do what it takes to make amends and to heal the breach, including acknowledging and listening to your pain, if that is helpful to you. And you who have been hurt need to be willing to explore whatever part you played in what happened, and then to express what you need to take steps toward rebuilding trust. This level of forgiveness is *reciprocal forgiveness*.

For most of us who have been cut off and dismissed, and replaced with someone new, such reciprocal forgiveness is not an option. Nevertheless, I include this ideal of reciprocal forgiveness to differentiate this potential for reconciliation between two people from the lofty ideal of spiritual forgiveness, and the more likely goal of acceptance.

Here is a litmus test for whether this approach may be an option for you. Is the offender approaching you with an attitude that includes the following two points? 1)"Please tell me what your life has been like since I left (cheated, lied, stole). Take as long as you need"; and 2) "I want to know what I can do to make it up to you." If he is not truly interested in your pain and in doing whatever it takes to help you heal, his apology may be insincere. An easy apology does not recognize the depth of the damage, or show willingness to commit time and energy to restoring trust.

If your betrayer does care about your pain and is willing to work with you to clear the past, give him credit for the strength that takes; and, if you want it, there is yet hope of mending the threads of your connection in some form. If, however, you are faced with a recalcitrant offender, who will not accept responsibility or make amends, any "forgiveness" that does not recognize the harm done denies the truth of the situation. It excuses rationalizations, half-truths, and obliviousness. Such premature, unearned, even unwanted forgiveness helps neither person to heal. Unlike reciprocal forgiveness, reconciling with or acceptance of the situation requires nothing from the offender, yet gives us what we need to reclaim our hearts, settle our minds and rebuild our lives. [7] We may yet reconcile with ourselves, with the event, and with God, if not with the other person.

Like many who hold out for a sincere apology, I found myself clinging to a false hope that Rob would one day arrive at my front door with an armful of pink roses, fall on his knees in tears, and say, "I am *so sorry.*" As you know, this was a fantastical leap from reality. Regardless of what Rob thought or how he treated me, in my many failures to forgive him, I was learning an important lesson. Sitting alone with the press of hurt and resentment humbled me. I wanted to do the right thing. But I did not know what "right action" or a right relationship to him or what happened would even look like anymore.

I firmly believed I could rise above the situation, heal myself, and forgive if I just applied myself diligently to the task. I found out how wrong I was. While I intended to say yes to the truth that tore apart my reality, it took grace to wear away the No! that came from the core of my being. I had to spend a long time in the valley of anger and tears before I could manage more than bringing Rob into my heart on a superficial level. Nonetheless, at times, I had glimmers of a healing light that gave me hope.

As a veteran of the inner wars of wishing to forgive but not being able to do so, I realize that it is not for any of us to tell anyone else that they should forgive. It is not for us to lay down a timetable or a method for them or us. If you choose not to even think about forgiving, that is your right and a legitimate step in regaining your ground and making sense of the situation. I wish I had done that from the start, instead of frustrating myself with an ideal I could not accomplish. Forgiveness is overrated!

Admitting that we cannot forgive may be the best action we can take for a long time. It implies we are listening to our truth, and that is already a significant step toward the acceptance and love of ourselves, just as we are, that opens the heart. Once I gave up on forgiveness, I satisfied both my higher and lower selves by regularly offering the prayer recommended in twelve-step programs for those who have harmed you: "God please help him—please heal him and give him whatever he deserves." And sometimes I added, "even if I am completely wrong about what that might be."

Sustained forgiveness? To this day I can only pray for that elevated state to take me over and will bow my head in thanks if it does. I am willing. Forgiveness, like faith and love, has become for me a prayer to be lived, a direction to face—no longer a goal to be attained. On the other hand, I have come a long way toward accepting this hand I have been dealt as what I needed to wake from many of my own delusions, and to recover the deepest yearnings of my heart.

CHAPTER 19

Finding Your North Star

And we are put on earth a little space,
that we may learn to bear the beams of love.
—William Blake

IN THE LONG INCUBATION of heartache, I developed an affection and reverence for the heart—her vulnerabilities to suffering, beauty, and love; the primordial grief held in her tissues; her rainbow qualities of gentleness, compassion, power, mystery, and wisdom. Nothing surpasses the quintessence of the heart for reviving, soothing, and healing the trauma-besieged soul. A few seconds of contact with her silent depths are like sunshine breaking through weeks of storm.

Previously, it had been rare for me to hear my own heartbeat, but as my nervous system calmed down, and I was quiet enough to pay attention, my physical heart was perceptible in a new way. This small pump seemed to be conveying subtle messages I needed to receive. When I listened closely, each beat radiated communion with life; each pulsing murmured, love, love, love, offering an infusion of radical love that I could barely contain but was thrilled to receive. In those graced moments, I realized that, right here in our own breast, lies everything we are looking for to recover our lives. The heart lives and breathes the miracle of life, *life is love is life is love is....*

The heart naturally cherishes and rejoices in the gift of living, exuding gratitude and humility, and constantly communicating the preciousness of existence to us—as long as we find a way to listen. When we listen, we know: I exist! I am here! To know oneself as an irreplaceable, unique expression of creation—for happiness, what more do we need? If only the awareness of this radical love were the ground for our daily life, how differently we would live. We have these moments: We remember, and then we forget.

Even as I was developing the faith to live more consistently in the light of the heart, I recall how often I remained distrustful of myself and other people.

Feeling safe and trusting life again after such a traumatic shattering takes time. After all, it was by trusting that you were so deeply hurt, so it is natural to be gun-shy about other people, and maybe especially about your own feelings and instincts. I would veer one day in this direction, the next day in that. In time, the alchemy of gentle awareness worked its magic, and my wariness softened, allowing the demons of fear, anger, and obsessiveness to loosen their grip. As the momentum of kindness toward myself grew, rivulets of conviction in the intrinsic goodness of life came more and more often to counter my ancient fears.

Finally, the scales tipped, my brain's rewiring flashed *Go*, and I said yes— yes to living, yes to now, yes to this terrible, wondrous existence, in whatever form it was taking.

I recall my elation when I felt the first decisive turn to a radical yes. It came in response to a dispiriting spell of loneliness. Bearing with the familiar, empty ache, I detected a pulsing aliveness in the disturbing sensations; and the lights went on. *Loneliness, too, is life.* Loneliness is God-force. Loneliness is full of spirit and wisdom and grace. I had been telling myself something like this all along. But, suddenly, no longer was "accepting" this feeling just a practice, intention, or good idea. Rather, I had begun to *trust this terrible feeling*.

My heart began to draw loneliness, this forever outcast of my psyche, into its embrace. Loneliness, too, belonged. Loneliness, too, deserved respect, warmth, curiosity, and openness. In that moment, my heart said yes to life just as it was. Even this searing isolation contained mystery and signaled loving creation at its core. I knew then what I had not previously understood and sighed aloud: So, *this is self-love*. I recalled the moment years before when I had a similar epiphany and said to myself: *So, this is what it is like to fall apart.* The connection between the two experiences was not lost on me.

At turning points such as these, I sensed my suffering had not been meaningless, after all. Maybe I was wrong about being inextricably flawed and hopeless. I am a once-only, not-to-be-replicated part of creation; I belong here for reasons beyond my comprehension; I deserve compassion, respect, and care for simply being here! And so does everyone else.

The seed of new receptivity to life and to myself had been planted and must have taken root without my realizing it. Now from the ground of the heart, the first buds of newborn trust had cracked into awareness. Not once and for all, but in increasingly frequent moments and varied situations, I was learning that even in suffering, the mystery of love can be found.

WHAT DOES THE HEART WANT?

The passage from the conditional love that depends on circumstances to the love of the mystic heart takes place in extraordinary liminal space. Heartache invites us to question our values, to discover what is most important in our lives. It jars us out of easy routines and living out priorities we inherited from our family or mindlessly adopted from our culture. It forces us to ask, "What do I really love?" and compels us to put our values into practice.

Even in the darkest, most despairing days, I intuited I was in the midst of something extraordinary (sometimes extraordinarily awful!). As Rilke suggested, I had been "living the questions." The one my psyche revolved around most—*What do I want in my deepest heart?*—gave a focus to my ruminations. Even though there were no easy answers to this question, I urgently needed one. I needed a reason to go on with a life that had been drained of meaning and no longer seemed worth living. Learning to listen to the heart, to receive its love, comes gradually as the darkness burns away the dense veils of lifelong resistance and defensiveness. In the dark, we are gestating answers to our vital questions, answers that bypass the mind and come straight from the heart.

When our world shatters, we yearn with uncommon passion to know the truth about who we are and what we want. For myself, I wondered, was there anything deep enough in me to take me beyond the sadness that the man to whom I had given my heart and taken into my body and soul had abandoned me, become an utter stranger, and was gone from my life? I did not want my world to revolve around this pathetic, self-involved question, but it was!—and I had to admit how important this was to me and what that meant.

I could no longer be satisfied with a concept of goodness, love, or God, or anything my mind told me I must still want, to counter the press of grief and loss. My surface emotions could not be counted on to answer; they were completely wrapped up with the heartbreak and not to be trusted. Only an answer arising from the intelligence of the heart would have enough substance to anchor my life now. I needed a lived experience to match the strength and power of this unrelenting longing from my emotional heart for her lost companion.

At times, I would have an insight; or a difficult emotion, like craving or rage, would transform into loving strength, and bring me a momentary lift in my spirits. But, I always asked my heart, "Is *this* what you want?" For a long time, no answers came in reply from that mysterious center of my being, just a blank, nothing. I could locate only the underlying sharp pain of yearning in my chest, the wound that would not heal, the reminder of the emptiness there and a hunger to have the lost parts of my soul restored. I took notice when

I heard James Finley say that the "jagged edges of our hurting heart are the boundaries of the Divine." His poetic way of putting it inspired me to keep on paying attention to the yearning.

I noticed, as time went on, that the question of what I wanted had taken a slight turn. Now, I was really asking, "What can I trust?" I felt how powerfully I needed to trust again to get back my life. Rob had been my safe ground. His departure had revealed the shakiness of this ground and how much my heart had sought its refuge in the wrong place. The shock had decimated my trust in just about everything—in him, in myself, in other people, in my aspirations, my experiences, my perceptions, in the goodness of life itself.

It can take years to let oneself feel the truth and extent of such a loss. Some young part of my soul held on and still believed he would show up in his integrity and restore the trust that gave meaning to my life. It is obvious now, but was too difficult to see when I was hurting, that I needed to establish contact with something more than he could ever provide to recover my faith and trust in life. Without consciously realizing it, that need drove me ever deeper into myself. In the grief and turmoil of betrayed love like this, ever so gently we are being "weaned from earthly things." (Rilke)

RENEWED INNOCENCE

A strange void began to call me as refuge from the stormy seas of my hurting heart and my turbulent emotions and thoughts. Each time I stopped to sink into the depths, I entered a disorienting emptiness, and my heart broke all over again. Tears flowed for no reason mixing joy with sorrow, sorrow with joy. I realized that, not only did I not know who I was, what I wanted, or whom to trust, I also had no idea who or what God or existence could possibly be. I was surrounded by mystery, and it broke me open each time I sensed the gap between that truth and my conditioned state of mind of certainty about it all.

What we normally trust in ourselves forms a veil over the knowing heart. In the shattered mind, our recycled self-images, primal emotions, and stale concepts float around like so many dust mites, until there is nowhere left for us to stand, and the truth of the groundlessness of our condition becomes clear. Our naïve trust in these images has to be destroyed to shift our allegiance from the past to the present, from the mind to the heart.

The dark night delivers us from being someone to being no one. Once we have passed through the shattering, waded through the detritus of dismemberment and the pain of dying, we lie in the tomb. It can feel like an endless night until we assent with all our heart to the free-floating uncertainty of being no one going nowhere. Getting past the terror of this seeming nonexistence can trip you up. Thus, in the descent, we need to spend a lot of time making friends with fear, discovering along the way how fear forms the bedrock of our ordinary way of being in the world. At least, that is how it was for me.

In those moments when our inner light shines through our armor of anxiousness, and we are graced to surrender into the sparkling, empty nothingness, love flows immediately toward us, as naturally as water flowing downhill. In place of my previous certainties, I was pierced, at times, with a subtle, delicate, innocence that made me feel fresh and young, as if I were looking in wonder at the world for the first time. The dawning mystic heart as it breaks into awareness could also be called the heart of innocence. A sense of renewal—that came to me in dreams and visions as images of white: unicorns, snow leopards, snowfall, blankets of foam—was rising from the ashes of the past. I experienced myself as a little child, full of curiosity and openness to life.

The touch of innocence, so ethereal as to be barely perceptible, soothed and mended my wounds. The caressing white gave me the strength to endure the anguish before a deeper form of nothingness arose. That inspired term, *the unbearable lightness of being,* best described the luminous, rich emptiness that was emerging. Sometimes I walked down the street as if in an invisibility cloak; "Sandy" roamed down Petaluma Avenue, but not in the familiar way. Through this animated clay form a unique stream of experience flowed: sights, sounds, and sensations of the moment, reaching out so much further than my body and mind; and I was all of it.

I felt as if I were born to absorb and live what was happening to me right at that moment. As Walt Whitman said, "This moment that comes to me out of the past decillions, there is none better than it and now."[1] While similar events might be happening to millions of other people, each of us experiences what comes to us in our own unique way. That I live life as fully as possible, as it passed through me, seemed important, crucial, holy work.

From the ground of innocence, I began to know, not merely conceptualize, that *I exist, I am here* as a singular presence connected to a living field of connectivity that wants and needs my participation. I intuited from my heart that, in trusting the moment, I was finally playing the part I was born to play in an alive, wondrous world. I felt I was sensing my place in the world soul, the *anima mundi,* about which the ancients had written. So began the rising from the ashes of a shattered life. Vulnerable and unsteady on this new ground, my sense-of-self continued to shift more often to include this translucent connection with the moment. When I paused to let it in, all around me a world glistened. In a given instant, strolling through the park, for example, from my own unbounded center of life a compelling curiosity arose.

What is it all about?—the willows over the creek, the children on the swings and slides, the myriad roses in different stages of bloom? That question brought an aliveness and wonder to brushing my teeth or peeling a cucumber for the salad. I sensed what it meant to trust with an entirely new faculty centered physically in my chest. With even a nanosecond of that trusting connection with my heart, a feeling of kinship with all-that-is-living flushed through me. I was playing my part just being here, and that was all I needed to make it contentedly through the day.

Faithfulness to the Heart

After months, or even years, of struggle in the land of betrayal, one day we realize that the past's hold over us has weakened. Through bearing with the trials of the trauma and the descent, hidden fears, resentments, and beliefs that we have lived with throughout our lives lose their sway over us. With each conscious breath, the insubstantiality of past memories, thoughts, and feelings smiles through more readily, and they simply do not mean what they used to mean to us. We have moved through the turbulent transitional space and find ourselves on new ground.

As the passions clear, the volume turns down on the obsessive preoccupation with what happened, and through the lingering pain, we can more readily hear the formerly faint melody of the true heart's song. Yearnings for our lost love, for life as we knew it, for the future we anticipated, take a slight but momentous turn as we begin to long, instead, *for faithfulness to our own awakening heart.*

You may be as surprised as I was to sense how this longing to be faithful to the deep heart has taken root in the ruins of your life. How did it happen? The intelligent heart that knows what to value arises from the burning grounds of betrayal like the mythological phoenix. The heart welcomes us to our true home and hearth to replace the imagined protective haven of our past love. I do not know how it happens—that remains for me another part of the mystery of betrayal I cannot solve. But, imperceptibly, as I grew accustomed to the rigors of the dark, my center of gravity was shifting.

In the midst of my daily routine, when I noticed the familiar aching sense that something, or more often *someone*, was missing, instead of automatically pining away for my lost love, I paused and breathed deeper into my heart's yearning—listening for the messages in the aching, beyond the thoughts in my mind. When I was depleted, angry, or lost, I found myself seeking refuge by *returning to that yearning* to listen, renew, and remember what I most wanted, as I would return to a caring friend. I turned to the pulsing heart to answer my questions, to quench my thirst, to ease my hunger pains, and to embrace me when loneliness threatened.

Breathing into my heart helped me recognize emptiness as my ally, no longer as the enemy. Instead of being swallowed by resentment or the tides of self-loathing and despair when the aching emptiness appeared, the waves of hollowness compelled my curious respect. Right in the center of these formerly unbearable torments, I found God calling.

A warm glow burst through the pain, like the sun bursting through a stormy sky, longing for freedom from the shackles of the senses. Mystery and flow streamed more regularly into my life. Although I had no idea what to expect next, I was falling in love with and beginning to trust my heart. What a quiet surprise: My most reliable companion was becoming my own heart. I was being led through loneliness, heartache, and despair *to trust the intelligence of my own heart.*

This new brand of trust was arising directly from the hurt and emptiness and began to spread its influence from heart to mind. Instead of the inflated certainty of my opinions, beliefs, and self-images, *not knowing* became the new sacred ground that deserved my deepest trust. This new trust sank its foundations in the big facts of life—the mystery that we exist at all; the potency of the moment; the living presence of the ground, of breath, of heart; the companionship of invisible guidance; and our looming mortality, infinitesimal size in the scheme of things, incalculable ignorance, and vast potential.

Staying anchored in the unfathomable life force in my heart, surrendering to whatever life presented in the moment, however horrible I deemed it to be, was becoming my most important undertaking. That surrender came from a new center of gravity: a point of light and mystery deep within. When and if that center came alive was not under my control. The guidance came and went, but I had claimed my new navigation point, the North Star that I trusted would guide my way home.

What the Heart Knows

In the lengthy crossing from despair to devotion, a heartbroken person develops many unanticipated strengths arising from the newfound capacity to allow the heart to break. The raw sensitivity that results from the injury of personal rejection can reveal, if we allow it, just how the heart's vulnerability connects us with all of life.

I had a friend who used to speak about having "foxhole buddies," referring to those we bond with while going through rough times together. From the perspective of the tender, open heart, just braving the human condition makes us all foxhole buddies. Making a pilgrimage through a dark night of the soul brings us home to others in a way that ignites the deepest compassion. Tendrils of the heart go out naturally to those around us; a sense of brother-and-sisterhood, of a shared fate, travels along those tendrils.

The wisdom heart feels into other hearts, and discerns who and what to trust. The heart knows how to discriminate, intuitively aware of the shrouds of anxiety, seduction, power, or indifference that mask another's suffering and can mislead you. As long as we listen, we find the heart offers protection as well as love. Spontaneously, we know when to say no and when to say yes. Shakespeare summed it up when he said, "To thine own self be true, and it must follow, as the night the day, thou canst not then be false to any man." In learning what to trust in ourselves, we become more trustworthy, and learn when others deserve our trust.

Immersion in the dark taught me the surprising lesson that the heart knows intuitively how best to be with people. The heart *relates* by its nature. We are born to bond, after all. With the eyes of the heart, we see the individual spark in others; we intuit their mystery, their beauty and divinity, as the most important thing about them. The heart rejoices simply sensing another's light. The light of his unique, irreplaceable being was what I missed most about Rob, and that is true of anyone we love. But as the grief of his loss lessened, I somehow found the courage to allow myself to feel into other hearts. They could not replace his particular music, but there were other lovely tunes, and they were everywhere! I found warmth of heart in friends and family, in store clerks, shoppers at Rite Aid, moms and children walking down the street.

Now that I knew how difficult life could be and how fragile we all are, I noticed, step by step, that respect and curiosity prevailed more often than anxiousness when I was around most other people, my compatriots in this challenging life. This is another way of saying that I was beginning to hold my dear old ego-self and those around me in greater kindness, instead of falling into the well-worn paranoia, judgment, cynicism, indifference, or a sense of superiority or unworthiness to cope.

More often I would sense beyond the irritating or hurtful behaviors of others a call for love. I would surprise myself when I bypassed my usual defenses to offer presence and nurturing where previously I would have shifted into some heady protection. As we feel more connection with people, we cannot help but move beyond fears about being hurt to wishing for their well-being. Not only that, but, as my strength returned, I also wanted to help; I especially wanted others not to hurt if I could help it. If you have been through this kind of hurt and have made it this far in this book, I imagine you know just what I mean.

The Wound That Does Not Heal

That we have come to know so intimately our own grief, longing, and broken-ness gives us eyes to see more readily the same hurts in others. Like the mytho-logical wounded healer Chiron, whose injury from Hercules' poisoned arrow would not mend, the wound itself becomes at once the source of misery and of our healing capacity, and opens the door to compassion. Whether or not we play the actual role in our outer lives, when we survive a serious betrayal, we become wounded healers.

Learning to live with the mystery of a heart broken by betrayal gives you the capacity to be a soothing haven for others who are suffering. The compas-sionate heart is a miracle worker that has already reclaimed outcast, exiled parts of our own nature. We could have died not knowing these parts of the soul, long walled off from our awareness by habit and fear. With the under-standing of how much of our own soul could have remained lost, the heart naturally extends its soul-stitching warmth and care to others.

Betrayal does leave its mark on the soul, a tender scar that threatens to keep us riveted to the ache; that is its dark gift. Nevertheless, the lingering ache offers a ready lifeline to the fertile mysteries of the heart. It is a wound that does not heal in the traditional sense of the pain going away. For years, I resented (and sometimes still do) being forced to live with the chronic vulner-ability of a tender wound. But as we learn to stop fighting it—imagining the hurt should be gone, or there must be something wrong—we recognize we now have in us an *automatic alarm clock* to remind us what is most important in life. The wound becomes the wake-up call from our everyday trance, alert-ing us to listen to the heart's deepest longings.

Here is the way one of my favorite writers, Anne Lamott, describes the continuing wound with an image that captures it well.

> You will lose someone you can't live without, and your heart will be badly broken, and the bad news is that you never completely get over the loss of your beloved. But this is also the good news. They live forever in your broken heart that doesn't seal back up. And you come through. It's like having a broken leg that never heals perfectly—that still hurts when the weather gets cold, but you learn to dance with the limp.[2]

Dancing at all after feeling so broken is a joy. The limp hardly interferes, and when it does, when we let ourselves feel the lingering wound with all our heart, automatically, we pray. The prayer in the longing ache calls to the invis-ible powers that guide our destiny, and itself forms the bridge that connects us with a world of mystery, freedom, and joy. I was astonished that grace entered right through the most insistent pain. I could not believe the day would come when, instead of recoiling when the cutting pangs of missing Rob came over me, I would turn to dance a little jig and, with thankfulness, stop to attend to this call of Spirit. I began to honor the preciousness of this "tragic," bitter hurt as the very place where the lasting love I longed for could most readily appear.

Slowly, I came to see the injury to my heart as a sacred event. I did not understand it. I still did not approve of betrayal as the method to inflict it; but I did, in faith, surrender to its truth and to its necessity. As I came to peace with a wound that did not heal, and listened to its daily calls for a deeper love, the hurt opened a passageway to a tender beauty in simple things and other people formerly inaccessible to me. I let Rebecca del Rio's poem "The Dark Stone" tell this tale as only a poet can.

> *There in the path, it waits*
> *The dark stone, in the center—*
> *The place we hoped never to arrive.*
>
> *Life is littered with so many losses,*
> *Dark stones, scattered in the fields and paths,*
> *Betrayals by death, dishonesty, disappointment.*
>
> *What happens if we meet that stone with wonder,*
> *Walk to its cruel center, sit in its*
> *Sorrowful presence?*
>
> *Here, yes here, in the heart of*
> *Fear, disillusion, chaos and*
> *Confusion, peace arrives, a soft surprise.*

When we are betrayed in love, our betrayer becomes both the carrier and the executioner of a precious, but all too human, love. Our human loves are beautiful gifts, but they pass away. Our hearts most long for that which will not pass away. For some of us, it takes suffering the betrayal of our human love to deliver us, torn and tattered—soft surprise—into the arms of the true Beloved.

The Return

Expect to have hope rekindled. Expect your prayers to be answered
in wondrous ways. The dry seasons in life do not last.
The spring rains will come again.
—Sarah Ban Breathnach

D ESPITE INFUSIONS OF GRACE from the compassionate heart along the way, the dark night that follows betrayal can feel as if it will never end. Finally, into the fourth year, I began to feel like a character in *Mission Impossible*. Moments of "mission accomplished" for simply surviving the worst torments slipped into the day. Storm clouds still hovered, but with less density; shafts of sunlight were breaking through. I was sleeping through the night, my weight had stabilized, my nervous system had calmed down. I engaged again with certain friends, and some days I could even laugh at the brooding on the past that could still carry me away.

I knew for sure a shift was coming when I actually did begin to enjoy dancing again. I used to love dancing, and Rob and I had danced often together. Perhaps because I knew he frequented dance venues to meet new partners, for a long time pain shot through me whenever I heard dance music or started to dance. Even so, one morning I turned on Pandora to the random setting. As I moved about my morning routine, I found myself waltzing around to Chopin, flowing into the music with pleasure and ease, then into Madonna and Julio Iglesias. It was a simple shift, but I teared up with gratitude that the joy of movement was coming back into my life, uncomplicated by sadness, after three long years of eclipse.

Around this time, I took a plane trip south. Looking out the window when we had reached cruising altitude, I felt a similar thankfulness for something that had long gone missing from my days. The sun breaking through behind mountains of cumulus clouds, sparkling on the waters of the Pacific, struck me as the most exquisite sight I had ever seen—perhaps a metaphor for the change of atmosphere inside me. In that moment, I realized that when my traumatized soul fled the premises, it had taken beauty with it. In my self-protective constriction, I had been closed to loveliness. Now, as this first drop of beauty reached my heart, I also wept quietly in relief. My heart had been thoroughly tenderized, and tears came now in response to many things.

Some days, I sensed myself in a field where everything exuded a startling aliveness: The chairs at the kitchen table kept me company, the hand-painted salt and pepper shakers smiled as I reached for them, the oak floor boards exuded a warm steadiness. I also noticed how my goals and incessant self-directions were diminishing, sometimes disappearing altogether. I stopped making lists of things to do and started to wait and watch to see what was next in the day. Going with the flow grew as a way of being, not just a good idea.

For no particular reason, going about my day I would break out in sponta-neous moments of laughter, wholehearted, where-did-that-come-from laugh-ter. With others, too, I was seeing the comic side of life more often. Even the betrayal, "the story of what happened to me," at times struck me as absurd and hilarious. Friends pointed out, "Look, you are joking about Rob, about that pain that almost killed you!" I had survived and, at moments, was even start-ing to thrive. With a new beginning seemingly close at hand, I did not realize I was entering the final test of this initiation. The return from the stormy night seas had finally begun.

I have spent most of this book detailing the shattering and the dark tran-sitional time in this rite of passage, this initiation of the heart that is betrayal. From the exile of descent, the day comes, as was happening for me, when you notice you are readying for incorporation, for *reentering* "normal" everyday life. At last, you have been evacuated from the churning pits of the dragon and tossed onto dry land. As if awakening from a dream, you look around and discover you are standing naked on a vaguely familiar, yet alien shore. Although you may feel relief, believing the greatest trials are over, reentry also brings tentativeness and great vulnerability.

You need time to adjust and to get to know yourself before you fully take on the requirements of the outer world. Transformed by the time in the under-world, you are no longer who you were. All the same, you find you must step back into the circle of community, family, and friends that knew you when. This can be the most challenging time of all.

If you are like me, you may not recognize yourself in your interactions with others, or if you do, you are likely to be filled with a sense of inauthentic-ity or strangeness. I was not sure how to express myself genuinely from this delicate, exposed place inside that I was coming to know as home. As the dark's shredding and shedding had softened my heart, I had a new sense of who I was and what was most important to me. At the same time, I was uncertain of myself. While the lengthening periods of normality gave me hope, I still needed to honor the vulnerability and the residual feelings from the ordeal. I needed to take baby steps when moving out toward others and come back frequently to regroup in the safety of my home base. During this time of reentry, I did have cause for celebration as well as for continued apprehension of danger. I had survived many trials and passed beyond the threshold of resistance into the transformative depths. Hooray! Well done, I would tell myself.

Nevertheless, the danger in the reentry period lies in being tempted to hurry the process. With signs that the suffering may be over, we are at risk of suppressing the lingering pain that still needs to be integrated. Like convalescents after a long illness, we are just plain tired of hurting, but are not yet fully functional or healed. Learning to live from the genuine heart means moving forward with a certain raw sensitivity. This is expected and natural. Building a new, more authentic identity that reflects what we have been through takes time and practice. Eager for the trials to be over, we may succumb to the temptation to move too quickly and put up our old barriers.

I recall the first time I spontaneously spoke in a group, for instance, after years of keeping mostly silent. Although I had led many groups and been in front of hundreds of classes, my chest felt raw and exposed, and my voice was shaky. Both the tenor of my voice and what I had to say surprised me. When later a few people spoke to me about how much I had added to the discussion, it struck me as odd. I was not sure whom they were talking to; it was as if "I" had not even spoken, yet something had come through me that was helpful. A wonder.

Newly Unfolded Wings

As we venture back into the demands of the larger world, we do well to remember that, in some ways, we are like a newborn, or a butterfly with freshly unfolded wings. Or we might picture ourselves as teenagers learning to take their newly hatched beings out into the world. If we do not allow for the social awkwardness, familiar defenses are likely to return to protect the core self, and it may discourage us from being with people at all. The newly tenderized heart has expanded our capacity for beauty, joy, and love, but these treasures are easily sacrificed when we pull ourselves together too soon to try to function with a breezy, cheerful, or competent front.

Solitude has given us the environment we needed to learn to listen and trust the wisdom of the heart. As far as trusting people again after a serious betrayal, we may need to start small. Taking that wisdom into the world of other people from the vulnerable ground of the newly opened heart comes later for many of us. When we have been badly hurt in relationship, we naturally shy away from being hurt again. It is expected that reconnecting with other people may be the biggest challenge of all. I found my way back to trusting other people gradually, with one or two friends, and through therapeutic relationships with professionals I knew I could rely on to support me as I wobbled my way into a new personality style.

Otherwise, when it came to reconnecting with most others, for a long time I dismayed of even taking the first steps. When traumatic shock makes safety our number one concern, we naturally tend to isolate and, if we are introverted to start with, it can become even more challenging to move toward others now. I could not believe how suspicious I had become of people's motives—especially men's—how I questioned everything they said, looking for the distortion, the manipulation, for their true, hidden feelings. I was especially spooked by touch. It took a long time for my body to recover from what it registered as a sexual assault. With the exception of one friend, it took more than three years before I would let a man touch me, even in the most casual way. My body learned to relax that unfair generalization by working with a compassionate and gifted male massage therapist.

For a long time, being with people asked too much of my mangled, discriminating faculties and was too scary to be worth the effort. I found it less complicated to simply keep to myself until I was more established in my new strengths. We are wise to be guarded around others until we get through retelling the trauma story, desensitizing to the shock, and restoring a sense of safety and calm to the nervous system.

Dwelling in the liminal land of in-between takes your full attention. During this time, your social persona has lots of cracks, as it is being dismantled and put back together again. During the descent and dissolving of the old nature, we still have little idea of what to trust in ourselves or anyone else.

During reentry, reverting to our old nature to get by can tempt at every turn. The defensive shield the psyche erects if we prematurely lift out of the shakiness can shut down our budding sensibilities, such as appreciating beauty and flow that may just now be coming back online. We are at risk for forming hard calluses of emotional scar tissue that can take the form of suspiciousness, cynicism, or superficiality and will prevent us from reconnecting authentically to others, with our hard-won delicacy of heart. We may also revert to detachment, insensitivity, manic busyness, boredom, or other defenses to "protect" from re-injury.[1] For myself, I did not like seeing how easily I could harden into judgment, or talk nonstop, to cover my shakiness about trusting people again.

To better solidify the person you have become, you may need to let go of certain former relationships and friendships and form new ones. My circle of friends had shifted in my long absence, and I wondered where I belonged. Some people were just more comfortable with who I had been than with who I had become. I found many others in my world had idealized me in a way that supported my inflated self-images of wisdom and spiritual maturity. Their expectations coupled with my habitual way of being with them could easily pull me away from my hard-won truths—how little I knew, how many pockets of emotional immaturity I harbored, and primarily, how much I felt I was a beginner in so many ways.

Having lived my former life governed too much by the opinions of others, I found working through betrayal dealt that tendency a mighty blow. The words of Thomas Aquinas imprinted on me as my friends and acquaintances fell away, "Whether they interpret well or ill of thee, thou art not therefore another (wo)man." The trials of humiliation, rejection, and misunderstanding reveal the shallowness of counterfeit connections based on people's good opinions. With fear of being alone no longer a demon driving us to connection, we can more easily choose to spend time with people we most enjoy, who are comfortable with our newfound vulnerability and who do not tempt us back into our old nature.

In my case, the struggle to reconnect with my true worth against the continuing, although weakening, pull of shame, was often triggered by reconnecting with people Rob and I both knew and who knew my history with him. And there were plenty around our town. After betrayal, the threat of taking the rejection to heart as a shamed victim identity tempts you again and again. It gave me plenty of practice in extending kindness to my lingering shame, that basic flaw that lurked ever ready to offer a handy place to anchor myself when stressed. Developing faithfulness to my heart had given me a better anchor, a new ground in reality than any grandiose or worthless self-image could; but being around these mutual friends and acquaintances, whew, what a test that was.

Emerging with our newly unfolded, wet, and fragile, wings, we need to be especially gentle with ourselves. With patience and care, we need not tighten back into our familiar cocoons. Yes, it may be awkward, but with what we have been through, we now know that other people's opinions matter so much less, and those that care for us will be there despite these lapses. After surviving such a dousing, we should get buttons made and pin them on our shirts: Vulnerability is strength! Broken is beautiful!

During the shaky re-entry time, there is always the refuge of nature. My trust in living beings had started to rebuild with tiny flowers. When the rest of the world still seemed ominous, dangerous, and overpowering, the innocence of the violas and miniature pink roses inspired me to let their beauty in. As if they were speaking directly to me in the silent language of flower-love, they were reknitting the threads of connection to the living world. Once the flowers had softened me, I noticed the oak tree in the front yard encouraging me to lean a while against its trunk. It filled me with its strength, generously offering its rooted spirit to steady my way back into the world of others. Finding a tree you enjoy sitting under is a reliable way to ground and connect with a living being.

When the time does come to reenter the world of relationship, if we do not prematurely force it, the heart's intelligences leads and protects us on our way. Simply pausing, taking a few breaths into my heart, looking at what was in front of me, and whispering, "Help," actually did help keep my alignment with a creative source that was open and fresh. When I was with people, I had to stop and ask myself when trying to speak more authentically from my heart: So what if I cry easily, have little to say, or stammer for the right words?

As I learned to lead from my vulnerability, I was often surprised to find the willingness to admit my limitations, the courage to stand up for what I most cherished, and the fierceness to honor what I loved, no matter what anyone else said or did.

If you have not already, maybe you will feel drawn to form another love attachment. But this time your newly honed, heart-powered discriminations will help guide you to a trustworthy and respectful soul. Navigating from the tenderized heart with discernment rather than distrust takes time, experimentation, and courage. For me, I went through such angst finding myself suddenly alone, when I did fall into a rhythm of life on my own, I so enjoyed the freedom to flow with the day, the intimacy with myself, and my newfound allegiance to my heart that I doubted whether another romantic relationship would be part of this next stage of my life. I was open; it was possible, but for now, the lessons of love had turned me in a different direction.

I was at a later phase of life. Someone said that aging is a symphony of loss; I had that music to attend to. Age is a great leveler for us all, with mortality knocking more and more loudly on the door. Along with assimilating the grief of this betrayal, I was adjusting to the many challenges that come with being an older woman in this culture. If ever there was a time to realize how important it was to find the way home, it was now.

THE PEARL

When the waves close over me, I dive down to fish for pearls.
—Masha Kaleko

While I was busy trying to figure out how to deal with my single life and the people in it, a newfound source of love was busy nourishing my spirit and humbling my overworked mind. The more we embrace our pain as a messenger calling us to love, and allow our suffering to melt into the wonder that we exist at all, the more we discover the ordinary riches we normally take for granted. The heart once broken opens ever more tenderly now as we pause to notice our world.

Quiet times revealed the simple wonders of my heart beating and my breath flowing. These steady companions saturated me with a delicate sweetness and caring I would not have noticed before the trials of the dark opened the eyes of my heart. From the beating of the heart and flow of the breath a life force emanates that can nourish us with a mystical, deep knowing.

It was in the graced moments when I became aware of these nourishing rhythms that I first tried my new wings. I could never have imagined such deliciousness in the sensations of pulse and breath as they opened me to their ever-present field of loving care, always available. "When in doubt, breathe," has become, more than ever, the best advice.

Opening to small difficulties as an integral part of life's flow also signals the shift of our center of gravity from a self-willed version of how things should be to the heart's humility and acceptance. After the marathon surrender and strength-training regime of betrayal we've gone through, the challenge of being cut off in traffic, getting e-mail hacked, or waiting for thirty minutes on hold for AT&T seems like a proverbial piece of cake.

Gradually, contentment entered more often into my days. At first in flashes, like the relief in waking from a nightmare, I would look around with a sigh wondering, *what was that? Oh, it was only a bad dream!* Later, the sense of waking from a dream came for hours or even days at a time.

Light now continued to return to my days most often from ordinary things. Besides my breath and heartbeat, I would marvel at the play of sunlight on the kitchen wall, the fall of the silken drapes as I pulled them open in the morning, the wonder of my hands at work as I cut the carrots. I had practiced yoga for years, and noticed how I was starting to connect more fully to the ground, and my strength was building. I could even do handstands and backbends again. Sometimes feeling the sap rising from what felt like the earth's center into my feet and legs and through my body filled me with support. I knew I belonged and was held by the earth. It seemed I would never tire or be let down, receiving her steady stream of nourishing strength.

As I attuned more often to the moment, the quiet flow of the heart's connecting charm kept me company and I learned to let its warmth imbue the events of the day. With the guidance of the heart, I found love in the most surprising places. People began to attract my curiosity, as I often perceived each as a unique expression of the mystery.

Maybe the most surprising place I found love was in my own mirror. Not the love of "Don't I look fabulous today?" but rather, while brushing my teeth or fixing my hair, even as I noticed a new wrinkle, I would soften at the beauty, and delight in the sparkle, of my own eyes. Startlingly, I would realize *I exist! What a wonder!* I saw the delightful being I first loved in Rob in myself. In these graced moments, I loved my own light as I had his. My prayers for love were being answered, though certainly not in the manner I had envisioned. I was coming to love myself as an amazing being among other amazing beings awash in pathos and mystery.

I knew that loved or rejected, humiliated or honored, successful or failing, we are here; we exist!—each of us a unique transforming station and inlet for a loving creation. From the ruins of my dreaded demise, a love for the mystery of life was blossoming. In those blessed moments of receptivity to life, I was love itself, as was everyone around me. The indwelling spirit captivates our allegiance with its compelling goodness, and recognizes us as its own.

The belly of the beast works in the dark to irritate us like the shell of an oyster to form the pearl of love—the "pearl of great price." Drinking the cup of sorrows we are handed all the way down allows the soul to glow with a wholly unanticipated new light. Abandoning myself to the rigors of the descent revealed right in the midst of my pain a longing that connected me to myself and to a larger life.

The little spark of "Sandy" existence had grieved its way out of the caverns of trauma and now stood resilient and willing to live in a tender new way. I feel certain the same will happen for you, if it has not already. Exposed and uncertain though I might have been, I felt more ready to receive the love all around me, to offer myself as the instrument of the Divine I was meant to be. I hope sharing the ins and outs of this strange passage helps in some way to light your way.

To Love...

I did not have all the answers I had hoped to find in my deep-diving excursions. I still do not know what love is. I expect to be living that question, learning the lessons of love, until my last days. As Rilke says, "It is also good to love: because love is difficult. For one human being to love another human being: that is perhaps the most difficult task that has been entrusted to us, the ultimate task, the final test and proof, the work for which all other work is merely preparation."² I had not found a way to resolve all my difficulties, to flow carefree through life, or to resolve or reconcile my torn relationship. At times, I still wondered what it had all been for.

This book I realized would be more a progress report than a summation. Yet I knew it was time to bring it to an end. In keeping with wanting to share my deepest truth, would I have to report to you that I must "leave you with a fine mess," as the mystic teacher Gurdjieff is reported to have said when he died? Would I leave you with no answers, or solutions, just the same lot of questions and conundrums with which we started? Those were the concerns my mind brooded over that kept me for a long time from completing this writing.

Finally, my heart had something to say on the subject. One day, in the middle of a visit by some inner demon, a simple reply came to the recurring questions that had haunted me during the darkest days: "What does my heart really want?" Bubbling up from the quiet ache within, I heard a voice saturated with authority echo through me...*to love God*...and a radiant warmth filled me with sure knowing. The voice spoke the longing to love the Divine in all things as the perfect answer, the last word, the motivating force for living. The longing itself I recognized as love. That I might better realize this longing as my lover and friend is what made me want to get up in the morning.

At moments of connection, like this, I wondered if drawing closer to communion with an invisible life that quickens and sustains us, had perhaps been the purpose of the betrayal all along. I sighed again, a sigh of relief. Maybe it all did make sense. If a greater alignment with the heart's mystery, where we taste the love of the Divine, requires that we plumb the depths of confusion and suffering, is not such a prize worth the cost?

In those blessed moments, the answer is obvious. When love brings us home like this, and we recognize in an instant what we have been living for and who we are, we naturally forgive our mistakes and those of anyone who has hurt us. Most significant, we forgive the mystery, we forgive God, for creating this painful, messy life that we can never hope to truly understand, but are astonished to be learning to love and trust with all our heart.

Tips for Tending Your Soul

ULTIMATELY, BETRAYAL IS A spiritual crisis that calls for spiritual healing. But, at first, and perhaps for a long time, the spiritual resources you previously relied on may seem to have evaporated with the shock of discovering the truth. This is to be expected. Our former foundation must crumble when we are being broken down and taken deeper into a fresher, less encumbered, more authentic relationship with life.

To get through a betrayal crisis, it is important, first of all, that you keep up your basic self-care. When you are in shock and hurting, you may not feel like doing these things, but they are the cornerstones for recovery: Eat well and moderately, exercise, avoid alcohol and drugs, get plenty of sleep, keep a journal, and reach out to family and friends.

As important as the basics are, you will also be longing for something to help you move beyond basic survival. I offer some suggestions for staying in touch with your deeper self during this challenging time. It is our connection to the invisible world, whether we are aware of it or not, that helps us most—not only to recover, but to transform our suffering into wisdom, strength, heart and compassion.

1. Tell your story. Your first order of business after a life-exploding betrayal is to directly address the trauma. One of the most proven ways to do this is to tell or write out your story. Through flashbacks and intrusions, your mind is already asking you to come to terms with what happened. Each time you purposely revisit the "scene of the crime" with awareness and support it helps reduce the charge that keeps pulling you into the painful past as if it were happening now.

You may find yourself needing to describe the traumatic event over and over again, and find it difficult to think or talk about anything else. Or, you may simply go on lockdown, as if nothing unusual has happened at all and push the feelings away. Either way, telling the story in a safe environment can help to unfreeze your traumatized brain.

2. Ask for help. But choose carefully who you trust with your vulnerability. Sharing your story and your pain with anyone who, however subtly, judges or blames you, gives you advice on getting over it, or is anxious to change the subject will only drive you further into your shell. Choose the best listener you know—preferably: 1) someone you trust cares about you; and 2) someone who has been through a similar experience. Many people may believe they know what you are going through, but do not; probe to learn more. Restrain your impulse to talk to anyone who will listen.

Recovering from shattered trust can be a long process. It is a lot to ask of a friend to hang in with you when you need to talk about what happened for the hundredth time. If possible, find a trained trauma specialist. Seek out a counselor with whom you feel safe, and ideally, who has lived through a similar experience. I found Somatic Experiencing very helpful. Many recommend EMDR. See my website for further resources: http://www.sandraleedennis. com/shattered-soul/

3. Ground yourself in the here and now. To give yourself a break from the story playing over in your head, you want to come into the current moment as much as possible. If you have a meditation practice, you know what to do. If you do not, now is an excellent time to start. Go to Tara Brach's website, listen to her guided meditations. Practice dropping intrusive thoughts, images, memories, and imaginary conversations. Shift your awareness to your five senses. Keep returning to the sounds, sights, and sensations around you. Do not worry if you consistently "fail," little slivers of current time will still slip through the trauma trance.

4. Take time out each day to be with your feelings. Make this a priority, as important as eating and sleeping; otherwise, the feelings may go underground and cause even more trouble. Treat yourself as if you are attending to a hurting child—because you are. Tending to feelings is not the same as being overwhelmed by them. If you can, follow your breath moving in and out to settle yourself. When the pain comes on, try for two minutes to allow the hurt in, a little at a time, on the in-breath. On the out- breath, send into the pain any hint of a pleasurable sensation you can locate—tenderness, warmth, or aliveness. Always be gentle, touch into the pain briefly, then regroup by shifting your attention to something soothing, then touch again into the pain.

5. Be curious and welcome your feelings. Try your best not to judge or resist any difficult emotions. Try this: Do not label your feelings at all, just stay with them when they arise, be curious and "listen." Ask, "What are you trying to tell me?" Listen for the messages in the feelings as if you are learning a new language. Higher, spiritual forces surround us and reach us most readily when we are cracked open and suffering. Listen for their guidance coming from the pain itself—not necessarily in words, but in images, sounds, insights. Befriend your feelings this way.

6. Try singing. If you simply cannot concentrate while attending to your feelings, which often happens with trauma, sing, hum, chant, or repeat to yourself a tune, prayer or mantra that inspires and soothes you. Try rocking yourself gently or climbing in a warm bathtub for additional calming. If the pain gets too intense, back off. Find a benign distraction. Look at a magazine, turn on a video, take a walk, play with your cat, call a friend. Always overcorrect in the direction of being patient and gentle with your self.

7. Reach for healing touch and let yourself be held. Touch helps, perhaps more than anything, to heal betrayal and abandonment wounds lodged deep in the body. It is important to let yourself receive reassuring warmth, hugs, and hand-holding from anyone you do still trust. Regular healing touch with a well-screened, recommended massage or body therapist can also be invaluable in helping to release the pain.

8. Choose a "name of God" that reminds you of your spiritual aspirations or highest good. This can be a word or a short phrase, or better yet, an image or memory that symbolizes the best life could bring. Use this image like a salve for your hurt and anger. Each time you notice a painful memory or obsessive thought, PAIR it with your word/phrase or image. Gradually the two will blend and your sense of the meaning and mystery of what has happened to you will deepen. Your narrative or story will subtly begin to change to include this quality.

9. Express your creativity: dance, paint, color, draw, sculpt, make a collage, write, create a website, cook. You are bubbling with creative energy unleashed by shock, now is the time to use it. Bring your feelings into form.

10. Listen to and read spiritual teachings. I found it helpful to listen to meditation teacher Pema Chodron's CD's. Keep inspiring books at hand. You might want to read Pema's book, "When Things Fall Apart". She specializes in teaching mindfulness in the midst of suffering. She lived through betrayal, and the kind wisdom in her voice soothes can soothe and take you deeper into the self-love you need now.

11. Exercise your body in nature. Spend as much time outdoors as possible, but at least twenty minutes, every day to focus on the wonders of the natural world. Walk around the block, sit in your garden, go to the park. Take in the trees, the flowers, the breeze, the sun, and the sky. Whenever possible make a trip to the ocean, a stream or a lake, the mountains, or a forest. Stop and give your attention to whatever attracts you for at least ten breaths (count! or you may slip back into trauma preoccupations). Feel into the grand forces of nature and let their warmth, inspiration, and support in.

12. Reassure your heart around others. After the shock of broken trust, everyone becomes an introvert for a while. If you are already introverted, you may need help to come out of your cave after being badly hurt. Do your best to stay connected with at least one person. It is also good just to be around other beating hearts for some part of each day. Join a group or class that does not demand your personal participation. If you are lonely and start to despair, go to the store, say hello to the clerk. You will feel better. Go anywhere where there is another human being. We are social animals. It is soothing just to show up around others. Our body registers: we are part of the human race. Oh, right!

13. Try "grace" with a new twist. Another way to bring your self out of isolation into more connection with the rest of humanity is to **pause for a minute before meals**. Picture the hundreds (likely thousands) of people whose labor and care went into bringing the food you are about to eat to you. In this way, eating itself becomes a powerful reminder of how we depend on and are connected with so many other people.

14. Throughout the day **make a mental note of ANYTHING good**, beautiful, kind or inspiring, no matter how small: a sip of warm tea, a helpful idea, a smile from a stranger, the blue of the sky, your feet on the ground. At the end of the day, go back and force yourself to recall these moments. When we have lost our love through deception, infidelity, or rejection, it can feel as if all good has gone out of life. Little by little, start rebuilding the reservoir of goodness in your soul by milking each tiny pleasure, kindness, or beauty for all it is worth.

15. Call on God, your higher power, as often as you can remember—even if it feels empty and meaningless to you now. Pray and ask for help. Put your rational mind on hold and tell yourself this practice is to help revive your heart. Just do it. Take at least five minutes morning and evening and whenever you can during the day to stop and take five deep breaths. On each breath, ask for help, whisper whatever name of God is most real for you. Help is already with you and soon enough, you will know the truth of being loved and supported by a love that will not fail you.

A Note to the Reader

IF, YEARS AFTER A serious betrayal, you are still wrestling with feelings that you cannot shake, an important piece may still be missing from the puzzle of what has happened to you. It is possible that you were involved with someone with anti-social, sociopathic, or narcissistic characteristics, or even a high-level personality disorder. Betrayed trust with a person like this may strike you particularly hard and even call your understanding of human nature into question.

If you are still feeling alienated, perplexed about the past and the depth and duration of your pain, please educate yourself about these disorders. Because there are many informative sources in print and online, I have not focused specifically on the subject in this book.[1] Yet, I want to call your attention to this possibility and encourage you to learn more, as it may help to fill in the remaining blanks for you.

People with these traits, in subconscious ways they may not recognize, routinely disregard the rights and feelings of others, with little or no conscience or remorse for the pain they cause. It can help to make sense of your own pain to recognize that the subtle abuse these individuals inflict on those who bond with them infiltrates deep in the psyche in a way that most people find difficult or impossible to understand.

There is a level of isolation and confusion that can continue even after you are long free of such a person. Because the experience of true pathology is so outside the realm of what most people experience in normal relationships, even very bad relationships, you sense no one will believe the enormity of what has happened to you. If you cringe and your heart sinks every time you hear someone say, "we've all been there"—you know intuitively that it is not true, but don't understand why—you may be dealing with the aftermath of such a relationship.

If this is the case, you likely feel very alone, but you are far from alone. As you do your research, you will discover legions of women, and some men, who know and understand what you are going through. Please educate yourself and do not hesitate to reach out for help. The validation and support will strengthen you in your quest to recover your heart and soul and to reclaim your precious life.

Endnotes

Chapter 1: On the Way to the Altar

[1] I have used a pseudonym in the narrative portions of the book for the man who was involved in my own experience of betrayal. But I use the real name of my late husband, Dennis. No, his full name was not Dennis Dennis. Throughout our marriage, I had been using my own surname, but as Dennis neared death, we decided I would use his name as my last to honor his memory.

[2] G. I. Gurdjieff was an influential spiritual teacher of the early to mid-20th century who taught that most humans live their lives in a state of hypnotic "waking sleep," but that it is possible to transcend to a higher state of consciousness and achieve full human potential. Gurdjieff developed a method for doing so, calling his discipline "The Work." He also described his teaching as *esoteric Christianity*. Work on oneself takes place in ordinary life and is also known as "The Fourth Way."

Chapter 2: Entering the Land of Betrayal

[1] Gerard May, *The Dark Night of the Soul: A Psychiatrist Explores the Connection Between Darkness and Spiritual Growth* (New York: Harper One, 2004), 133.

[2] Jeanette Winterson, *Why Be Happy When You Could Be Normal?*, (New York: Grove Press, 2011), 9.

[3] Ibid., 8.

[4] Jerry Sittser, *A Grace Disguised* (Grand Rapids, MI: Zondervan, 1995).

Chapter 3: When Trust Shatters

[1] Hillman, "Betrayal Part 2 (of 3)." *Black Sun Journal* (March, 2002). http://www.blacksunjournal.com/psychology/21_betrayal-part-2-of-3_2002.html

[2] John Amodeo, *Love & Betrayal: Broken Trust in Intimate Relationships* (New York: Ballantine Books, 1994), 16.

[3] "Betrayal at any stage of the socio-developmental cycle results in extreme bio-psychosocial distress far beyond the event itself.... Planful problem-solving, coping strategies often become non-viable, resulting in activation of primitive biologically based, amygdala-driven coping mechanisms that are often long-term maladaptive." Alan Hensley, "Betrayal Trauma: Insidious Purveyor of PTSD," *Return to Equilibrium: The Proceedings of the 7th Rocky Mountain Region Disaster Mental Health Conference,* ed. George W. Doherty (Laramie, WY: Rocky Mountain Region Disaster Mental Health Institute, 2009), 149-170.

[4] George Eliot, *Romola* (New York: John W. Lovell, 1901).

[5] John Milton, *Paradise Lost and Paradise Regained* (New York: Penguin Books, 1968), Book III, Lines 682-684, 118.

[6] Susan Piver, *The Wisdom of a Broken Heart* (New York: Free Press, 2012), 80.

[7] James Hillman, "Betrayal Part 3 (of 3)," *Black Sun Journal* (April, 2002).

[8] Narcissism is the individual and collective diagnosis of our times, one that is becoming overused, often to point a finger at anyone we do not like. Still, this personality style deserves consideration in the context of betrayal. The psychological manipulations that are a hallmark of someone with sociopathic or extreme narcissistic tendencies or a personality disorder are often cited as a major cause of the emotional damage of betrayal.

We all have narcissistic parts of ourselves, places of wounding where our early needs for love, affection, attention, and mirroring were neglected. It helps to picture narcissistic traits on a continuum from normal and mild to sociopathic and destructive. In a young child, a deep early wound to one's sense of self-worth causes unbearable pain and shame. For an extreme narcissist, fending off this pain by passing it on to others has become a way of life.

Unfortunately, except for the most obvious, self-centered, grandiose types, narcissists can be difficult to detect. They often come across as more charming, caring and compassionate than most. But the truth is, they cannot help relating to people as objects and using them for their purposes. It is beyond the scope of this book to explore this subject specifically. If you suspect you have been or are in relationship with a destructive narcissist, you can find websites, Facebook groups, videos, blogs, books and articles that abound on the subject of this disorder. For more information, you can find posts on the subject plus links to helpful sites at www.sandraleedennis.com.

The best resources for learning about these disorders are by people who have lived through this experience. Here are a few to start with: *Psychopath Free* by Peace, *People of the Lie* by Scott Peck, *The Sociopath Next Door* by Martha Stout, *Without Conscience* by Robert Hare, and *Stalking the Soul* by Marie-France Hirigoyen. An often-quoted, popular book full of frequently-asked questions on the subject and written by a self-avowed narcissist is *Malignant Self-Love* by Sam Vaknin. Books written by psychotherapists using case studies describing narcissism include: *Freeing Yourself from the Narcissist in Your Life* by Linda Martinez-Lewi, *Why is it Always About You?* by Sandy Hotchkiss, and *Disarming the Narcissist* by Wendy T. Behary, which offers a cognitive approach.

[9] Spiritual teacher A. H. Almaas discusses what happens when we are overtaken by primal survival instincts. "The animal drives for shelter, survival, pleasure, and sex… can instantly become inhumanly brutal…When our survival or objects of desire are threatened, we can lose all heart and rationality, and become so primitive, cruel and insensitive that it would be difficult to find such behavior in the animal kingdom." A. H. Almaas, *The Inner Journey Home* (Boston, MA: Shambhala, 2004), 142.

[10] Piver, 80.

[11] Diane Cousineau Brutsche, "Betrayal of the Self, Self-Betrayal, and the Leap of Trust: The Book of Job, a Tale of Individuation," in *Trust and Betrayal: Dawnings of Consciousness,* ed. Isabelle Meier, Stacy Wirth, and John Hill (New Orleans, LA: Spring Journal Books, 2011),

[12] Aldo Cartotenuto, *To Love, To Betray* (Wilmette: IL, 1996), 86.

[13] Michael Fox, *The Emotional Rape Syndrome* (Tucson, AZ: Tucson Publishing, 2001), 2.

[14] Hillman, quoting Jean Genet, according to Sartre. "Betrayal Part 2 (of 3)."

15 Therapists who are inclined to support rationalizations and distortions in their charming, "victimized" male clients without ever meeting their partners or considering the impact of betrayal, please take note: "If you are a clinician: survey your caseload, you may be surprised to realize how many people have arrived at your office to process the existential horror (as well as the post-traumatic response) that follows an encounter with either transitory or characterological sociopathy, victimized by a large or small volitional act of evil that has called their very understanding of humanity into question. They are often confused, in a state of horrified paralysis, mystified, enraged, numb, bewildered. For some it generates a special spiritual crisis, an existential shock." Martha Crawford, LCSW, "Deliver Us: Thoughts on Evil and Psychotherapy," http://whatashrinkthinks. com/2012/02/06/deliver-us-thoughts-on-evil-and-psychotherapy.

Chapter 4: Falling Apart

1 Donald Kalsched, *The Inner World of Trauma: Archetypal Defenses of the Personal Spirit* (New York: Routledge, 1996), 1.

2 See Foreword by Stephen Cope in David Emerson and Elizabeth Hopper, *Overcoming Trauma through Yoga* (Berkeley, CA: North Atlantic Books, 2011), xiii.

3 Natural and technological disasters, criminal violence, rape, child abuse, and domestic violence name some of the most obvious external causes. Esther Giller, "What is Psychological Trauma?" Sidran Institute, 1999, http://www.sidran.org/ sub.cfm?contentID=88&sectionid=4.

4 The impact depends to some degree on the resilience of the affected person. Though everyone has a breaking point, a very small minority of people appear relatively invulnerable to extreme events. Judith Herman, *Trauma and Recovery* (New York: Basic Books) 57.

5 See Onno van der Hart, Ellert R. S. Nijenhuis, and Kathy Steele. *The Haunted Self: Structural Dissociation and the Treatment of Chronic Traumatization* (New York: W. W. Norton, 2006), 24, and Robert C. Scaer, *The Body Bears the Burden*, (New York: Hawthorne Press, 2001), *xx*.

6 Herman. *Trauma and Recovery*, 52.

7 See Helen E. Fisher, et al., "Reward, Addiction and Emotion Regulation Systems Associated with Rejection in Love," *Journal of Neurophysiology*, July 2010.

8 Diane Cousineau Brutsche, "Betrayal of the Self, Self-Betrayal, and the Leap of Trust: The Book of Job, a Tale of Individuation," in *Trust and Betrayal: Dawnings of Consciousness*, ed. Isabelle Meier, Stacy Wirth, and John Hill (New Orleans, LA: Spring Journal Books, 2011), 24.

9 Ginette Paris, *Heartbreak: Recovering from Lost Love and Mourning* (Minneapolis, MN: Mill City Press, 2011), xviii.

10 Herman, *Trauma and Recovery*, 55.

11 Ibid., 36.

12 Ibid., 55.

13 Sandra Ingerman, *Soul Retrieval: Mending the Fragmented Self* (New York: Harper Collins, 1991), 11.

[14] Christa Mackinnon, *Shamanism and Spirituality in Therapeutic Practice*, (London: Singing Dragon), 2012.

[15] Pema Chodron, *The Places that Scare You: A Guide to Fearlessness in Difficult Times* (Boston: Shambhala, 2001), 10.

[16] For a helpful discussion on various uses of "ego," see Deborah Bowman, "Slang, Freud and Buddhist Psychology: Clarifying the Term 'Ego' in Popular, Psychodynamic and Spiritual Contexts," http://www.luminousbuddha.com/lb/Articles/Entries/2011/11/5_Slang,_Freud_and_Buddhist_Psychology.html.

[17] Donald Winnicott, "Fear of Breakdown," *International Review of Psycho-Analysis*, 1 (1974), 103-107. Winnicott believed panic was a defense against this unbearable distress. He used the impulse to suicide to describe the inexpressible angst of the infantile psyche left "in the dark" without the container of the mother to help modulate overwhelming emotion. Discussed in more detail by Mark Epstein in *The Trauma of Everyday Life* (New York: Penguin Books, 2013), 30.

[18] Mark Epstein, MD, *Thoughts without a Thinker* (Cambridge: Basic Books, 1995), 210-211.

[19] Hillman, "Betrayal, Part 3 (of 3)."

[20] James Finley, audiotape, "Transforming Trauma," 2011, http://contemplativeway.org/books/freerecordings.html.

Chapter 5: A Spiritual Crisis

[1] Eliot, *Romola*.

[2] Steven Foster and Meredith Little, *The Book of the Vision Quest: Personal Transformation in the Wilderness* (New York: Fireside, 1992), 30.

Chapter 6: The Subtle-Body Connection

[1] Robert Romanyshyn, *The Soul in Grief: Love, Death, and Transformation* (Berkeley, CA: North Atlantic Books, 1999), 7.

[2] Ken Wilber and Grace Treya, *Grace and Grit* (Boston: Shambhala, 1991), 396.

[3] Walt Whitman, *Leaves of Grass,* from "Out of the Cradle Endlessly Rocking" (New York: Modern Library, n.d.).

[4] Many birds mate for life, including albatross, crows, ravens, macaws, sea eagles, doves, ospreys, hawks, bald eagles, cranes, swans, condors, vultures, and owls. When a mate dies or is killed, the other bird grieves, and some may even grieve themselves to death. "Do Birds Mate for Life?" by Melissa Mayntz. See: http://birding.about.com/od/birdingbasics/a/mateforlife.htm.

Stories about birds grieving the loss of their mates are mainly anecdotal. For several accounts, see http://www.peopleforanimalsindia.org/articles-by-maneka-gandhi/158-birds-too-mourn-when-their-loved-ones-die.html.

[5] To be haunted, according to the Oxford English Dictionary, is to be "much visited by spirits, imaginary beings, etc." The authors of *The Haunted Self* use this definition in their conceptualization of the dissociative after-effects of severe trauma. They show that trauma survivors experience shadowy "others" in their internal world, but the authors take pains in their discussion to avoid concretizing these spirits into persons or personalities. Primarily, they show how the traumatized psyche splits into an "apparently normal" persona that avoids reminders of the trauma at all costs,

and the hypervigilant, threatened part that is immersed in the trauma as if it was still happening. Onno van der Hart, Ellert R. S. Nijenhuis, and Kathy Steele, *The Haunted Self: Structural Dissociation and the Treatment of Chronic Traumatization* (New York: W. W. Norton, 2006).

6 Mary Oliver, "Wild Geese," in *Dream Work* (New York: Atlantic Monthly Press, 1986).

7 For an overview of descriptions of the subtle body in psychological literature, see Sandra Lee Dennis, *Embrace of the Daimon* (York Beach, Maine: Nicholas-Hayes, 2001), 19-38.

8 Cyndi Dale and Richard Wehrman, *The Subtle Body: An Encyclopedia of Your Energetic Anatomy* (Boulder, CO: Sounds True, 2009).

9 G. R. S. Mead, *The Doctrine of the Subtle Body in the Western Tradition* (London: Solos Press, 1919), 71 (quotes Synesius, a neo-Platonist from the first century AD, in his discussion of the ancient roots of the concept of the subtle body).

10 Henry Corbin, "*Mundus Imaginalis* or the Imaginary and the Imaginal," *Spring*, (1972), 9.

11 C. G. Jung, "Psychology and Alchemy," *The Collected Works of C. G. Jung*, vol. 12, ed. Gerhard Adler et al., trans. R. F. Hull, Bollingen Series No. 20. (Princeton, NJ: Princeton University Press, 1968), par. 400.

12 Nathan Schwartz-Salant, *On the Subtle Body Concept in Clinical Practice* (San Francisco CA: San Francisco Jung Institute, n.d.), audiotape.

13 Richard Tarnas, *The Passion of the Western Mind* (New York: Ballantine, 1991), 441-442.

14 We take it for granted, but women have only had the right to vote since 1920, been guaranteed equal pay and employment opportunities since the 1960s, and had the right to make decisions about their own body (abortion rights) since the 1970s. See http://www.thefreelibrary.com/A+striking+disconnect%3A+marital+rape+law's+failure+to+ keep+up+with...-a0295551332.

15 Fortunately for us, Eastern modalities of self-knowledge and healing—such as yoga, acupuncture, shiatsu, and the Hindu chakra system—have recognized the existence of subtle planes for thousands of years. That knowledge is now readily accessible and growing in the mainstream.

Chapter 7: Sex & Erotic Entanglement

1 Rainer Maria Rilke, *The Duino Elegies*, trans. C. F. MacIntyre (Berkeley, CA: University of California Press, 1968).

2 That stimulus might even be a fantasy, a pornographic image, or whatever fetish turns you on, as well as another person. When something gives us pleasure, we, like Pavlov's dog, become conditioned to associate the stimulus with the reward.

3 The Eucharist is the Christian rite of Holy Communion.

4 Cynthia Bourgeault, *The Meaning of Mary Magdalene* (Boston: Shambhala, 2010), 145. The quote continues: "[the primary function of sexual love may be] (my brackets) a more subtle exchange of substances that…possess a subtle materiality that is nourished not only by the partners' faithful love but by the actual commingling of their substances during sexual intercourse, carried out primarily by the exchange of seminal fluids."

[5] When we participate in these mysteries, we enter compelling but dangerous territory. The pleasures of connection can take us into blissful states of consciousness, what the Buddhists call the realm of the gods, and Jungian thought refers to as partial *coniunctios* (unions). The danger of opening to such expansive experiences at the sacred borderlands of consciousness lies in inflation—we are tempted to identify with the experiences of delight, beauty, and surrender, as if this is who we are. Touching into this much light eventually calls forth deeper levels of the unconscious shadow. Only then is our grandiosity revealed, and we suffer to see how quickly and easily we fall from ecstasy into the agonies of the hell realm.

[6] New research on "mirror neurons" suggests how partners become more alike with time. See "Mirror Neurons: Resonant Circuitry in Brain," January 18, 2010, http:// physiology-physics.blogspot.com/2010/01/mirror-neurons-resonant-circuitry-in. html

[7] Bourgeault, *The Meaning of Mary Magdalene*, 152.

[8] Quoted in Barbara Bradley Hagerty, "Can Positive Thoughts Help Heal Another Person?" May 21, 2009, http://www.dailygood.org/more.php?n=5017.

[9] "IONS' Pioneering Work on 'Distant Healing' Suggests Further Study Warranted," http://www.noetic.org/about/case-studies/love-study/.

[10] Jung was so taken with the *Rosarium* images that he wrote a 430-page volume, *Mysterium Coniunctionis,* on the mystery of the sacred marriage. This text began with his well-known statement: "The factors which come together in the *coniunctio* are conceived as opposites, either confronting one another in enmity or attracting one another in love"—an apt description of most intimate relationships. Jung, *Collected Works,* vol. 14, par. 1.

[11] Admittedly, many modern practicing and former Catholics consider this a regressive viewpoint, rooted in patriarchal prejudice. The related phrases in the Bible "What God has joined together, let no man tear asunder" (Mark 10:9) and "The two shall become one flesh" (Mark 10:8) sound arcane and out of touch today, especially considering the fifty-percent divorce rate. However, despite my agreement that this view can be dogmatic, these two biblical phrases resonate with my lived experience of subtle-body marriage bonds. King James version.

Chapter 8: Desecration

[1] Scaer, *The Body Bears the Burden*, 194.

Chapter 9: Coping with Cultural Blindness

[1] The phrase "blaming the victim" was coined in the early seventies and adopted by advocates for crime victims, especially rape victims, who were held responsible for their victimization. In 1947, Theodor Adorno defined what would be later called "blaming the victim" as "one of the most sinister features of the Fascist character." T. W. Adorno, "Wagner, Nietzsche and Hitler," *Kenyon Review,* ix (1) (1947), 158, https://en.wikipedia.org/wiki/Victim_blaming.

[2] Aldo Carotenuto, *To Love, to Betray* (Wilmette, IL: Chiron, 1996), 95.

[3] If you or your partner were born before 1960, you came of age before the women's movement brought unconscious sexism into mainstream awareness. It takes a conscious effort to bring these attitudes to awareness and not act out these sexual prejudices.

4 There have been an average of thirty wars going on globally every year in the twentieth century where human beings have killed 200 million people. Since the beginning of recorded history over 14,500 major wars have killed four billion people.   http://filipspagnoli.wordpress.com/stats-on-human-rights/statistics-on-war-conflict/statistics-on-violent-conflict/

5 For a discussion of the possible roots of male violence see Robert Scaer, *The Trauma Spectrum: Hidden Wounds and Human Resiliency*, (New York: W. W. Norton, 2005), 133.

6 In a 2010 report based on data from the ten states with the highest female victim/male offender homicide rates, 94 percent of female victims (1,571 out of 1,669) were murdered by a male they knew. Sixty-five percent (1,017) of female homicide victims were wives or intimate acquaintances of their killers. Sixteen times as many females were murdered by a male they knew (1,571 victims) than were killed by male strangers (98 victims). Violence Policy Center, *When Men Murder Women: An Analysis of 2010 Homicide Data* (Washington, DC, September 2012).

Another study reports that while it is estimated that less than 50 percent of rapes are reported, three in four women (76 percent) who reported they had been raped and/or physically assaulted since age 18 said that an intimate partner (current or former husband, cohabiting partner, or date) committed the assault. U.S. Department of Justice, *Prevalence, Incidence, and Consequences of Violence Against Women: Findings from the National Violence Against Women Survey*, November 1998.

7 Sheri Stritof and Bob Stritof, "Is marital rape a crime?" *About.com Marriage*, http://marriage.about.com/cs/maritalrape/f/maritalrape10.htm.

8 Domestic violence injuries outnumber car accidents, muggings, and rapes combined. The 1994 Violence Against Women Act was one of the first federal programs that outlined programs to prevent violence against women, Kathleen Szeluga, "A History of Domestic Violence Law and Legislation," *Suite 101*, http://suite101.com/article/a-history-of-domestic-violence-law-and-legislation-a401353.

Before this time, domestic violence was routinely treated as "family squabbles" and transferred to family court where no criminal charges could be pressed. Assault was downplayed and treated with indifference by the criminal justice system. Battered women were considered "masochistic." The first law making it illegal for men to rape their wives was not passed until 1976. See http://www.thefreelibrary.com/A+striking3A+marital+rape+law's+failure+to+keep+up+with...-a0295551332.

9 We might recall that it was not that long ago when wife beating was not only legal, but also considered useful and necessary as long as the husband could prove that "she deserved it." The stereotype that the woman deserves to be mistreated still holds sway from the days when it was legal for a husband to kill his spouse, as long as he could prove he had "just cause." The most likely time for a man to become physically violent is at the point of abandonment—when the woman leaves him or is found with another man.

10 Herman, *Trauma and Recovery*, 7-8.

11 Veronica Goodchild, *Songlines of the Soul: Pathways to a New Vision for a New Century*, (Lakeworth, FL: Nicolas-Hayes, 2012), 6.

Chapter 10: The Weight of Projection

1 Mark Twain, *Mark Twain's Notebooks, 1898*. http://www.twainquotes.com/Life.html

²   Thomas Keating, *Invitation to Love* (New York: Continuum, 1999), 88.

³   Splitting and projection are the psychological dynamics that justify genocide, torture, and war.

⁴   C. G. Jung, *Nietzsche's Zarathustra: Notes of the Seminar Given in 1934-1939*, vol. 1, ed. J. L. Jarrett (Princeton, NJ: Princeton University Press, 1988), 1, 495.

⁵   This *Huffington Post* excerpt from an article by Rabbi Moredecai Finley that discusses divorce describes how easily we take on projections, often in the form of "toxic emotional dumps." Rabbi Mordecai Finley, "The Toxic Dump," *The Huffington Post*, November 8, 2012, http://www.huffingtonpost.com/rabbi-mordecai-finley/the-toxic-dump_b_778922.html.

Chapter 11: Facing the Trauma

¹   Susan Anderson, *Journey from Abandonment to Healing* (Berkeley, CA: Berkeley Trade, 2000).

²   See J. Douglas Bremmer. "Traumatic Stress: Effects on the Brain," *Dialogues in Clinical Neuroscience* (December 2006) 8(4), 445-461. http://www.ncbi.nlm.nih.gov/pmc/articles/PMC3181836/

³   Ethan Kross et al., "Social Rejection Shares Somatosensory Representations with Physical Pain," *Proceedings of the National Academy of Sciences* (2011), 108(15), 6270-6275. For instance, scientists from the University of Michigan made network news recently with a study published originally in the *Proceedings of the National Academy of Sciences*. These researchers reported that significant interpersonal rejection (loss of love) and physical pain share a common neuro-circuitry. While you cannot ethically recreate torture in the laboratory, they found that a hot coffee burn and looking at a picture of an abandoning former partner lit up the same center in the brain—the secondary somatosensory cortex and the dorsal insula—producing similar sensations.

⁴   Paris, *Heartbreak*, 121. Her full quote: "Dr. Rich, the cardiologist from the Mayo clinic who educated the public about this syndrome has this to say: 'apical ballooning syndrome (ABS) is a unique reversible cardiomyopathy that is frequently precipitated by a stressful event, and has a clinical presentation that is indistinguishable from a myocardial infarction. [...] The term *Broken Heart Syndrome* may not be the best name for this syndrome, as one typically thinks of a broken heart as something that occurs after receiving a Dear John letter, rather than something that happens after seeing a loaded .44 magnum shoved in one's face. Nonetheless, this terminology has resulted in lots of publicity, and the knowledge of this new syndrome consequently has been rapidly and widely disseminated. And that widespread awareness is good. The symptoms of BHS are so severe that it is nearly inconceivable that anyone who develops it will fail to seek medical help [...].'" She references, for further information, http://www.hopkinsmedicine.org/asc/.

⁵   Fisher, *Journal of Neurophysiology*, July 2010. See also: Daniel G. Amen, MD. *The Brain in Love* (New York: Three Rivers Press, 2007), 68. Dr. Amen asserts, "When we love someone, they come to live in the emotional or limbic centers of our brain. They actually occupy nerve-cell pathways and physically live in the neurons and synapses of the brain. When we lose someone through a breakup our brain gets disoriented. Since the person lives in neural memory connectors, we expect to see them, hear them, feel them and touch them. When we cannot touch or talk to them

as we usually do, the brain centers where they live become inflamed looking for them."

6 For elaboration of the idea that in trauma, spiritual energies are recruited for defensive purposes in a "self-care system," see: Donald Kalsched, *Trauma and the Soul: A Psycho-spiritual Approach to Human Development and Its Interruption* (London: Routledge, 2013).

7 Anderson, *Journey from Abandonment to Healing*, 87.

8 Helen Fisher, "Lost Love: The Nature of Romantic Rejection," in *Cut Loose*, ed. Nan Bauer-Maglin (New Brunswick, NJ: Rutgers University Press, 2006), and Helen Fisher, *Why We Love* (New York: Henry Holt, 2004).

9 Patrick J. Carnes, *The Betrayal Bond* (Deer Beach, FL: Health Communications, 1997).

10 Fear-based bonds—commonly recognized in domestic violence—can sneak up on anyone in an ongoing relationship. Through minor, everyday insults, the alternating of warmth and coldness gradually wears away at a person's self-worth and confidence. The longer the abuser intersperses periods of warmth and affection with disrespect, disparaging, or withdrawal, the stronger the fearful attachment grows. In order not to threaten this source of "protection," you start to find it easier to turn a blind eye to the abuse and rationalize inexcusable behaviors.

11 See Lundy Bancroft's illuminating discussion of the many different styles abusive men adopt. You may be surprised to learn that the most insidious forms of abuse of power are the most subtle, and the most difficult men to treat are those who appear to be the most "sensitive," vulnerable, or wounded. These are often men who couch their manipulations and systematic dehumanizing in the language of New Age or pop psychology. They love to use the language of feelings, discussing their issues and weakness and to "work on the relationship." The closer they get to you, the more vulnerable you become, and the more apt they are to use their knowledge of your vulnerabilities to control or hurt you. Lundy Bancroft, *Why Does He Do That: Inside the Minds of Angry and Controlling Men* (New York: Berkeley Books, 2002).

12 Helen Fisher, "Lust, Attraction, Attachment: Biology and Evolution of the Three Primary Emotion Systems for Mating, Reproduction, and Parenting," *Journal of Sex Education and Therapy* (2000), 25(1), 99.

13 My strategies included journaling, affirmations, singing, visualizations, chanting, dancing, taking lessons (golf and drumming), attending classes (French and opera), biking and hiking, yoga, volunteer counseling, and more. In addition, I took to consulting multiple healers—spiritual directors, priests, ministers, and numerous psychics—astrologers, tarot readers, intuitives—for suggestions and help; I attended grief rituals, tried Eye Movement Desensitization and Reprocessing (EMDR) sessions, trauma therapy (Somatic Experiencing and Core Energetics), as well as conventional therapy, and I continued acupuncture, pressure-point and Reiki healing. I also tried aromatherapy, homeopathic and flower essence remedies, and depression-fighting supplements such as 5-HTP and St. John's wort.

I participated in two different psycho-spiritual groups each month. For more than two years, I practiced forgiveness and loving-kindness meditations daily, attended a weekly *Course in Miracles* group, and worked my way twice through the 365 daily exercises in that book. I engaged in various other psychological exercises, including Gestalt dialog, squares and polarities, owning my projections. I attended several five-to-fifteen-day meditation and prayer retreats and a wilderness quest. I even briefly tried online dating. I traveled and left town for extended periods to visit friends. You see why it took so much to give up my belief I could heal myself!

[14] The healing of trauma is a skill set many therapists do not have. Seek out someone specifically trained to treat trauma and familiar with the added complications of betrayal—particularly the creeping, corrosive impact it has on the capacity to trust and to feel safe in close connection. The classic approach to treatment is for the traumatized person to retell the trauma story in an atmosphere of safety. Replaying the trauma eventually desensitizes you to the shock. Recent research shows that trauma responds best to a combination of physical engagement, such as movement and body-sensation focus, and psychological attention, as well as story retelling. Physical touch is also recommended as it communicates safety to the brain stem, where the traumatic imprints have the greatest hold and resonate with injuries from earlier in life. You might start your search with Peter Levine's Somatic Experiencing website: http://www.traumahealing.com/somatic-experiencing/practitioner-directory.html

Chapter 12: An Archeological Dig into the Past

[1] The dominant theoretical approach today in understanding how we form relationship ties is attachment theory. British psychiatrist John Bowlby formulated attachment theory in the 1960s and 1970s. His work grew out of object relations theory (Otto Rank, Ronald Fairbairn, Melanie Klein, Donald Winnicott) and supports the view that our earliest relationship patterns determine our sense of self and our typical ways of relating to others. According to attachment theory, infants seek proximity to their caretaker in situations of distress in order to survive. The response of those caretakers during the critical learning period of six months to two years of age determines our expectations and style of attachment in future relationships.

[2] Margaret Mahler's separation-individuation theory also grew out of psychodynamic object relations theory. *Dual-unity* is the term that Mahler used to describe the mother/infant imprint in our psyche: "that state of undifferentiation, of fusion with mother, in which the 'I' is not yet differentiated from the 'not-I' and in which inside and outside are only gradually coming to be sensed as different." Internal "objects" (of ourselves and others) are formed by these patterns of our early caretaking environment. Expecting these patterns to recur, we project them into all of our relationships, although these patterns may or may not turn out be accurate representations of the actual, external others. From this perspective, we live our entire egoic lives reenacting our past relationships. Margaret S. Mahler et al., *The Psychological Birth of the Human Infant* (New York: Basic Books, 1975), 44.

[3] Sexual intimacy recapitulates the physical closeness and warmth, the interpenetration of physical and subtle bodies of our first relationship. On one hand, deep sex creates an atmosphere for dissolving ego boundaries that can be ecstatic; but on the other, it threatens to expose our early pain, and undermine our ego self.

[4] Judith Viorst, *Necessary Losses: The Loves, Illusions, Dependencies, and Impossible Expectations That All of Us Have to Give up in Order to Grow* (New York: Simon & Schuster, 1986), 23.

[5] Ibid., 23.

[6] Carotenuto, *To Love, To Betray*, 72.

7 An infant, totally dependent on its mother, registers any minor need that is not immediately fulfilled—hunger, thirst, the desire for contact—as abandonment. In the infant brain, even seemingly minor lapses in care can be felt as traumatic, life-threatening events.

8 This empty yearning may be the core wound of what has been described as our culture of narcissism. See Mark Epstein's classic, *Thoughts Without a Thinker*, (New York: Basic Books, 1995) for a fascinating development of this theme in the context of psychotherapy and meditation.

9 Attachment theory teaches there are two phases in a child's reaction to separation from the mother: protest, then despair. Judith Viorst, in *Necessary Losses* (p. 26) explains: "Take a child under three from his mother to be with strangers. He will scream, he will weep, he will thrash about. He will eagerly, desperately search for his missing mother. He will protest because he has hope, but after a while, when she does not come…and doesn't come…protest will turn to despair, to a state of muted, *low-key yearning that may harbor an unutterable sorrow*" (my italics). Abandoned adults pass through similar stages.

10 Milan Kundera, *Testaments Betrayed* (New York: Harper Perennial, 1996), 263.

11 James Hillman, *Re-visioning Psychology* (New York: Harper & Row, 1975), 47.

12 Jacqueline Wright, "In Love." Jung Society Newsletter Articles in *C. G. Jung Society of Atlanta*, 2006, 6-8, http://www.jungatlanta.com/articles.html.

Chapter 13: The Problem of Pain

1 Chodron, *The Places That Scare You*, 10.

2 Chogyam Trungpa, *The Myth of Freedom* (Boston: Shambhala, 2002), 14.

3 Ibid., 12.

4 Annie Dillard, *Teaching a Stone to Talk* (New York: Harper & Row, 1982), 65.

5 Hillman, "Betrayal Part 2 (of 3)." Hillman builds his case on the prevalence of betrayal in human life and, beyond the personal, in the myths and symbols of the culture.

6 I am indebted to former monastic and contemplative psychotherapist, James Finley for this idea, shared at his Contemplative Prayer retreat, October 25-27, 2013, at Mercy Center, Burlingame.

7 Tara Brach's phrase from *Radical Acceptance: Embracing Your Life with the Heart of a Buddha* (New York: Bantam, 2003).

8 St. John of the Cross, *Dark Night of the Soul*, trans. E. Allison Peers (New York: Image Books, 1959).

9 Jung, "*The Psychology of the Transference*," *The Practice of Psychotherapy*, Collected Works, vol. 16, par. 455.

10 The goal of alchemical operations was "turning lead into gold," which we interpret now as transforming the lead of fixated or attached states of mind to the gold of refined spiritual light. The *nigredo is* the essential first step of transformation, when one is broken down, crushed, and demolished to prepare for renewal. Jung found in medieval alchemy a map of psychological and spiritual development that describes with astounding precision the structure of the ego and the processes it goes through in the growth of consciousness. He devoted three volumes, two-thirds of his writings, and two thousand pages to the study of alchemy.

¹¹ C. G. Jung, "The Relations between the Ego and the Unconscious," *Two Essays on Analytical Psychology*, Collected Works, vol. 7, par 431.

¹² F. Scott Fitzgerald, *The Crack-up* (New York: Charles Scribner's & Sons, 1931).

¹³ In the Christian tradition, they call the searing of attachments *salvation*, being set free from bondage, or being forgiven for our sins. *Sin* in this sense refers to the lack of love that comes when we are imprisoned by belief in our separateness. Gerard May, *The Dark Night of the Soul*, 182.

¹⁴ Heide M. Kolb, "Ariadne and the Minotaur," *Heide Kolb's Blog* (blog), April 11, 2010, http://jungianwork.wordpress.com/2010/04/11/ariadne-and-the-minotaur-lovetrauma-abandonment-a-jungian-perspective/.

¹⁵ Ibid.

¹⁶ The word "attachment" as I use it here, refers to the ways we continually limit and constrict ourselves by believing we are less than we are. Often we mistake attachments as our highest good, since they gratify and enhance our identity, and our sense of what is important and meaningful. But our attachments tie up our goodness—our ability to receive and give love. The things we attach our life force to can be outside us, such as the body, money, job, fame, health, appearance, creative success, and, of course, relationships. However, we form the most persistent and pernicious attachments to the passing phenomena of our inner life, also considered "things" in the world of spirit: thoughts, feelings, moods, dreams, understandings, fantasies, compulsive behaviors, sensations (such as pleasure and pain), beliefs, energetic experiences, opinions, images, and, most important, the ever-present ego sense of self. All the attachments subtly enhance our ego self and limit our capacity to love and be free.

Chapter 14: Resentment Is the Altar Where We Go to Pray

¹ Paris, *Heartbreak*, 132.

² Ibid., 104.

³ Herman, *Trauma and Recovery*, 189.

⁴ Franciscan priest and men's group leader Richard Rohr supports my observations: "The ego moves forward by contraction, self-protection, and refusal. Sad to say, contraction gives you focus, purpose, direction,...superiority and a strange kind of security...Contraction allows you to eliminate another person, write them off, exclude them, torture them, at least in your mind, and somehow expel them. This immediately gives you a sense of being in control. Hatred or mean-spiritedness gives one a superior sense of identity, even if it is totally untrue...Hatred is a false way of taking away the doubt and free-floating anxiety that comes with the fragility of human existence..." Richard Rohr, *A Lever and a Place to Stand* (Mahwah, NJ: Hidden Spring, 2011), 69-70.

Chapter 15: Conscience and the Pilgrimage of the Heart

¹ Scientists are making great strides in establishing the importance and complexity of the heart. Researchers at the HeartMath Institute have shown that the heart has an intricate and far-reaching intelligence. The heart is a powerful sensory organ with its own internal nervous system that registers, learns and remembers independent of the brain. Significantly, the heart influences the brain more than the other way

around. The heart's rhythm affects the brain and the entire body neurologically, biochemically, biophysically, and energetically. See Institute of HeartMath, www. heartmath.org

2 Michael Green, *Celtic Blessings Calendar 2007* (Portland, OR: Amber Lotus, 2007).

3 Chodron, *The Places that Scare You*, 4.

4 Bourgeault, *The Wisdom Way of Knowing*, 34.

5 Some traditions use a mantra, sacred word, or calling on the name of God as a method of focusing the mind, and quieting the surface heart to learn to listen to the messages of the subtle heart. The Desert Fathers of the fifth century, whose writings can be found in the *Philokalia*, recommended aligning the breath with the heart while calling on the name of God, to awaken to the constant presence of God in the heart. The fourteenth-century *Cloud of Unknowing* recommends a similar heart-centered practice.

6 Valentin Tomburg, *Meditations on the Tarot: A Journey into Christian Hermeticism*, trans. Robert Powell (New York: Tarcher, 1985).

7 Liz Greene, *Saturn: A New Look at an Old Devil* (New York: Samuel Weiser, 1976), 11.

8 Psalms 44:19, King James version.

9 "Dweller on the threshold," *Wikipedia*, http://en.wikipedia.org/wiki/Dweller_on_the_threshold.

10 "It was in solitude that they could live, i.e., develop spiritual temperature, breathe spiritual air, quench their spiritual thirst, and satisfy their spiritual hunger." Valentin Tomburg, *Meditations on the Tarot: A Journey into Christian Hermeticism*, trans. Robert Powell (New York: Tarcher, 1985), 307-308.

11 François Fénelon, *The Spiritual Letters of Archbishop Fenelon: Letters to Women*, trans. H. L. Sidney Lear (New York: Longmans, Green, 1921), 29.

Chapter 16: Grieving and the Veils of the Heart

1 Francis Weller, *Entering the Healing Ground* (Santa Rosa, CA: WisdomBridge Press, 2011). Weller regularly conducts community grief rituals to encourage the ongoing practice of deepening into soul life through acknowledging one's grief.

2 Cynthia Bourgeault, *The Wisdom Jesus* (Boston: Shambhala, 2008), 43.

3 Weller, *Entering the Healing Ground*, 6.

4 Paris, *Heartbreak*, 60.

5 Romanyshyn, *The Soul in Grief*, 16.

6 Oscar Wilde, *De Profundis: The Ballad of Reading Gaol and Other Writings* (Hertfordshire, UK: Wordsworth Classics, 1999), 64-66.

7 While grieving holds a key to deep currents of living, I do not want to romanticize grief. Robert Romanyshyn, describes the painfully slow work of mourning, how this painful necessity can feel like "a continual tearing at an open wound." We may question our motives, accuse ourselves of indulgence, or refuse to "let go" of resisting life. When we find ourselves frozen by unbidden memories and stuck in the past, it is almost as if they provide us with a refuge from the dissolving that comes with grieving, rather than a giving in to it. It is difficult to discern the difference. Romanyshyn, *The Soul in Grief*, 20.

[8]   Bourgeault, *The Wisdom Jesus*, 43.

[9]   Helen Luke, *Old Age, Journey into Simplicity* (Great Barrington, MA: Lindisfarne, 2010), 109.

Chapter 17: Surrendering to Grace

[1]   "The Man Watching" by Rainer Maria Rilke, English translation by Robert Bly, http://www.poetry-chaikhana.com/Poets/R/RilkeRainerM/ManWatching/index.html.

[2]   Cynthia Bourgeault, *The Wisdom Way of Knowing* (San Francisco: Jossey-Bass, 2003), 72-73.

[3]   Jerry Sittser, *When God Doesn't Answer Your Prayer* (Grand Rapids, MI: Zondervan, 2003), 19.

[4]   Ibid., 42.

[5]   Paul Brunton, *Meditations for People in Crisis,* eds. Sam Cohen and Leslie Cohen (Burdett, NY: Larson Publications, 1996), 57.

[6]   About this time, I came across Centering Prayer—the contemporary mystical Christian community's answer to Eastern meditation with roots in the medieval works, such as *The Cloud of Unknowing*. The writings of Cynthia Bourgeault and Thomas Keating, who revived this form of prayer, speak the language of psychology, Eastern religion, and modern physics, grounded in Christianity. What they described as prayer of the heart had already been arising spontaneously in my inner world.

[7]   This was not the first time the cross had appeared in my inner life. Many years before, a cross was the central image in a vision I described in *Embrace of the Daimon*. Going into the dark this time, I no longer so much needed the mediating images that occupied me in that work to filter my encounter with the daimonic depths. Instead, I was taken directly into the core of the primal agonies for the spiritualizing, transformative work. For the earlier imagery of the serpent and the cross and the Rose Cross, see Dennis, *Embrace of the Daimon*, 173.

[8]   C. G. Jung, *The Psychology of the Transference* (London: Routledge, 1998), 100.

Chapter 18: The Holy Grail of Forgiveness

[1]   Herman, *Trauma and Recovery,* 189-190.

[2]   Hillman, "Betrayal Part 3 (of 3)."

[3]   Ibid.

[4]   A. H. Almaas explains this natural process of letting go: "You don't let go of anything or anybody by trying to let go. The letting go is a natural process of dropping away when the situation is understood completely. But you never let go. I never experienced myself letting go, never in my life—eventually certain parts start dissolving…and what you're feeling right now becomes the important thing." A. H. Almaas, *Brilliancy: The Essence of Intelligence* (Boston: Shambhala, 2006), 144.

[5]   "And if he trespass against thee seven times in a day, and seven times in a day turn again to thee, *saying, I repent; thou shalt forgive him.*" Luke: 17:4 King James version, Cambridge Edition. (my italics)

[6] Hillman, op. cit. Quoting Jung, Hillman tells us that to carry a "sin," such as betraying another, means we are willing to take responsibility for it ourselves, and not unload it onto others to carry for us.

[7] For a full discussion of "acceptance" and "genuine forgiveness" see Janis Abrahms Spring, *How Can I Forgive You?* (New York: Harper Collins, 2004). Her approach is especially useful if you are working with the person who hurt you to try to heal the relationship. She offers practical, step-by-step advice for the offender, too.

Chapter 19: Finding Your North Star

[1] Whitman, *Leaves of Grass*, from "Song of Myself."

[2] Anne Lamott, "Wisdom of the Ages," *Tribe*, March 30, 2005.

http://womenonly.tribe.net/thread/48115c4b-a0c7-4418-8325-0fc5e8596193

Chapter 20: The Return

[1] Anderson, *Journey from Abandonment to Healing*, 218-219.

[2] Rainier Maria Rilke, Letter Seven (14 May 1904), *Letters to a Young Poet*, trans. Stephen Mitchell (New York: Vintage, 1986).

Note to the Reader

[1] See endnote #8, chapter 3.

Selected References

Aanavi, Michael. 2012. *The Trusting Heart: Addiction, Recovery, and Intergenerational Trauma*. Wilmette, IL: Chiron Publications.

Almaas, A. H. 1998. *The Pearl Beyond Price: Integration of Personality into Being: An Object Relations Approach*. Berkeley, CA: Diamond Books.

———. 2004. *The Inner Journey Home: Soul's Realization of the Unity of Reality*. Boston: Shambhala.

———. 2006. *Brilliancy: The Essence of Intelligence*. Boston: Shambhala.

Amen, Daniel G. 2007. *The Brain in Love*. New York: Three Rivers Press.

Amodeo, John. 1994. *Love & Betrayal: Broken Trust in Intimate Relationships*. New York: Ballantine Books.

Anderson, Susan. 2000. *The Journey from Abandonment to Healing*. New York: Berkley Publishing Group.

Anonymous. (Valentin Tomberg) 1985. *Meditations on the Tarot: A Journey into Christian Hermeticism*. Trans. Robert Powell. New York: Tarcher.

Bancroft, Lundy. 2002. *Why Does He Do That? Inside the Minds of Angry and Controlling Men*. New York: Berkley Books.

Bayda, Ezra. 2002. *Being Zen, Bringing Meditation to Life*. Boston: Shambhala.

Bourgeault, Cynthia. 2001. *Mystical Hope*. Cambridge, MA: Cowley Publications.

———. 2003. *The Wisdom Way of Knowing*. San Francisco: John Wiley & Sons (Jossey-Bass).

———. 2004. *Centering Prayer and Inner Awakening*. Lanham, MD: Cowley Publications.

———. 2008. *The Wisdom Jesus*. Boston: Shambhala.

———. 2010. *The Meaning of Mary Magdalene*. Boston, Shambhala.

Brach, Tara. 2003. *Radical Acceptance: Embracing your Life with the Heart of a Buddha*. New York: Bantam Books.

Brown, Byron. 1999. *Soul Without Shame*. Boston: Shambhala.

Carnes, Patrick J. 1997. *The Betrayal Bond*. Deer Beach, FL: Health Communications.

Carotenuto, Aldo. 1996. *To Love, To Betray: Life as Betrayal*. Wilmette, IL: Chiron.

Chodron, Pema. 1997. *When Things Fall Apart, Heart Advice for Difficult Times*. Boston: Shambhala.

———. 2001. *The Places That Scare You: A Guide to Fearlessness in Difficult Times*. Boston, Shambhala.

———. 2005. *No Time to Lose: A Timely Guide to the Way of the Bodhisattva*. Boston: Shambhala.

Corbin, Henry. 1969. *Creative Imagination in the Sufism of Ibn'Arabi*. Trans. Ralph Manheim. Princeton, NJ: Princeton University Press.

Courtois, Christine A., and Julian D. Ford, eds. 2009. *Treating Complex Traumatic Stress Disorders: An Evidence-Based Guide*. New York: Guilford Press.

Cozolino, Louis. 2002/2012. *The Neuroscience of Psychotherapy*, 2nd ed. New York: W. W. Norton.

Dennis, Sandra Lee. 2001/2013. *Embrace of the Daimon: Healing through the Subtle Energy Body: Jungian Psychology & the Dark Feminine*, 2nd ed. Petaluma, CA: LC Enterprises.

Edinger, Edward F. 1994. *The Mystery of the Coniunctio: Alchemical Image of Individuation*. Toronto: Inner City Books.

Emerson, David, and Elizabeth Hopper. 2011. *Overcoming Trauma through Yoga*. Berkeley, CA: North Atlantic Books.

Epstein, Mark. 1995. *Thoughts without a Thinker: Psychotherapy from a Buddhist Perspective*. New York: Basic Books.

———. 2013. *The Trauma of Everyday Life*. New York: Penguin Books.

Finley, James. 2004. *Christian Meditation: Experiencing the Presence of God*. San Francisco: Harper.

Freyd, Jennifer, and Pamela Birrell. 2013. *Blind to Betrayal*. Hoboken, NJ: John Wiley & Sons.

Hedva, Beth. 1992. *Journey from Betrayal to Trust*. Berkeley, CA: Celestial Arts.

———. 2013. Betrayal, Trust and Forgiveness: A Guide to Emotional Healing and Self-Renewal (3rd edition). Bonners Ferry, ID: Wynword Press.

Helminski, Kabir. 1992. *Living Presence: A Sufi Way to Mindfulness and the Essential Self*. New York: Tarcher/Putnam.

Herman, Judith Lewis. 1992. *Trauma and Recovery*. New York: Basic Books.

Hillman, James. 2001-2002. "Betrayal Parts 1-3." *Black Sun Journal* (December, 2001; March, April 2002). Originally published in *Loose Ends* (Spring Publications, 1975). http://www.blacksunjournal.com/psychology/18_betrayal-part-1-of-3-by-james-hillman_2001.html

Ingerman, Sandra. 1991. *Soul Retrieval: Mending the Fragmented Self*. New York: HarperOne.

Jung, C. G. 1954. *The Collected Works of C. G. Jung*, vol. 7. *Two Essays on Analytical Psychology*. Ed. Gerard Adler, et al., trans. R. F. Hull. Bollingen Series No. 20. Princeton, NJ: Princeton University Press.

———. 1968. *Collected Works of C. G. Jung*, vol. 12. *Psychology and Alchemy*. Princeton, NJ: Princeton University Press.

———. 1970. *Collected Works of C. G. Jung*, vol. 14. *Mysterium Coniunctionis*. Princeton, NJ: Princeton University Press.

———. 1973. *Answer to Job*. Trans. R. F. C. Hull. Princeton, NJ: Bollingen Press.

———. 1988. *Nietzsche's Zarathustra*, vol. 1. Ed. J. L. Jarrett. Princeton, NJ: Princeton University Press.

———1998. *Collected Works of C. G. Jung*, vol. 16. *The Practice of Psychotherapy*. Princeton, NJ: Princeton University Press.

———. 1998. *The Psychology of the Transference*. London: Routledge.

Kalsched, Donald. 1996. *The Inner World of Trauma: Archetypal Defences of the Personal Spirit*. London: Routledge.

————. 2013. *Trauma and the Soul: A Psycho-spiritual Approach to Human Development and Its Interruption.* London: Routledge.

Karr-Morse, Robin. 2012. *Scared Sick: The Role of Childhood Trauma in Adult Disease.* With Meredith S. Wiley. New York: Basic Books.

Keating, Thomas. 1994. *Intimacy with God.* New York: Crossroad.

————. 1999. *Invitation to Love.* New York: Continuum.

————. 2009. *Divine Therapy and Addiction.* New York: Lantern Books.

Kolb, Heide M. 2010. "Ariadne & the Minotaur—Love, Trauma & Abandonment —A Jungian Perspective." *Heidekolb's Blog* (blog). See: http://jungianwork .wordpress.com/2010/04/11/ariadne-and-the-minotaur-lovetrauma-abandonment-a-jungian-perspective/

Kornfield, Jack. 1993. *A Path with Heart: A Guide through the Perils and Promises of Spiritual Life.* New York: Bantam Books.

Laird, Martin. 2006. *Into the Silent Land: A Guide to the Christian Practice of Contemplation.* New York: Oxford University Press.

Lesser, Elizabeth. 2004. *Broken Open: How Difficult Times Can Help Us Grow.* New York: Villard.

Levine, Stephen. 2005. *Unattended Sorrow: Recovering from Loss and Reviving the Heart.* Emmaus, PA: Rodale.

Lewis, C. S. 1940/2006. *The Problem of Pain.* New York: Harper Collins.

Lewis, Thomas, Fari Amini, and Richard Lannon. 2000. *A General Theory of Love.* New York: Random House.

Luke, Helen M. 2010. *Old Age: Journey into Simplicity.* Barrington, MA: Lindisfarne Books.

Mackinnon, Christa. 2012. *Shamanism and Spirituality in Therapeutic Practice.* London: Singing Dragon.

Marlan, Stanton. 2005. *The Black Sun: The Alchemy and Art of Darkness.* College Station, TX: Texas A&M University Press.

May, Gerald G. 2004. *The Dark Night of the Soul.* San Francisco, CA: HarperSanFrancisco.

McGilchrist, Iain. 2009. *The Master and his Emissary.* New Haven, CT: Yale University Press.

Mead, G. R. S. 1919. *The Doctrine of the Subtle Body in the Western Tradition.* London: Solos Press.

Meier, Isabelle, Stacy Wirth, and John Hill, eds. 2010. *Trust and Betrayal: Dawnings of Consciousness.* Jungian Odyssey Series, Vol. III. New Orleans, LA: Spring Journal Books.

Milton, John. 1968. *Paradise Lost and Paradise Regained.* New York: Penguin Books.

Mindell, Arnold. 1982. *Dreambody.* Boston: Sigo Press.

Paris, Ginette. 2012. *Heartbreak: New Approaches to Healing.* Minneapolis, MN: Mill City Press.

Pennington, M. Basil. 1982. *Centering Prayer.* New York: Image Books.

Piver, Susan. 2010. *The Wisdom of a Broken Heart.* New York: Free Press.

Rohr, Richard. 2011. *A Lever and a Place to Stand.* Mahwah, NJ: Hidden Spring.

Romanyshyn, Robert. 1999. *The Soul in Grief: Love, Death and Transformation.* Berkeley, CA: Frog Limited.

Sardello, Robert. 2006. *Silence: The Mystery of Wholeness.* Berkeley, CA: Goldenstone Press.

Scaer, Robert C. 2001. *The Body Bears the Burden: Trauma, Dissociation, and Disease.* New York: Haworth Medical Press.

———. 2005. *The Trauma Spectrum: Hidden Wounds and Human Resiliency,* New York: W. W. Norton.

Schore, Allan N. 2012. *The Science of the Art of Psychotherapy.* New York: W. W. Norton.

Schwartz-Salant, Nathan. 1995. *Jung on Alchemy.* Princeton, NJ: Princeton University Press.

Sittser, Jerry. 1995. *A Grace Disguised: How the Soul Grows Through Loss.* Grand Rapids, MI: Zondervan.

———. 2003. *When God Doesn't Answer Your Prayer.* Grand Rapids, MI: Zondervan.

Tarnas, Richard. 1991. *The Passion of the Western Mind.* New York: Ballantine.

Temple-Thurston, Leslie. 2000. *The Marriage of Spirit: Enlightened Living in Today's World.* With Brad Laughlin. Santa Fe, NM: CoreLight Publishing.

Tolle, Eckhart. 1997. *The Power of Now: A Guide to Spiritual Enlightenment.* Vancouver, BC: Namaste Publishing.

———. 2006. *The New Earth: Awakening to Your Life's Purpose.* New York: Plume.

Trungpa, Chogyam. 2002. *The Myth of Freedom and the Way of Meditation.* Ed. John Baker and Marvin Casper. Boston: Shambhala.

Trungpa, Chogyam. 2009. *Smile at Fear: Awakening the True Heart of Bravery.* Ed. Carolyn Rose Gimina. Boston: Shambhala.

Van der Hart, Onno, Ellert R. S. Nijenhuis, and Kathy Steele. 2006. *The Haunted Self: Structural Dissociation and the Treatment of Chronic Traumatization.* New York: W. W. Norton.

Viorst, Judith. 1986. *Necessary Losses: The Loves, Illusions, Dependencies, and Impossible Expectations That All of Us Have to Give Up in Order to Grow.* New York: Simon & Schuster.

Wallin, David J. 2007. *Attachment in Psychotherapy.* New York: Guilford Press.

Weller, Francis. 2011. *Entering the Healing Ground.* Santa Rosa, CA: WisdomBridge Press.

Wikman, Monika. 2004. *Pregnant Darkness: Alchemy and the Rebirth of Consciousness.* Berwick, ME: Nicolas-Hays.

Wilbur, Ken, and Treya Wilbur. 1991. *Grace and Grit.* Boston: Shambhala.

Wilde, Oscar. 1962/1999. *De Profundis: The Ballad of Reading Gaol & Other Writings.* Hertfordshire: Wordsworth Classics.

Acknowledgments

FOR THE PAST FIVE years, I have lived and breathed this book—it has been a healing ritual, a compulsion, a spiritual practice, a lifeline, and a labor of love. This is a book I never set out to write. More than ten years ago, after revising my dissertation for publication, I swore that I would never again undertake the extraordinary demands of crafting another book. Despite my intentions, this time, I seemed to have had little say in the matter.

In the world of astrological symbology, a configuration exists called a "finger of God." This lineup of heavenly indicators point to an area of life where unconscious forces drive a person to turn in a wholly unanticipated direction to accomplish something in the outer world. You come to a crossroads and find yourself suddenly engaged, often even against your conscious intentions, in an undertaking you had not planned. I felt such an unexpected turn in writing this book. As if I had no choice, the finger of God pointed me to my desk, and said "write!" For the sustaining grace that swept through me and moved me to write and to persevere, I am grateful. Without those hours of flow and surprise at what was pouring onto the page, I could never have kept at it and finished the task.

Many wonderful people also helped me during this long labor to whom I want to express my love and gratitude. First, I am indebted to those who supported me through the many iterations of the manuscript: To my web designer and assistant, Leila Rand, for holding my hand, talking things through when nothing made sense, and managing the details while I worked on the manuscript. To my editors: foremost, Elianne Obadia, whose keen intelligence and inspired suggestions helped shape the arc of the book; to David Carr, Stephanie Marohn, Karen Gordon, Kristen Nicolaisen, and Joan Wilcox for their able editing, critiques, and comments; and to Stephanie Beavers for her attention to the final details.

To those dedicated readers of the early drafts: Jill Friedlander for her unfailing empathy, her recognition of the value of the narrative, and her intuition about what worked and what did not; to Martina Hutchins, who reviewed the first draft; to my daughter, Rachael Kojan, who helped me cut through my academic stuffiness and find my voice; to Fran Carbonaro, a sister in the struggle of the heart. Thank you, Fran, for your warmth, your flair with words, and your sense of humor. And thanks go to the men who tackled selected chapters, for their insightful comments: John Amodeo, Charlie Fisher, and Gary Rosenthal. Thanks also to Joel Friedlander for his encouragement, his insider publishing advice, and his cover design. I am grateful to the many people who responded with understanding and compassion to the initial sharing of "the story" on my website and to the many others who shared their experiences of abandonment and betrayal with me and helped shape my thinking.

The book would never have been completed without the healers who helped me through the trauma. Thank you Annie O'Connor for your heartfelt listening, for diving with me into the chaos, for your love, patience and warmth; Bas Molenkamp, your body work proved that your heart truly does live in your hands; Ruah Bull for believing in me, and for helping me keep the lines to spirit open; Cornelia Gerken, you faced the raw trauma with generosity, compassion and care; Rick Russell, soulful Jin Shin friend for holding me safely in the early, worst days; Yurgen Welka, you wise soul and wizard with acupuncture needles; and Suzie Gruber. Thank you Deborah Riverbend and the Naka-Ima community for your warmth and understanding; Leslie Temple Thurston; Ray Castellino and the womb surround group; James Finley for speaking to my heart; Hameed Ali, Jessica Britt, and the Diamond Heart community for your dedication to the work; Miranda Macpherson and the Santa Rosa circle for your love, support, and inspiration.

I appreciate many others who helped to draw me back into community: Michelle and Barry Vesser, Charlie Fisher, and Mike Shea; Francis Weller, for your community grief work; Mark Zaifman, financial advisor extraordinaire; the Wanderwomen who accepted me despite my absentee norm; The *Course in Miracles* group, who allowed me to just listen for so long; Scott Eberle and Betty Perluss for that first Vision Quest; Zuza and Scott Engler and the Soul Motion community—when I was finally ready to dance it out, you were there with play, wisdom, and soul. Thanks to Karl Frederick, your warmth, handkerchiefs, and kind heart sustained me through many tears; to Jane and Leslie Locke for welcoming me into your hearts and home when I was most on the edge; to Glenn Lenox, for taking me in with kind caring; and to dear friends Sarah Kahn-Heick, Chris and Melissa Baker, Lew McFarland, Sara Harris, Kaylee Powell, Susie and Patrick Troccolo, and the Kocjan family: I knew you were always there.

Finally, I thank my family for their patience and support. To my great blessing, my daughter, Rachael—your goodness and *joie de vivre* light my life and give me hope on the darkest day. To my parents, Roy and Nettajo Morter, your vitality and zest for living, perseverance through tough times, love, and sacrifices to make our lives richer fill me with appreciation; to my sisters, Terry Petersen, Cathryn Selchow, and Vicky Morter and your families for your love. Vick, you never fail to show up when most needed. Thank you all for gracing my life and making this book possible.

About the Author

SANDRA LEE DENNIS, PhD obtained her MA in Social Psychology from the University of Michigan and her doctorate in Integral Studies/ Psychology and Religion from the California Institute of Integral Studies. She is an author, teacher and explorer of the interplay of depth psychology and spiritual experience.

A teacher in the Gurdjieff tradition for many years, a long-time student of Diamond Heart work, and an Ananda yoga instructor, Sandra has also been on the faculty at Portland State University, the University of Hawaii, the California Institute of Integral Studies and the C.G. Jung Institute of San Francisco. She spends her time writing, reading, gardening and luxuriating in the beauty of the Bay Area.

Her first book, *Embrace of the Daimon: Healing through the Subtle Energy Body/Jungian Psychology & the Dark Feminine,* presents a practical method for healing the dangerous split between body, soul, and spirit that afflicts our times. Cultural historian Richard Tarnas described her work as a "significant contribution to the phenomenology of altered states of consciousness."

In her latest book *Love and the Mystery of Betrayal,* Sandra dives again into dark recesses of the psyche that traditionally resist description, this time to explore abandonment, trauma, pain and heartache. Casting betrayal as a profound initiation of the heart, she shares her own story while taking us through the classic stages of a dark night of the soul. She puts flesh on the bones of existing theories about betrayal, trust, and forgiveness to help those journeying through this little underrated trauma and those who would help them reclaim their lives.

If you found this book helpful, would you consider leaving a review on Amazon or Goodreads? Thank you!